| exploring |

Adobe
Photoshop CS5

P9-CCJ-306

exploring

Adobe
Photoshop CS5

Annesa Hartman

DELMAR
CENGAGE Learning

Australia • Brazil • Japan • Korea • Mexico • Singapore • Spain • United Kingdom • United States

DELMAR
CENGAGE Learning™

Exploring Adobe Photoshop CS5
Annesa Hartman

Vice President, Career and Professional
 Editorial: Dave Garza

Director of Learning Solutions: Sandy Clark

Senior Acquisitions Editor: Jim Gish

Managing Editor: Larry Main

Associate Product Manager: Meaghan O'Brien

Editorial Assistant: Sarah L. Timm

Vice President, Career and Professional
 Marketing: Jennifer Baker

Marketing Director: Deborah S. Yarnell

Marketing Manager: Erin Brennan

Marketing Coordinator: Erin Deangelo

Production Director: Wendy Troeger

Senior Content Project Manager: Glenn Castle

Senior Art Director: Joy Kocsis

Technology Product Manager: Christopher
 Catalina

Cover design: Steven Brower and
 Lisa Marie Pompilio

Cover Illustration: Stephanie Dalton

© 2011, Delmar, Cengage Learning

ALL RIGHTS RESERVED. No part of this work covered by the copyright herein may be reproduced, transmitted, stored, or used in any form or by any means graphic, electronic, or mechanical, including but not limited to photocopying, recording, scanning, digitizing, taping, Web distribution, information networks, or information storage and retrieval systems, except as permitted under Section 107 or 108 of the 1976 United States Copyright Act, without the prior written permission of the publisher.

For product information and technology assistance, contact us at
**Professional Group Cengage Learning Customer & Sales Support,
1-800-354-9706**
For permission to use material from this text or product, submit all requests online at **www.cengage.com/permissions**
Further permissions questions can be e-mailed to
permissionrequest@cengage.com

Adobe® Photoshop® are trademarks or registered trademarks of Adobe Systems, Inc. in the United States and/or other countries. Third party products, services, company names, logos, design, titles, words, or phrases within these materials may be trademarks of their respective owners.

Library of Congress Control Number: 2010921544
ISBN-13: 978-1-111-13034-3
ISBN-10: 1-111-13034-5

Delmar
5 Maxwell Drive
Clifton Park, NY 12065-2919
USA

Cengage Learning is a leading provider of customized learning solutions with office locations around the globe, including Singapore, the United Kingdom, Australia, Mexico, Brazil, and Japan. Locate your local office at: **international. cengage.com/region**

Cengage Learning products are represented in Canada by Nelson Education, Ltd.

To learn more about Delmar, visit www.cengage.com/delmar

Purchase any of our products at your local college store or at our preferred online store **www.CengageBrain.com**

Notice to the Reader
Publisher does not warrant or guarantee any of the products described herein or perform any independent analysis in connection with any of the product information contained herein. Publisher does not assume, and expressly disclaims, any obligation to obtain and include information other than that provided to it by the manufacturer. The reader is expressly warned to consider and adopt all safety precautions that might be indicated by the activities described herein and to avoid all potential hazards. By following the instructions contained herein, the reader willingly assumes all risks in connection with such instructions. The publisher makes no representations or warranties of any kind, including but not limited to, the warranties of fitness for particular purpose or merchantability, nor are any such representations implied with respect to the material set forth herein, and the publisher takes no responsibility with respect to such material. The publisher shall not be liable for any special, consequential, or exemplary damages resulting, in whole or part, from the readers' use of, or reliance upon, this material.

Printed in the United States of America
1 2 3 4 5 XX 12 11 10

For my mother, Carolyn Murov

| Contents |

| Contents |

| Contents |

| Preface |

"The universe is full of magical things, patiently waiting for our wits to grow sharper."

—Eden Phillpotts

intended audience

Quick, grab a seat. The show is about to begin, and it is full of a wonderfully mischievous cast of characters you do not want to miss. They call them "pixels," magical spirits brought to life by digital mayhem and transported by light. They are the muses of the digital artist, the star performers on the Photoshop stage, and the lead actors in this book, *Exploring Adobe Photoshop CS5*.

Whether a new student to computer graphics, a computer arts educator, a professional visualizer, animator, designer, illustrator, photographer, or just plain curious dabbler, *Exploring Adobe Photoshop CS5* has something for you. It offers a practical and straightforward introduction to the essentials of digital image creation, compositing, and photo retouching; comprehensive step-by-step lessons; easy reference to commonly used tools and features of Photoshop; and plenty of encouragement for artistic exploration.

emerging trends

In today's world, the amount of data that moves through our consciousness is overwhelming. Some of this information we manage to absorb into knowledge and understanding, and it enhances and improves our lives. Other data comes to us as fluff; we hold on to or let go of it as our interest wanes. More so than ever, graphic designers have the tools and resources to bring data to visual life in diverse ways.

Thomas L. Friedman, author of *The World Is Flat*, says, "The world is being flattened. . . . we are now connecting all the knowledge centers on the planet together into a single global network . . . , which could usher in an amazing era of prosperity, innovation and collaboration. . . ."

A high-speed flow of digital information is prevalent and far-reaching to all corners of the world like never before. In our case—as graphic designers, artists, developers, students, and educators—this digitally connected world opens up a level playing field, where we can explore endless new ways to research, use, and effectively design our creative visions.

The need to find the best solutions for the effective, horizontal flow of data is not being overlooked. Adobe's new creative software suites are designed for easy transfer of visual and textual content between different software programs, allowing quick workflow processes between various designers and developers. An illustrator can draw a logo in Illustrator, add effects to it in Photoshop, and then send it to an animator. The animator can make it move in Flash or After Effects, and then send it to a printer, the Web, or a mobile device content developer.

Furthermore, today's successful graphic artists realize the importance of not just having a foundation in design principles and knowing the tools, but also having the skills to communicate clearly and collaboratively with others in the innovation process. The artists highlighted in this book were asked, "What suggestions for success would you give to the emerging graphic artist?" All emphasized the need for one to be adaptable to change and alterations; to be professional, organized, and prompt in all matters of his or her business; to be personable to others, and yet persistent in self-promotion; and to keep learning, exploring, and engaging with all that this expansive world offers.

background of this text

"Any sufficiently advanced technology is indistinguishable from magic," says Arthur C. Clarke, author of *2001: A Space Odyssey* (1968) and astrophysicist.

Aptly, Photoshop is an example of such a technology. For Photoshop, or any other current computer graphics software program, it is not uncommon to describe what it can do and how it is embraced by the user as anything but amazing, magical. Without lessening the impact Photoshop has made in the graphics and photographic industries, and the continual advancements occurring with each new version, this book is intended to demystify what ostensibly seems complicated but is really quite engaging and accessible. After all, as automated as the program can appear, it is still a product of the mortal mindset, which we can assume understands some method to the madness.

As is the purpose all the books in the Delmar Cengage Learning's Design Exploration series, the objective of this text is to be clear and no-nonsense in approach, never negating the practical—yet vastly experiential—aspects of the program. You could say it is the "Penn and Teller" method of instruction. Yes, for the outside viewer it appears all magic (and we want to keep it that way!), but for the magician it really is just practiced tricks that can be easily explained and enacted.

Textbook Organization

As you learn in Chapter 1, Photoshop is a "must-know" program for the graphic artist, with the ability to retouch, blend, composite, layer, and add effects to photos and digital imagery, draw and paint, and save in different image formats for different purposes, such as for use on the Web, for print, or in other programs.

This book has been conceptualized and organized with the following intentions:

▶ Explore the questions that face today's Photoshop artist and provide some educated answers through the use of Adobe Photoshop's digital tools and features

▶ Offer process-oriented lessons developed from actual implementation in the classroom and production firms

▶ Develop an understanding of core concepts related to digital artwork and image creation through fundamental design principles and methods

▶ Provide an inside look at how artists working in the field come up with ideas and inspirations

▶ And, most importantly, open the door for continued, self-guided discovery

The textbook contains common features found in each of the Design Exploration books, but specifically this material is presented in a need-to-know basis and so each chapter builds upon itself. This eliminates the amount of information the reader must know to successfully complete a task. Each chapter also accommodates those who appreciate alternative methods of learning information, providing both textually and visually succinct explanations of important concepts, step-by-step experiences; or for those who prefer to wander around, final project files, samples, and a section for further exploration. The following is a brief rundown of what is learned in each chapter:

Chapter 1: A Discovery Tour Right away, retouch a photo in Photoshop and discover the purpose of the Photoshop program.

Chapter 2: The Staging Area Take center stage and explore the workspace and navigational features of the program.

Chapter 3: Image Essentials Get the "know-how" on bitmap and vector graphics, bit depth, resolution, and image formats.

Chapter 4: Selecting and Transforming Using Photoshop's varied selection tools and transform commands, get up-close-and-personal with selecting and transforming image pixels—the most fundamental of procedures in Photoshop.

Chapter 5: Working with Color Uncover fundamental concepts of color, such as how color is reproduced, color modes, and a hands-on study with color models. Additionally, explore important aspects of color specifically related to Photoshop, such as tips for managing color, channels, and using the color application tools.

Chapter 6: Image Correction Learn, step by step, fundamental techniques in the image-correction process such as adjusting tonal levels, retouching, and adding effects.

Chapter 7: Drawing and Painting Get a thorough introduction to the drawing and painting tools and options, advancing your creative possibilities to a whole new level.

Chapter 8: Masking Discover techniques for hiding and revealing areas of an image while preserving its integrity. Includes practice with layer, vector, type, clipping, and quick masks.

Chapter 9: Layers, Compositing, and Process Uncover the process and methods by which to composite, link, blend, merge, and organize graphical elements into complex images or graphic layouts.

Chapter 10: Print Publishing Learn about the different print processes and what it takes to prepare your digital images for print.

Chapter 11: Web Publishing Learn about image optimization and what it takes to prepare your digital images for the Web. Also learn how to slice and animate images for Web output.

Chapter 12: A New Dimension (for Photoshop CS5 Extended version users) Discover how Photoshop Extended supports transformation, material editing, and texture mapping on simple 3D objects available within the program or imported from 3D authoring programs.

Features

The following list provides some of the salient features of the text:

▶ Learning goals are clearly stated at the beginning of each chapter.

▶ Written to meet the needs of design students and professionals for a visually oriented introduction to image composition and the functions and tools of Photoshop.

▶ Client projects and Adventures in Design involve tools and techniques a designer might encounter on the job.

▶ Full-color format provides the most accurate depictions of software screen shots.

▶ Explorer Pages highlight Photoshop artists, their artwork, and personal accounts of their design process.

▶ Exploring on Your Own sections offer suggestions and sample lessons for further study of content covered in each chapter.

▶ In Review sections are provided at the end of each chapter to quiz a reader's understanding and retention of the material covered.

▶ A CD-ROM at the back of the book contains the support files to complete the exercises and audio interviews with the book's contributing artists.

New! In *Exploring Adobe Photoshop CS5*

▶ Two new Explorer Pages featuring two new professional illustrators working in the field today

▶ Coverage of CS Live, which provides online services and resources that you can access directly from Photoshop.

▶ New coverage of the Mini Bridge tools, which makes the power of the Bridge program accessible directly within Photoshop

▶ Improved painting and 3D features

▶ New icons for several Photoshop tools

Instructor Resources

This CD was developed to assist instructors in planning and implementing their instructional programs. It includes sample syllabi for using this book in either an 11- or 15-week semester. It also provides answers to the "In Review" questions, PowerPoint slides highlighting the main topics, and additional instructor resources. To order, please call 1-800-347-7707.

ISBN: 1-111-13035-3

File Setup

Located at the back of this book is a CD-ROM containing all files for completing the lessons. These lesson files are compatible with Photoshop CS5. For a trial version of Photoshop CS5, visit *http://www.adobe.com/downloads/*.

Before starting the lessons, create a folder on your local computer. Name it **My Lessons** (or whatever name you prefer). From the CD, drag a copy of the lesson files to the folder. As you work on the lessons, open the lessons, assets, and sample files from this location. You can save your work in the same place.

About the Author

Annesa Hartman holds a Masters in Teaching with Internet Technologies, focusing her attention on instructional design for online technologies, and Web and graphic design concepts and programs. Currently, she is a Content Developer for Kaplan University, where she designs and develops online courses for educators. For over 15 years she also has taught computer graphic courses and is a freelance graphic designer with clients from around the world. She is the author of *Exploring Adobe Photoshop CS4*, *Exploring Adobe Illustrator CS5*, *Exploring Adobe Flash CS5*, and *Producing Interactive Television*. When she is not pushing pixels, she is performing in community theater and teaching yoga classes.

Why is Annesa turned upside down and twice? The upside down versions might look a bit strange, but turn them right-side up (flip this book over). One photo looks normal, the other not so much (scary!). It's a trick on the eyes. This author photo is an illusion created using Photoshop. You can do it too – take a photo of your face and flip the eyes and mouth using Photoshop's selection tools that you learn about in Chapter 4.

Visit where this idea came from — the Mona Lisa version on the Exploratorium Web site — at *http://www.exploratorium.edu/ exhibits/mona/mona.html*

Acknowledgments

It's quite remarkable that this book is now in its fifth edition. And not unlike any momentous task, it would not have happened without the help of my friends, colleagues, and students. Many, many thanks to all those who contributed content for the book's lessons, visual examples, "Adventures in Design" and "Explorer Pages", including Ruth Marx, Kevin Burke, Jim Carroll, Max Ruse, Geoff Burgess, Karen Kamenetzky, Bruce and Linda Lord, Terry Hartman, Darrel Anderson, Joel Hagen, Michael Dwyer, Glenn Mitsui, Joe Summerhays, Natascha Roeoesli, Tim Warnock, Dave Garcez, Jeffrey Moring, Brian Sinclair, David Julian, and Charlene Chua.

For their patient persistence (if there is such a thing), I also thank the staff at Delmar Cengage Learning. What a comfort to know that you are out there in full force promoting the Design Exploration series and making this experience worthwhile. Last, I would like to thank my mother, Carolyn Murov, whose photographic talent supplied many of the images found in the pages of this book.

Delmar Cengage Learning and the author would also like to thank Toni Toland for her invaluable suggestions and quick eye in reviewing the technical accuracy of this text.

Questions and Feedback

Delmar Cengage Learning and the author welcome your questions and feedback. If you have suggestions you think others would benefit from, please let us know and we will try to include them in the next edition.

To send us your questions and/or feedback, contact the publisher at:

Delmar Cengage Learning
Executive Woods
5 Maxwell Drive
Clifton Park, NY 12065
Attn: Media Arts & Design Team
800-998-7498

Or Annesa Hartman at:

Kaplan University
Content Developer
P.O. Box 83
Saxtons River, Vermont 05154
ahartman@kaplan.edu

How To Use This Text

The features discussed in the following sections are found in the book.

▶ ## Charting Your Course and Goals

The introduction and chapter objectives start off each chapter. They describe the competencies the reader should achieve upon completing the chapter.

▶ ## Don't Go There

These boxes highlight common pitfalls and explain ways to avoid them.

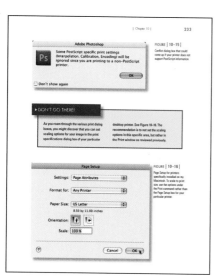

▶ ## Explorer Pages

These sections showcase the imagery, insights, and workflow processes of successful graphic artists.

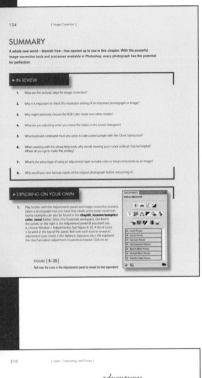

▶ In Review and Exploring on Your Own

Review questions are located at the end of each chapter. They allow readers to assess their understanding of the chapter. The section Exploring on Your Own contains exercises that reinforce chapter material through practical application.

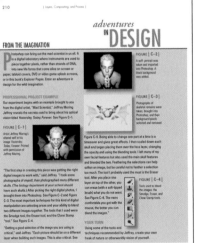

▶ Adventures in Design

These pages contain client assignments showing readers how to approach a design project using the tools and design concepts taught in the book.

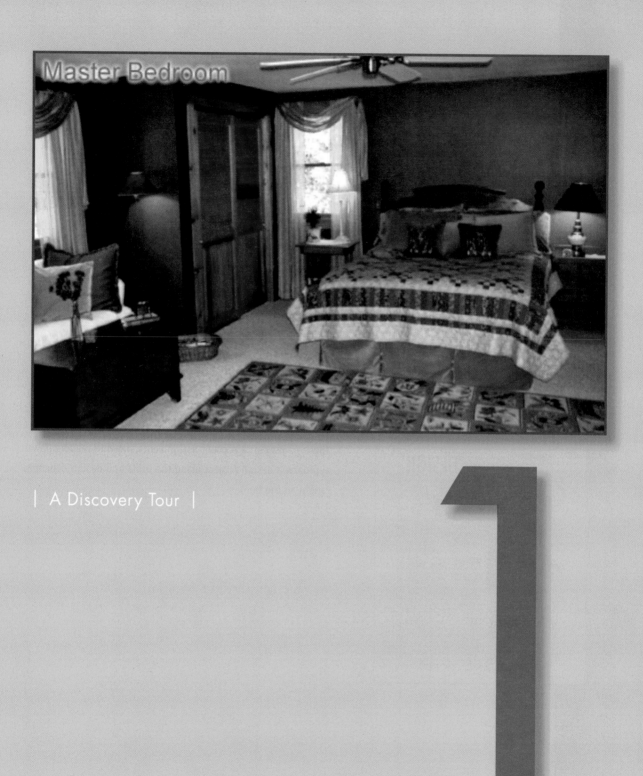

| A Discovery Tour |

1

charting your course

I hope you have brushed up on your "ta-das," because you are in for a Harry Houdini of an experience—a venture into the digital wizardry of Adobe Photoshop. If there is only one program you should know as a graphic artist, Photoshop is it. And, if I begin to sound a bit highfalutin about its prospects, well, it is because I am. You can say Photoshop is the pinnacle (the Big Daddy) of all computer graphic programs, proven to handle in numerous ways just about any type of graphic and photographic image. In this chapter you will get hands-on practice with Photoshop and experience a first taste of its illusionary talents. Depending on your learning style, you can choose to "do" the lesson, "read" the lesson, or both. The trick is to get you started on the experience of Photoshop and then show you what makes it so magical.

goals

In this chapter you will:

- ▶ *Discover the purpose of Photoshop*
- ▶ *Get excited about Photoshop*
- ▶ *Fix a bad photo and optimize it for the Web*
- ▶ *Explore some of Photoshop's tools and features*

A MAGIC TOUR

No matter what kind of multimedia project you might be up against, Photoshop more often than not is going to play a pivotal role in the creation process. Think of it as the Swiss Army knife of the digital imaging world. It will come to your rescue when the lighting for those wedding pictures is less than perfect—to remove the unwanted blemish on the bride's cheek, or superimpose the indisposed from the family portrait. Take, for instance, the photograph shown on the left in Figure 1–1, which was taken by a point-and-shoot camera. The film was digitized on a CD and later handed to me to put on the Web. To tell you the truth, the photo quality was dreadful. However, with my bag of tricks (Photoshop), a wave of the magic wand (computer mouse), and $50 added to my client's invoice, I produced what looked like the real thing: a room in a fine country inn, not a room in a rundown shack. OK, so maybe the differences in the two photos are not that extreme, but my point is that with a little magic, and about 15 minutes of your time, you can make a "ho-hum" image look "oh wow" and prepared to download fast from the Web.

LESSON: THE 15-MINUTE PHOTO MAKEOVER

It is said that a magician never reveals her tricks—until now. In this lesson you will learn how I fixed up the country inn photo (see Figure 1–1) and made it Web-ready. I will not get into too many specifics about the program just yet; there is plenty of that to come. However, you will learn enough secrets to realize that Photoshop is not mere hocus-pocus.

FIGURE | 1–1 |

The original photo of a room in a country inn (left), and a 15-minute makeover version using Photoshop (right).

Importing and Cropping the Photo

1. Open the Photoshop program. (A trial version is available for download at *http://www.adobe.com/products/photoshop/compare/*. There are two program versions you can choose from—CS5 and CS5 Extended. To complete Chapter 12 of this book you will need CS5 Extended.) Install the program version of your choice onto your hard drive.

2. Choose File > Open from the menu bar, and on your local hard drive browse for the Exploring Photoshop CS5 **lessons/chap01_lessons/assets** folder. Open the file **masterbed.tif.**

> Note: *As mentioned in the Preface, to save your work, you must make a copy of the chapter lessons to your local hard drive and select files from that location.*

3. Press Shift-Tab to hide unnecessary window panels (at least for the time being). Your imported image of **masterbed.tif** should be visible, with the toolbox to the left of the interface, and the menu bars located at the top. See Figure 1–2.

FIGURE | 1–2 |

The Photoshop interface (Mac).

4. From the menu bar at the top of the screen, choose View > Fit on Screen to enlarge the photo to the Photoshop window size.

5. Select Photoshop > Preferences > Units & Rulers (Mac), or Edit > Preferences > Units & Rulers (Windows), from the menu bar.

6. In the Preferences dialog box, set the Rulers units to "pixels" and click OK. See Figure 1–3. (If the rulers are not showing, select View > Rulers (Command+R for Mac or Ctrl+R for Windows).)

FIGURE | 1–3 |

Set the Rulers units to pixels.

FIGURE | 1–4 |

Select the Crop tool
in the toolbox.

7. Select the Crop tool in the toolbox. See Figure 1–4. With the Crop tool you can delete unnecessary or unflattering parts from an image.

8. In the Options bar found along the top of your image, under the menu bar, type in the following parameters for the Crop tool. After entering a value, press the Tab key to move the cursor to the next field (see Figure 1–5).

  ▸ *Width: 550 pixels*

  ▸ *Height: 350 pixels*

  ▸ *Resolution: 72 pixels/inch*

FIGURE | 1–5 |

Enter parameters for the Crop tool in the Options bar. (Tip: to quickly move from field to field to enter each parameter, choose Tab on the keyboard.)

> Note: *When entering numbers numerically in the Options bar, it's helpful to type in "pixels" or "px" after the number entered, otherwise Photoshop might default to a measurement you don't want, like 550 inches!*

9. From the upper left corner of the image, click and drag with the Crop tool to the lower right corner of the image. Select the entire image except for the unwanted section along the right edge. See Figure 1–6. If you feel the area was not cropped properly, press ESC and try again.

FIGURE | 1–6 |

Crop the image.

10. Click on the Crop tool icon in the toolbox to bring up the Crop dialog box. See Figure 1–7. Select the Crop option to execute the crop. (Alternatively, you can double-click inside the selected area or press Return (Mac) or Enter (Windows) to execute the crop.)

FIGURE | 1–7 |

Execute the crop action.

Adobe Photoshop

Crop the image?

Ps

Don't Crop   Cancel   Crop

> Note: *Argh! What if you make a mistake? From the menu bar, select Window > History to open the History panel, if it is not already opened. Each step you perform in Photoshop is recorded in the History panel (up to 20 states by default). To go back a step, click on the state above the step you just made. For instance, from the Crop state, click up to the Open state to return the image to its original state. See Figure 1–8. You can also press Command-Z (Mac) or Ctrl-Z (Windows) to undo your last step.*

11. Choose View > Actual Pixels to see the final cropped image.

12. Choose File > Save As. Make sure you are set to save in your **chap01_lessons** folder (copied from the text's CD) when the Save As menu pops up. For Format, choose Photoshop (top of the list). Your file name should read **masterbed.psd** (the native file format for Photoshop).

FIGURE | 1–8 |

The History panel—a life saver!

Fixing the Color

1. You have probably noticed that the color of this image is too red. This can be fixed in one easy step: choose Image > Auto Color. Ta-da!

2. To lighten the image, choose Image > Adjustments > Levels. The Levels histogram comes up. This determines the lights and darks (brightness and contrast) in an image. You will learn more about levels in later chapters. Right now, move the white arrow (on the lower right side of the graph) inward until you get 200 in the Input Levels right box. Click OK. See Figure 1–9.

FIGURE | 1–9 |

Adjust the photograph's brightness and contrast using Levels.

> Note: *You may have noticed the Brightness/Contrast choice found under Image > Adjustments. I chose not to use this, as Levels gives us more control over our image.*

FIGURE | 1–10 |

The photo is located on one layer: the default layer called "Background."

Creating a Shadow and Border Effect

1. Choose Window > Layers to open the Layers panel. Layers organize information in Photoshop. Right now we only have one layer: our photo. See Figure 1–10.

2. In the Layers palette, double-click on the Background layer that contains the photo. The New Layer dialog box comes up. Type in **master bedroom** and click OK. (This renames the Background layer and unlocks it for further editing.)

FIGURE | 1–11 |

Increase the canvas size.

3. From the menu bar, choose Image > Canvas Size. Select the Relative option. Then, for Width type in 20 pixels and for Height, type in 20 pixels. This will increase each side of the canvas by 20 pixels. On a side note, the Anchor box allows you to position where the current image will be on the new canvas. Let's keep it in the center for now. Click OK. See Figure 1–11.

4. From the menu bar, choose Layer > Layer Style > Drop Shadow. Select "Preview" on the right side of the Layer Style window, so you can view the changes you make in the dialog box directly on the document. Enter the following parameters and remember to use the Tab key to move among them quickly (see Figure 1–12):

FIGURE | 1–12 |

Create a drop shadow.

▶ *Angle: 120 degrees*

▶ *Distance: 10 pixels*

▶ *Spread: 20%*

▶ *Size: 10 pixels*

Leave the other settings at their default.

5. Click OK.

Note: *In the Layers panel, notice the small "fx" icon next to the layer name. This indicates that there are effects (i.e., the drop shadow) on the image. To edit the effects, simply double-click on the "fx" icon to open the Layer Style dialog box.*

6. Now, let's select just the photo and not the background, which can be tricky. In the Layers panel, place the cursor over the layer thumbnail (the small image to the left of the layer name). A pointer hand icon will appear. Press Command (Mac) or Ctrl (Windows) and click on the thumbnail. The photo (the object in the selected layer) will be selected in the document. This is indicated by a series of moving, dashed lines around the edge of the photo, also known as "marching ants." See Figure 1–13.

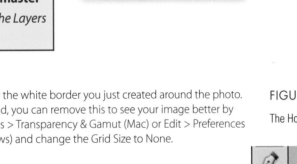

FIGURE | 1–13 |

Marching ants indicate a selected area.

7. From the menu bar, choose Edit > Stroke. Enter the following parameters (see Figure 1–14):

   ▶ *Width: 4 pixels*

   ▶ *Color: Click on the color box to open the Color Picker and choose white.*

   ▶ *Location: Center*

FIGURE | 1–14 |

The Stroke options box.

Note: *If Edit > Stroke is dimmed and therefore unavailable, be sure the* **master bedroom** *layer is highlighted in the Layers panel.*

8. Click OK.

9. Choose Select > Deselect to view the white border you just created around the photo. If you see a checkered background, you can remove this to see your image better by going to Photoshop > Preferences > Transparency & Gamut (Mac) or Edit > Preferences > Transparency & Gamut (Windows) and change the Grid Size to None.

FIGURE | 1–15 |

The Horizontal Type tool.

10. Save your file.

Note: *If you receive a Maximize Compatibility Photoshop Format option dialog box, keep the option selected to ensure compatibility of this file with previous versions of Photoshop.*

Creating a Title Effect

1. Select the Horizontal Type tool in the toolbox. See Figure 1–15.

2. In the Options bar, set the typeface to Arial or Verdana, depending on what is available on your computer. Set the type size to 24 points. For color, click the color box in the Options bar (see Figure 1–16) to open the Color Picker.

FIGURE | 1–16 |

Change the typeface and type size, and set the text color.

FIGURE | 1–17 |

FIGURE | 1–17 |

The Eyedropper tool takes a sampling of color from the photograph.

3. Move the Color Picker dialog box to the right side of the screen, so you can see your image. With the Color Picker open, notice that your cursor changes to an eyedropper when you move it over the photo area. See Figure 1–17.

4. Move the Eyedropper tool over a light-brown area of the closet door frame in the photo and click to take a sample of the color (see Figure 1–17). The color is recorded in the Color Picker. Click OK to close the Color Picker.

5. With the Horizontal Type tool, click in the upper left corner of the document. A blinking cursor will appear. Type in **Master Bedroom.**

FIGURE | 1–18 |

The final, glowing title.

6. Choose Layer > Layer Style > Outer Glow. Leave the default setting for the outer glow (unless you want to play on your own!) and click OK. See Figure 1–18.

7. Select the Move tool in the toolbox (see Figure 1–19). Place the Move tool over the text and click and drag it to a position of your liking on the photograph.

8. Save your file. You're almost there.

Optimizing the Image for the Web

1. OK, one last detail. Let's prepare this photograph so it can be used on the Web. We need to do two things: make the file size smaller (compress it), so it will download quickly for those of us with slow Internet connections, and save it in JPEG format, which is a file format the Web can display (you will learn more about that in Chapter 11). For now, choose File > Save for Web & Devices. The document opens up in a new window.

FIGURE | 1–19 |

The Move tool.

2. Select the 2-Up option (see Figure 1–20). At the top is your original image. On the bottom is the image you will compress for the Web. By having them side-by-side, you can compare the quality of the Web image with the original as you adjust the compression settings.

3. In the Optimize panel to the right of the images, set the image quality to JPEG Low, next to the word Preset (see Figure 1–21). Note how the quality of the image on the bottom deteriorates compared to the image at the top. Look closely at the title text in particular.

Note: *If you are having difficulty seeing parts of an image, use the Hand tool on the left side of the window to navigate the image view right, left, up, or down.*

FIGURE | 1–20 |

Select the 2-Up option
in the Save for Web &
Devices window.

4. Now, set the quality
to JPEG High. Much
better. I know you're
wondering why you
should ever use the
JPEG Low setting. Look
at the box with numbers
right below the two
images. Note that the
lower the setting, the
smaller the number,
allowing for a faster
download (more on this
in Chapter 11).

FIGURE | 1–21 |

The Optimize panel properly
prepares the image for
Web publication.

5. Take a look at the estimated download
time of the lower image at the bottom of
the image's window. See Figure 1–22.

FIGURE | 1–22 |

View the size and estimated
download time of the
Web-formatted image.

6. Click Save and save the
masterbed.jpg
file in your **lessons**
folder—Photoshop
automatically adds
the jpg extension for
you. The image is now
ready to be placed
on a Web page. See
the completed image,
shown in Figure 1–23.

FIGURE | 1–23 |

The completed
photograph—it's magic!

> **Note:** *For fun, view your JPEG image in a Web browser. Open a Web browser of your choosing (e.g., Firefox, Internet Explorer, or Safari). Choose File > Open File and browse for the* **masterbed.jpg** *that you just saved to your lessons folder. The file will appear in the browser window. Alternatively, try opening the original TIF image (***lessons/chap01_lessons/assets/masterbed.tif***). The browser doesn't recognize this type of image format. More on image formats in Chapter 3.*

7. Select File > Save to save the final Photoshop (.psd) file. You did it!

PHOTOSHOP—IN BRIEF

As you have probably surmised by its name, fixing up photos is the essence of what Photoshop can do. That's what it was originally designed to do from its inception in 1987 with the brothers Thomas and John Knoll and in 1990 when Adobe first licensed the product. Now Photoshop and its immense toolset have grown to be a vital part of any magician's repertoire—something you will discover in the lessons of this book. No animator, illustrator, game developer, scientist, multimedia developer, or Web designer could survive without Photoshop. It has a way of working with one of the main ingredients of digital image construction: pixels. These are the tiny picture elements that, when placed together in a grid, make all the images we see on a computer screen. Chapter 3 gets into greater detail about pixels, among other important graphic essentials. For now, I can sum up what Photoshop does best in four simple bullet points:

- *Manipulates photographs and other digital imagery, such as select, cut, paste, clone, colorize, compress, erase, transform, and mask, and adds special effects*
- *Composites, layers, and blends photographs and images*
- *Draws and paints*
- *Converts photographs and illustrations into different formats for different purposes, such as for use on the Web, for video, for print, and to import into other programs*

SUMMARY

Photoshop is the "must know" of all computer graphic software packages. For the successful graphic artist, it is as vital a prop as a deck of cards and a white rabbit to a magician. In this chapter you discovered one of Photoshop's greatest and most used secrets: how it can fix a badly exposed photograph and make it Web-presentable. From here, there is only more magic to come.

▶ IN REVIEW

1. What does the command Shift-Tab do?

2. What is so great about the History panel?

3. In general, what are levels in Photoshop?

4. What are layers? How are they useful?

5. What are "marching ants"?

6. Name at least three uses for Photoshop.

▶ EXPLORING ON YOUR OWN

1. Visit the Photoshop area of the Adobe site at http://www.adobe.com/products/photoshop/photoshop/.

2. The programmers of software packages such as Photoshop love to play tricks and hide fun, little surprises within the programs they create. These surprises are called "Easter eggs," and you can find them in Photoshop if you know where to look and what to do.

   Here is how to find the infamous magician Merlin. In Photoshop, go to Window > Layers (if not already open). Click on the small arrow with four lines in the upper right corner of the Layers window to open the layer options. Hold down Option/Alt and click on Panel Options in the drop-down menu. Merlin lives!

Tyrone

©2007 Carolyn Murov

| The Staging Area |

2

charting your course

If you were at a carnival, Chapter 1 would be the enticing gypsy beckoning you into the tent of digital enchantment. It was only a teaser, offering a small taste of what Photoshop has to offer. In this chapter you will pull back the curtain, step inside the tent, adjust your eyes to the darkness, and become a part of the performance rather than remain a spectator. Here, you take center stage— where all the action happens—and explore the workspace and navigational features of the program.

goals

In this chapter you will:

▶ *Get comfortable with the Photoshop interface*

▶ *Set and delete preferences*

▶ *Navigate the workspace*

STAGING

Before you produce your first Photoshop masterpiece, it helps to get acquainted with the program's interface, or work area, and set it up to your desired specifications. In theater, this process is called staging. First, you will get familiar with such props as the document area, toolbox, menu bar, panels, and workspace. Second, you will practice using the navigational tools, avoiding any chance of getting lost among the bright lights of your virtual stage.

LESSON 1: INTERFACE HIGHLIGHTS

Learn your way around in this lesson.

Identifying Props

1. Open Photoshop.

2. Choose File > New from menu bar. Enter the following information (see Figure 2–1):

    ► *Name:* Type **myfile**
    ► *Preset:* Default Photoshop Size
    ► *Color Mode:* RGB Color, 8 bit
    ► *Background Contents:* White

FIGURE | 2–1 |

New Document options box.

3. The Photoshop interface may look different depending on whether you are a Macintosh or a Windows user. The main props, however, are the same. Compare your Photoshop interface with Figure 2–2 (Mac) and Figure 2–3 (Windows), and note where the various parts of the program are located.

FIGURE | 2–2 |

The Photoshop interface (Mac).

> ▶ *Document Area:* When you created a new file in step 2, you specified properties for a document area. This is the blank area in the center of the interface where you do all of your work (consider this your canvas or stage). At the top of the document area is a document tab, which provides information about the document (file), such as its name, current magnification, color mode, and bit depth. Each file you open or create in Photoshop will have different information in its document tab. See Figure 2–4. It is likely you will have many document windows open at the same time. All open documents are seen as tabs at the top of the document area. See Figure 2–5. To view a document, click on the document tab at the top of the document area to bring the document forward in the window. To close a document, click the X icon on its tab.

> ▶ *Menu Bar:* Along the top of the interface is the menu bar, which contains all of the commands to perform certain tasks: File, Edit, Image, Layer, Select, Filter, Analysis, 3D, View, Window, and Help. The commands are categorized so you

FIGURE | 2–3 |

The Photoshop interface (Windows).

myfile.psd @ 100% (RGB/8)

FIGURE | 2–4 |

The document title tab shows specific information about an open document.

can find them easily (so do not bother memorizing them all!). For example, if you want to open a panel window, click the Window menu and a list of options will pop up. To make global adjustments to an image, go to Image. To edit, go to Edit. You get the idea.

▶ *Application Bar:* A recent feature in all Adobe Creative Suite applications is the Application bar. The bar extends along the top of the program below the menu bar ON the Macintosh interface and as part of the menu bar on the Windows interface. It contains universal commands found across the Creative Suite programs, such as the application's icon, a link to Bridge (more on that below), and setting and tool options for how you might like to view a file in the Document Area, such as show Grids, Guides and Rulers, Zoom level, Arrange Documents, and Screen Mode. See Figure 2–6. Also on the Application bar are workspace options. Workspaces are predefined panel sets for particular tasks in Photoshop. The Essentials workspace is the default, but there are other preset workspaces to

⊗ myfile.psd @ 100% (RGB/8)   ⊗ example_file @ 200% (RGB/8)   ⊗ another_file @ 66.7% (RGB/8)

FIGURE | 2–5 |

Open documents are seen as tabs at the top of the document area.

Macintosh Application Bar

Windows Application Bar

FIGURE | 2–6 |

The Application Bar for Mac and Windows.

meet your image creation needs, such as Design and Painting. A more detailed exploration of workspaces is covered in the Exploring on Your Own section at the end of this chapter. Furthermore, you can have the option to Access CS Live from the Application bar. CS Live provides online services that you can access directly from Photoshop to accomplish such tasks as color matching, data conferencing, and online document creation, as well as other resources to aid your creative workflow. Finally, the Application bar also provides access to the Adobe Bridge and Mini Bridge programs, stand-alone applications for file browsing and management across Adobe's Creative Suite programs. Alternatively, open the Bridge program by choosing File > Browse in Bridge. Among many features, Bridge allows you to quickly browse for a file on your local hard drive, and it even provides a visual thumbnail of the file for easy selection. Check it out! See Figure 2–7.

FIGURE | 2–7 |

The really cool Adobe Bridge. Find a file quickly and visually!

Switch Toolbar Layout

Marquee Tool(s) — M

Quick Selection Tool
(Magic Wand) — W

Eyedropper Tool
(Color Sampler|Ruler|Note|Count) — I

Brush Tool
(Pencil|Color Replacement|Mixer) — B

History Brush Tool
(Art History Brush) — Y

Gradient Tool
(Paint Bucket) — G

Dodge Tool
(Burn|Sponge) — O

Type Tool(s) — T

Shape Tool(s) — U

3D View Tool(s) — N

Zoom Tool — Z

Default Foreground & Background Colors — D
Set Foreground Color

Edit in Quick Mask Mode — Q

V — Move Tool

L — Lasso Tool(s)

C — Crop Tool
(Slice Tool(s))

J — Spot Healing Brush Tool
(Healing|Patch|Red Eye)

S — Clone Stamp Tool
(Pattern Stamp)

E — Eraser Tool(s)

R — Blur Tool
(Sharpen|Smudge)

P — Pen Tool(s)
(Point Tool(s))

A — Path Selection Tool
(Direct Selection)

K — 3D Object Tool(s)

H — Hand Tool
Rotate View Tool (R)

X — Switch Foreground & Background Colors

Set Background Color

FIGURE | 2–8 |

The Photoshop CS5 toolbox.

FIGURE | 2–9 |

The classic toolbox.

▶ *Tools Panel/Toolbox:* Located by default to the left of the work area is the toolbox. This is where you choose the tools you need to select, edit, modify, and create your Photoshop masterpiece (see Figure 2–8 for tool names and shortcut keys). In CS5, the toolbox is displayed in a long, single column. If you wish to use the double-column toolbox from prior versions of Photoshop, click on the light gray double arrow at the top of the toolbox. This will toggle between the new toolbox (see Figure 2–8) and the classic toolbox (see Figure 2–9). Tool icons with a black arrow in the corner contain hidden, related tools. With your cursor, click and hold down on a tool's icon to reveal the other tool choices (see Figure 2–10). You will be using the toolbox a lot, so always keep it handy. If you close it by mistake you can reopen it from the Window menu. You will learn about most of the tools in the next chapters, but if you are the curious type and cannot wait, choose Help > Photoshop Help on the menu bar, select the section Workspace, and review Tools.

▶ *Options Bar/Control Panel:* Most of the tools selected in the toolbox have options. These are displayed in the Options bar (also referred to as the Control Panel), located along the top of the document window, below the Application bar. The Options bar is context-sensitive, which means it displays different information depending on what tool is selected. Try it out: select some tools in the toolbox and watch the content change in the Options bar with each new selection.

FIGURE | 2–10 |

Reveal hidden tools in the toolbox.

▶ *Panels:* Panels (referred to as palettes in previous versions of Photoshop), usually located to the right of the work area, help you modify and monitor your images. By default, panels are tabbed together in like-minded groups that can, in turn, be placed in docks. However, you can separate them. Simply click on their title tabs and drag them to another area of the workspace. Of course, you can dock any panel back into a group by dragging its title bar over the desired panel group. See Figure 2–11 and Figure 2–12. If you want your panels out of the way, so you can better see your workspace, just hide them by pressing Shift-Tab. To bring them back, press Shift-Tab again. If you don't see a particular panel, go to Window on the menu bar and select the panel name. Panel names with checks by them are already open. To uncheck a panel, go to Window on the menu bar and select the checked panel name to toggle it off—close it from view.

FIGURE | 2–11 |

Panels are grouped by similar topic. Select a tab to bring a panel forward.

▶ *Docks:* Photoshop CS5 offers a handy way to organize your favorite panels, called docks. Docks are located on the right and/or left sides of the screen and can hold a single panel or groups of panels. To familiarize yourself with using the docks, try the following:

1. Choose Window > Workspace > Reset Essentials to set the Essentials workspace area to its default arrangement.

FIGURE | 2–12 |

A panel can be separated from its group by clicking and dragging the title tab to a different area of the workspace.

FIGURE | 2–13 |

Undock the Swatches panel.

FIGURE | 2–14 |

Collapse a panel.

2. Undock the Swatches panel: click in the title bar of the panel and drag it into the document area. See Figure 2–13.

3. Expand or collapse a dock: click on the double arrow in the title bar of a panel. See Figures 2–14 and 2–15.

4. To close the Swatches panel, click on the Close icon on the left (Mac) or right (Windows) side of the title bar. See Figure 2–16.

5. Choose Window > Swatches to reopen the Swatches panel.

FIGURE | 2–15 |

Expand a panel.

FIGURE | 2–16 |

Close a panel.

6. To re-dock the Swatches panel, click in the title bar of the panel and drag it over the Swatches and Styles panel already docked on the right side of the screen until you see a blue outlined dock shadow appear. See Figure 2–17.

7. Close the panel by clicking the black arrow with horizontal lines in the upper-right corner of the panel's title bar and choosing Close Tab Group, or Ctrl-click (Mac) or right-click (Windows) over a title bar and choose Close or Close Tab Group.

> **Note:** *When a panel is docked the Close icon is not visible in the panel's title bar, as it is when the panel is undocked. You can also close panel groups by unchecking them under the Window menu.*

FIGURE | 2–17 |

Drag a panel into a panel set.

8. Choose Window > Swatches to reopen the Swatches panel. Notice that the panel set remains docked.

▶ *Status bar:* The status bar is located at the bottom left edge of the document window. It shows you information about a document's size and dimensions, the current tool being used and its magnification level, and more. See Figure 2–18.

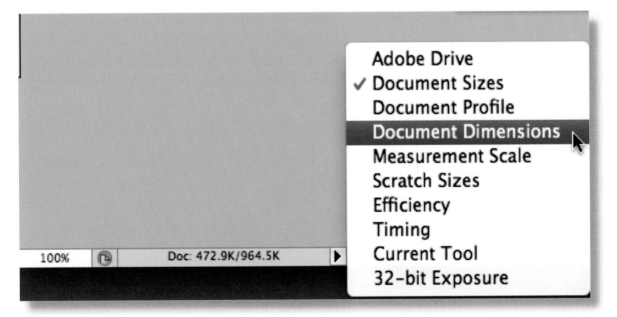

FIGURE | 2–18 |

The Status bar reveals information about a document.

▶ *Context menus:* Context menus appear when you Ctrl-click (Mac) or right-click your mouse (Windows) in the document area. They are drop-down menus that give you quick access to various features of any tool you are currently using. See Figure 2–19.

Marking the Stage

1. Place the cursor (do not click!) over the Rectangle tool in the toolbox. Note that a text equivalent of the tool name appears. This is called a tool tip. Next to the tool name there is also a shortcut key indicated. See Figure 2–20. (If your tool tips are not showing, you can turn them on using Photoshop > Preferences > Interface (Mac) or Edit > Preferences > Interface (Windows).)

FIGURE | 2–19 |

Context menu for the Marquee tool. Ctrl-click (Mac) or Right-click (Windows) to get to the context menus.

FIGURE | 2–20 |

The tool tip for the Rectangle tool is revealed.

FIGURE | 2–21 |

Click and hold on the Rectangle tool to reveal other shape options.

2. Click and hold on the Rectangle tool to open other shape tool options. See Figure 2–21. Select the Ellipse tool.

3. Click on the Foreground color swatch in the toolbox to choose a color. See Figure 2–22.

FIGURE | 2–22 |

Set a foreground color.

4. Select a color in the Color Picker and click OK. See Figure 2–23.

FIGURE | 2–23 |

Select a color from
the Color Picker.

5. To create an ellipse filled with color and have it
    automatically placed on its own layer, be sure to
    select the "Shape layers" option in the Options bar.
    See Figure 2–24.

6. Place your ellipse tool over the document window.
    Click and drag on the document window to create
    an elliptical shape. Draw four or five shapes of
    different sizes. To create a perfect circle, hold down
    Shift as you click and drag to make the shape. See
    Figure 2–25.

FIGURE | 2–24 |

Select the Shape layers option in the Options bar.

FIGURE | 2–25 |

Create elliptical shapes.

7. Unless you are up for playing around some more with this file, we are done with marking up the stage. However, save the file for use in the next lesson. Choose File > Save As. For Format, choose Photoshop. Name the file **myfile.psd** and save it to your **lessons** folder.

> Note: *You might be wondering, "What's the '.psd' at the end of my filename?" This is the native file extension for all Photoshop files. If you see a file with this extension on the end, you know it was created in Adobe Photoshop.*

LESSON 2: CUSTOMIZE YOUR EXPERIENCE

Photoshop is smart; it remembers what you like. Every time you open it and do things like drag panels into your dock, set ruler units, or change your cursor display, Photoshop saves these preferences in a Preferences file located on your hard drive. This is great when you want to reopen the program on your computer and have everything exactly where you left it. Let me show you how this works.

> Note: *You can also save the arrangement of your favorite workspaces—the setup of panels, menus, and keyboard shortcuts—to your liking (see No. 1 of the Exploring on Your Own section at the end of this chapter).*

Setting Preferences

1. Open Photoshop.

2. Click on the double arrow at the top right of the Application bar and choose Reset Essentials to set the workspace back to its default settings. See Figure 2–26.

3. Choose File > Open and find the file **myfile.psd** that you created in the last step of Lesson 1.

4. Choose Shift-Tab on the keyboard to close all the panels on the right side of the interface.

> Note: *If you do not have myfile.psd, open chap2L2.psd in the chap02_lessons folder instead.*

5. Choose Window > Layers to open only the Layers panel.

6. Select the layer called **Shape 1**.

7. In the Layers panel, click the black arrow with four horizontal lines in the upper-right corner of the window to open the panel's options. Choose Blending Options from the drop-down menu. See Figure 2–27.

FIGURE | 2–26 |

Check that the workspace is set to Essentials.

FIGURE | 2–27 |

Located at the top right of any panel is a sub menu (also referred to as a "flyout" menu) containing more options.

8. In the Layer Style dialog box, choose the Drop Shadow and Bevel and Emboss style options. See Figure 2–28. Be sure Preview is selected in the dialog box so you can see the styles applied automatically to the document. Click OK.

9. Select other layers (**Shape 2, Shape 3, Shape 4**, etc.) and apply other styles found in the Layer Styles dialog box. For example, try the Outer Glow and Satin styles.

> Note: *Yes, I know, the Layer Style dialog box can be overwhelming—no worries. I guarantee this will eventually be one of your favorite places to visit in Photoshop.*

10. Without really knowing it, you have already been setting some file preferences. To set some more use the Preferences dialog box. Choose Photoshop > Preferences > Cursors (Mac) or Edit > Preferences > Cursors (Windows). Any change you make in this box is recorded in a preferences file for the next time you open the program. There are many preference options. We will only tinker with a few. However, it is a good idea to look through all of them in case you want to make a change later.

11. Under the Cursors option, go to Other Cursors and select Precise. This changes the cursor of a selected tool from its standard icon to a more precise, crosshair indicator. See Figure 2–29. This crosshair indicates a precision cursor; that is, the center of the cursor is the exact spot where you will select, draw, or edit. This is

FIGURE | 2–28 |

Select a style option.

FIGURE | 2–29 |

Change preferences in the Preferences dialog box.

much more accurate than an icon cursor. What if you like working with both cursors? Simple! Choose the Standard cursor in Other Cursors and use the Caps Lock key to toggle between the crosshair indicator and the regular cursor. For now, let's keep it on Precise to show the advantage of Preferences.

12. Click OK to close the Preferences window.

13. Save your file as **myfile2.psd**.

14. Choose Photoshop > Quit Photoshop (Mac) or File > Exit (Windows) to shut down the program.

15. Reopen the program and your saved **myfile2.psd**. Note that your preferences have not changed. Precise cursors are still indicated in the Preferences dialog box, and the Layers panel is still open on your workspace.

Deleting Preferences

1. If you want to go back to Photoshop's default Preferences settings, first close Photoshop by choosing Photoshop > Quit Photoshop (Mac) or File > Exit (Windows).

2. Now, depending if you are on a Mac or a Windows computer, do one of the following:

> ▶ *Press and hold Option-Command-Shift (Mac OS) or Alt-Control-Shift (Windows) while you launch Photoshop. You will be prompted to delete the current settings file. See Figure 2–30.*

FIGURE | 2–30 |

The delete file prompt.

Alternatively:

> ▶ *In Windows, go to the* **Documents and Settings\username\Application Data\Adobe\Adobe Photoshop CS5\Adobe Photoshop CS5 Settings** *folder. Move a copy of the* **Adobe Photoshop CS5 Prefs.psp** *file to your desktop as a backup and then delete the one in the Settings folder.*

> ▶ *In Mac OS, go to Users, then your username folder, and choose* **Library > Preferences > Adobe Photoshop CS5 Settings > Adobe Photoshop CS5 Prefs.psp.** *Move a copy of the* **Adobe Photoshop CS5 Prefs.psp** *file to your desktop as a backup and then delete the one in the Settings folder.*

3. Once you have deleted the preferences file, reopen Photoshop to view the default setup. It will look something like that shown in Figure 2–31.

SEEING IS BELIEVING

Have you ever been in the unfortunate situation where you paid $60 to see your favorite rock star in concert only to find yourself in the last row of the concert hall wishing you had remembered to bring your binoculars? Well, you will be happy

FIGURE | 2–31 |

Photoshop with default setup.

to know that you will never have that problem working in Photoshop. No matter how many layers of objects you find yourself accumulating, there is a tool to help you see clearly where you are and what you are doing. In this next lesson, you will get up-close-and-personal with Photoshop's navigational features, such as the Hand and Zoom tools, the Navigator panel, and the screen and view modes.

LESSON 3: NAVIGATIONAL FEATURES

Magnification Tools

1. In Photoshop, open the file **chap2L3.psd** in the **chap02_lessons** folder.

> Note: *If you receive a dialog box stating, "Some text layers might need to be updated…" choose Update.*

2. Choose View > Fit on Screen to magnify the image to fit in the window area. Note that the document title bar indicates the current magnification of the image. See Figure 2–32. This number varies depending on what view you have indicated for the document. For example, choose View > Print Size, which shows you the image size if it were to be printed (a number of factors influence how an image is viewed on screen, which will be covered in Chapter 3).

chap2L3.psd @ 66.7% (photo, RGB/8#)

FIGURE | 2–32 |

The document title bar indicates the current magnification of the image.

3. Choose View > Actual Pixels. This shows you the image size at 100% of the screen resolution (you will learn more about resolution in Chapter 3).

4. Select the Zoom tool in the toolbox. See Figure 2–33.

FIGURE | 2–33 |

The Zoom tool.

5. Click once with the Zoom tool over the image. It zooms in. Click again to zoom even closer.

6. Hold down Option (Mac) or Alt (Windows) to reverse the Zoom tool (note the minus sign in the Zoom tool cursor). Continue to hold down Option/Alt as you click once on the artwork to zoom back out. Click three more times to zoom out even farther.

7. OK, let's try a different (very cool!) method. With the Zoom tool click and hold the mouse button down over the image—it animates the magnification smoothly toward you. Now, hold down the Option (Mac) or Alt (Windows) and hold the mouse button to animate the magnification smoothly away from you. This zoom feature is playfully called "Scrubby Zoom." You can turn this feature off by unchecking the option in the Options panel of the Zoom tool.

8. Let's zoom into a particular area of the photograph. With the Zoom tool selected, click once over the copyright notice in the lower-left corner of the document. Click again in the same spot to zoom into the area even closer. See Figure 2–34.

FIGURE | 2–34 |

Select an area to zoom close.

9. Select the Horizontal Type tool in the toolbox. Then click and drag over the text **2003** to select it (you will know when you can select type because the cursor changes from an I-beam with a box around it to a plain I-beam). Change the text to **2010**. See Figure 2–35.

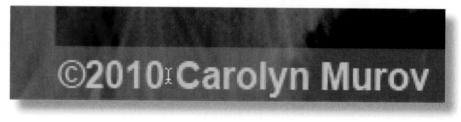

FIGURE | 2–35 |

Change the text.

10. Select the Hand tool in the toolbox (the tool right next to the Zoom tool in classic view, or just above it in single-column view). Click and drag with the Hand tool over the document, pushing it down until you see the **Tyrone** text at the top of the photo.

11. In the Layers panel, select the layer called **Tyrone**. Change the blending mode for the text layer from Normal to Color Burn. See Figure 2–36. Note that the text blends with the background colors of the photo.

FIGURE | 2–36 |

Located at the top right of the Layers panel is the drop-down menu to change the blending modes of a layer.

> Note: *There are many different types of blending modes for layers, as well as the painting tools. Feel free to explore the others (such as Difference and Luminosity). Blending modes are used a lot, so this will not be the last time you get to play with them.*

12. Be sure the Hand tool is selected in the toolbox. Note the options available for the Hand tool in the Options bar right below the Application bar. In the Options bar, select Fit Screen (alternatively, you can choose View > Fit Screen from the menu bar, or double-click on the Hand tool in the toolbox, or press Command 0 (Mac) or Ctrl 0 (Windows)). See Figure 2–37.

FIGURE | 2–37 |

The Options bar for the Hand tool.

The Navigator Panel

1. The Navigator is another way to get a good view of your work. Choose Window > Navigator to open the Navigator panel (if it is not already open). Note in the panel window a small view of the image with a red border around it. See Figure 2–38.

FIGURE | 2–38 |

The Navigator panel.

2. In the Navigator panel, slide the small arrow in the lower part of the window to the right to magnify your view or to the left to reduce it. Note that the red border adjusts in the viewing window to indicate what area is viewable in the document.

> Note: *As an alternative to moving the slider to zoom in and out, you can click on the mountain-looking icons on each side of the slider. You can also type in a zoom percentage in the lower-left corner of the Navigator panel.*

3. Magnify the image by sliding the arrow in the Navigator panel to the right. The red box in the Navigator window should grow smaller.

4. Locate a specific area of the image by placing the cursor over the red box in the Navigator panel (note that the cursor changes to the Hand tool). Now, click and drag the red border area.

Screen Modes

1. With the Hand tool still selected, choose View > Fit on Screen to see the complete image.

2. In the Application bar, click the Screen Mode button and select the Full Screen Mode option. See Figure 2–39. You will receive a warning that all panels will be hidden in this mode. Choose the Full Screen button. Press ESC or F on the keyboard to exit Full Screen Mode.

FIGURE | 2–39 |

There are three screen mode options located on the Application bar: Standard Screen Mode, Full Screen Mode with Menu Bar, and Full Screen Mode (no menu bar).

3. From the Application bar, try Full Screen Mode with Menu Bar.

4. Go back to Standard Screen Mode by once again clicking on the monitor icon on the Application bar.

5. Close the file. You are done with this lesson.

SUMMARY

This chapter familiarized you with the Photoshop staging area—the workspace and navigational elements of the program. You also learned how to set your own preferences and, if necessary, delete them. Additionally, you gained insight into how easy (dare we say "magical"?) it is to do such useful things as change your cursor icon, create a drop shadow behind a shape, and blend the colors of two layers.

▶ IN REVIEW

1. What does Shift-Tab do?

2. What does .psd at the end of a filename indicate?

3. What is Adobe Bridge? How is it useful?

4. What is the difference between View > Fit on Screen and View > Print Size?

5. What is a precise cursor? How can you change the cursor from Standard to Precise Mode?

6. What are two ways to reset your preferences to the default settings?

7. What is the purpose of the Navigator panel?

▶ EXPLORING ON YOUR OWN

1. There are many ways to customize your experience in Photoshop. Explore the various options for how your workspace could be set up by choosing Window > Workspace (or, for some features, the Workspace button on the Applications Bar). See Figure 2–40. Keep in mind, however, that you do not want to customize too much while you are doing the lessons in this book, or things might get confusing; the lessons are based on the default arrangement of the workspace and keyboard shortcuts. Options include:

   ▶ *New/Delete Workspace:* Allows you to create, save, and delete your favorite workspace setup (panels, menus, and keyboard shortcuts) for quick access every time you use the program.
   ▶ *Reset Essentials:* Resets the Photoshop interface to its default arrangement and closes any open panels.
   ▶ *Keyboard Shortcuts & Menus:* Allows you to customize keyboard shortcuts for opening application menus, panels, and tools.

Window Help

Arrange   ▶

Workspace   ▶   ✓ Essentials (Default)
                       New in CS5

Extensions   ▶
                       3D
3D   Design
Actions   ⌥F9   Motion
Adjustments   Painting
Animation   Photography
Brush   F5
Brush Presets   Reset Essentials
Channels   New Workspace...
Character   Delete Workspace...
Character Styles
Clone Source   Keyboard Shortcuts & Menus...
Color   F6
Histogram
History
Info   F8
Layer Comps
✓ Layers   F7
Masks
Measurement Log
✓ Navigator
Notes
Paragraph
Paragraph Styles
Paths
Styles
✓ Swatches
Tool Presets

FIGURE | 2–40 |

Customize your workspaces under Window > Workspace on
the menu bar.

File Edit Image Layer Select Fil

New...   ⌘N
Open...   ⌘O
Browse in Bridge...   ⌥⌘O
Browse in Mini Bridge...
Open As Smart Object...
Open Recent   ▶

Share My Screen...
Create New Review...
Device Central...

Close   ⌘W
Close All   ⌥⌘W
Close and Go To Bridge...   ⇧⌘W
Save   ⌘S
Save As...   ⇧⌘S
Check In...
Save for Web & Devices...   ⌥⇧⌘S
Revert   F12

Place...

Import   ▶
Export   ▶

Automate   ▶
Scripts   ▶

File Info...   ⌥⇧⌘I

Print...   ⌘P
Print One Copy   ⌥⇧⌘P

FIGURE | 2–41 |

When New in CS5 is selected,
context specific menu items are color
highlighted for certain workspaces.

▶ *New in CS5:* When selected, new features of CS5
will be highlighted in blue on the menu bar.
See Figure 2–41.

▶ 3D, Design, Motion, Painting, and Photography are preset workspaces designed for
a specific task within the program. When selected, panel sets associated with the
particular task are made available. For example, choose the 3D workspace option
(Window > Workspace > 3D) or from the drop-down menu in the upper right corner of
the Application bar, and note that the panel sets change to reflect that workspace.

▶ For more information on Workspaces in Photoshop, go to Help > Photoshop
Help and read the section Workspace > Workspace basics.

2. Create a new file. Use the Rectangle and Ellipse tools to make shapes. Fill each shape with a
different color (Note: to have each shape created on its own layer choose the Shape layers option
in the Options bar.) Use the Zoom and/or Navigator panel to practice zooming in and out of
the document window. Move the file around with the Hand tool. Reset your preferences.

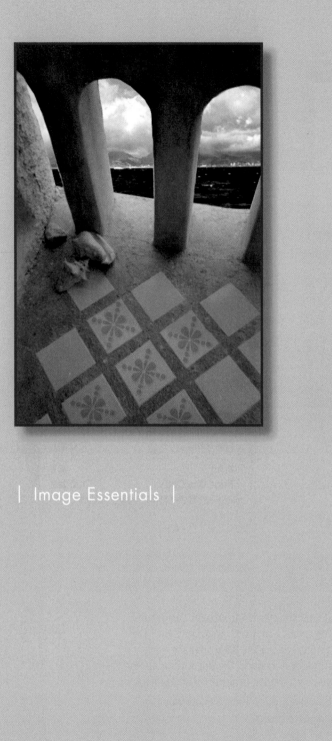

| Image Essentials |

3

charting your course

Getting acquainted with the Photoshop staging area was the essence of Chapter 2. It allowed you to get comfortable in the space so the real show can begin. As you might already know, any well-trained artist has a background in the classics. If you are an actor, you study Shakespeare's works; a painter, Renaissance art; a musician, Mozart's symphonies; a dancer, ballet. The study of the classics not only provides some perspective from the past, but, more importantly, becomes a fundamental sounding board to grow creatively. Such a sounding board for a graphic artist would be an understanding of how computer graphics are generated, and that is what this chapter is about. Your classical training begins with a study of vectors and bitmaps, with an emphasis on bitmaps, since that is what Photoshop knows best. It also begins with other vital information, such as bit depth, resolution, and image formats. In addition, you will get more practice working with Photoshop's main ingredient: pixels.

goals

In this chapter you will:

▶ *Develop a firm grasp of the two types of digital images: vector and bitmap*

▶ *Discover the meaning of zeros and ones*

▶ *Master some tricks to make resolution your friend*

▶ *Learn about image formats and get an overview of common image format types*

▶ *Explore how images are created and edited using pixels*

▶ *Explore more tricks of the program with bitmaps and pixels in mind*

IMAGE CONSTRUCTION

No doubt you are eagerly waiting to get your hands on Photoshop again. However, it would not be right to send you on the next phase of the journey ill-equipped. It would be like placing a light saber in your hand without guiding you in the art of "the Force"; you would survive a little while, probably create some really star-studded stuff, but eventually you would want finesse. Filters and effects only get you so far. The real goal is to become one with the program—to know exactly what makes it tick. This applies not just to Photoshop but to any computer graphics program. Your training begins with an overview of how images are constructed in the digital world. They come in two forms: bitmap (or raster) and vector.

THE BRIEF ON BITMAPPED IMAGES

Let's start by examining a basic black-and-white photograph. See Figure 3–1. Reproducing this image on paper is pretty straightforward: some black ink is deposited dot-by-dot on white paper. But how is this photo reproduced on a computer? Imagine this image is formed from a mosaic of tiles. However, instead of each tile being made of ceramic or glass, it is made of pixels—rectangular or square-shaped elements. When lined up side-by-side in a grid, these pixels form a complete image or pattern. See Figure 3–2. This grid of pixels is called a bitmap, and it is the manipulation of bitmapped images that is the heart of Photoshop.

FIGURE | 3–1 |

A photograph reduced to black and white.

FIGURE | 3–2 |

A photograph constructed from a grid of pixels.

Bit Depth

Two important concepts related to bitmaps are bit depth and image resolution. Let's start with bit depth. Going back to our black-and-white visual in Figure 3–1, how does the computer know which part of the visual is black and which is white? Let me explain without getting too "techie." First, you must know that the brain of the computer knows only two numbers: zero and one. Yep, no deep math here—just zeros and ones. Amazingly, how the computer calculates different combinations (or strings) of zeros and ones produces every image, letter, and movement made on the computer. For instance, if you type **shazam** on your keyboard, the computer translates that word into its own language of zeros and ones—a string of data that looks something like 0111001101101000011000010111101001100001011011010000110100001010.

Here is where it gets interesting. A single zero (0) or a single one (1) has a measurement called a "bit." Furthermore, a certain number of zeros and ones (bits) is represented in each pixel (tile) of a bitmapped image. (Are you still with us? Hang in there; it will soon be made clear.) This representation is an image's *bit depth*. In the instance of the black-and-white photo, a white pixel you see (or do not see) is translated as zero (off) in the computer brain and a black pixel is translated as one (on). Each pixel in this example is equal to one bit of color information, which can be either black or white.

Not surprisingly, a black-and-white image is sometimes referred to as a *one-bit image*. We will discuss the relationship of image color to bit depth in Chapter 5. For now, just remember that the larger an image's bit depth (accumulation of zeros and ones), the more variations of color it contains. See Figure 3–3. In general, a larger bit depth also produces a more detailed image with a larger file size.

FIGURE | 3–3 |

The larger an image's bit depth, the more variations of color (for example, shades of gray) it contains.

1-bit   4-bit   8-bit

Resolution

Resolution plays an important role in Photoshop, and the concept of resolution is going to crop up several times throughout this book. It is something of an elusive term because it can be discussed in many different contexts, depending on how an image is being used and where it is being viewed. Ultimately, though, resolution works as a measurement of how much information a file contains. For our purposes right now, resolution is a way to describe the amount of pixels in an image, which corresponds to the size (in dimensions and/or in file weight) an image might be when reproduced for print or the screen (i.e., the Web).

In Photoshop, an image with a resolution of 72 pixels per inch (ppi) and measuring 72 pixels in width and 72 pixels in height equals a 1-inch-by-1-inch image when set to a magnification of 100%. This makes an image with a total of 5,184 pixels. Huh? See Figure 3–4 for a visual.

Why 72? Well, that is the default screen resolution (the resolution set for viewing images on a screen) when creating a new document in Photoshop. If you don't believe me, go to Photoshop > Preferences > Units & Rulers (Mac) or Edit > Preferences > Units & Rulers (Windows) and see for yourself

72ppi / 72ppi / 72 x 72 = 5,184

FIGURE | 3–4 |

A 1-inch-by-1-inch image in Photoshop is set, by default, at a resolution of 72 ppi.

(or see Figure 3–5). Do not mess around with this screen resolution setting. Keep it at 72 ppi, which is the average resolution of Web images. This makes sense as Web images are viewed via a screen. (I know you're wondering, "Will my picture look better if I increase the screen resolution?" The answer is no. You are just squeezing more zeros and ones (bits) into the same area. The only thing you would be doing is making your file larger in size.)

FIGURE | 3–5 |

The Preferences dialog box for setting screen resolution.

Now, by default, Photoshop views images at 100% based on the 72 ppi screen resolution. However, if you wanted to create an image that would print 1 inch by 1 inch, the resolution needed would depend on the resolution of the output device (i.e., your printer). Let's say you wanted to create an image that needed to be 144 ppi. What would it look like in Photoshop if set to a screen resolution of 72 ppi? Let's find out:

1. Open Photoshop.

2. Choose File > New and enter the following information:

   ▶ *Name:* res_72

   ▶ *Preset:* Custom

- ▸ *Width:* 1 inch
- ▸ *Height:* 1 inch
- ▸ *Resolution:* 72 pixels/inch
- ▸ *Color Mode:* RGB Color, 8 bit
- ▸ *Background Contents:* White

3. Click OK.

4. Choose View > Actual Pixels to ensure the document is at 100% magnification. You should see a blank document that is approximately 1 inch by 1 inch. See Figure 3–6.

Note: *If you do not see rulers around the image, choose View > Rulers from the main menu.*

5. Keeping your **res_72** document open, choose File > New and enter the following information:

- ▸ *Name:* res_144
- ▸ *Preset:* Custom
- ▸ *Width:* 1 inch
- ▸ *Height:* 1 inch
- ▸ *Resolution:* 144 pixels/inch
- ▸ *Color Mode:* RGB Color, 8 bit
- ▸ *Background Contents:* White

6. Click OK.

7. Choose View > Actual Pixels to ensure the document is at 100% magnification. You should see a blank document, but compared to the first document (**res_72**), it is visually four times the size. See Figure 3–7. Even though its dimensions were set to 1 inch by 1 inch like **res_72**, it appears bigger because you are viewing it at the default 72 ppi screen resolution (remember that setting in the Photoshop preferences?). To show all the pixels for **res_144** set at 144 ppi (a total of 20,736 pixels) at a screen resolution of 72, the document must visually expand its size, precisely four times the size of **res_72**.

8. Moreover, when the file **res_144** gets to its final output source (a printer, which in this case requires an image of 144 ppi), it will print at the intended 1-inch-by-1-inch size. Choose View > Print Size to see this calculation.

FIGURE | 3–6 |

A 1-inch-by-1-inch document with a resolution of 72 ppi, 100% magnification, in Photoshop.

FIGURE | 3–7 |

Compare the size of a 72-ppi document to a 144-ppi document at 100% magnification.

> Note: *One more thing to be aware of is the file size of each of the documents created. The file size of res_144 is four times larger (61K) than res_72 (15K).*

I completely understand if you are still unsure about the concept of resolution. Perhaps you even feel the urge to slam this book shut. Before you do, however, bookmark this page; you will probably want to refer to it again, as well as the "more on resolution" resource links found in the Exploring on Your Own section at the end of this chapter. If it is of any comfort, this whole resolution idea really begins to sink in when you find yourself in an actual predicament (or two or three) using the program. Until such a predicament arrives, you will get plenty of practice with resolution throughout the lessons in this book.

THE BRIEF ON VECTOR GRAPHICS

As you have discovered, when dealing with bitmap images, an image's resolution and pixel dimensions are interdependent. Adjusting the amount of pixels per inch in a bitmap image affects its resolution, not to mention its visual quality, and vice versa. There is no way around it, unless you are working in vectors. Vectors are another way of constructing digital images. As part of your classical training, it is important to cover vectors, but only briefly. Photoshop does have some vector support (which comes in handy when you need some flexibility with free-form drawing or when importing vector-based graphics created in other programs, such as Adobe Illustrator), but, as you know, bitmaps, not vectors, are at the heart of Photoshop.

Vector graphics are comprised of points and lines that describe an object's outline or shape. See Figure 3–8. Instead of being composed of a grid of square pixels (see Figure 3–2), a vector image is drawn based on mathematical calculations of X and Y coordinates. This means vectors are resolution independent: they can be scaled large (billboard size) or small (postage stamp size) and printed to any output device without loss of detail or clarity. If so, why not use vectors for all digital images? I hate to break it to you, but there is no one-stop shop. Vector graphics are great for a certain type of image design and for free-form drawing, including bold and illustrative types of graphics (i.e., logos and text treatments that can be easily scaled while retaining crisp lines and solid colors). On the flip side, bitmaps are a great way to represent continuous-tone images, such as photographs or digital paintings that have subtle gradations of color and shading.

FIGURE | 3–8 |

Anatomy of a vector graphic from full-shade view to outline view.

SEEING ALL SIDES

Now that you have gotten an idea of the differences between bitmap and vector graphics, I must confess it is not all black and white. With the proliferation of so many kinds of computer graphic software programs, you might find yourself sifting through a lot of digitized gray matter. Programs such as Adobe Photoshop, Adobe Fireworks, and GIMP are designed to work specifically with bitmap-constructed images. Adobe Illustrator, Adobe Flash, and CorelDRAW are designed to work with vector-based graphics. However, most programs, to some extent, have the ability to import and translate both vector and bitmap graphics. At first this convergence of image types might seem confusing, but once you understand how digital images are constructed, your work as a graphic artist will become more productive.

Before moving on, you should know that there are different image formats for different types of images. A format is described by an extension at the end of the filename, as in **image.jpg** or **mywork.tif**. An image's format identifies whether it is comprised of bitmaps or vectors. It also determines an image's file size and visual quality. There are many kinds of image file formats, depending on where you are going to use the image (i.e., print or Web, or exporting for use in another program).

Most graphic programs support the use of the following:

Bitmap-only Formats

- ▶ *BMP:* Limited bitmap file format not suitable for Web or prepress
- ▶ *GIF:* Compressed format mainly used for Internet graphics with solid colors and crisp lines
- ▶ *JPEG:* Compressed format used for Internet graphics, particularly photographs
- ▶ *PNG:* Versatile, bitmap-compressed format used mainly for Internet graphics
- ▶ *TIFF:* Uncompressed format for saving bitmapped images (although in Photoshop there are some options for compression capability, with LZW being the best choice for compression with no loss in quality); most popular for artwork going to print

Vector and Bitmap-based Formats

- ▶ *EPS:* Flexible file format that can contain both bitmap and vector data; most vector images are saved in this format
- ▶ *PICT:* Used on Macintosh computers and can contain both vector and bitmap data
- ▶ *SWF:* The Macromedia Flash output format; a common vector-based graphics file format for the creation of scalable, compact graphics for the Web and hand-held devices
- ▶ *SVG (Scalable Vector Graphics):* An XML-based vector format for the creation of scalable, compact graphics for the Web and handheld devices

IMPORTING AND EXPORTING

In Photoshop, you can import (place) images and files saved in many types of formats. To import files into Photoshop and to view a list of the readable documents it supports, choose File > Place to place a file inside a currently open file or File > Open (All Readable Documents or All Formats) to open a file in a separate window.

You can also export (save) your Photoshop work to different formats depending on where it will go next in the design process (printed, published to the Web, or imported into another program). To export a file, choose File > Save As and select the format type you want to export.

PIXELS: THE MAIN INGREDIENT

Photoshop manipulates pixels like a sculptor molds clay. Pixels are the main ingredient from which all images are formed in the program. Just as a sculptor has various implements to mold his vision, the tools in Photoshop's toolbox are designed to shape pixels. For example, the Magic Wand tool selects pixels, the Crop tool deletes them, the Smudge tool smudges them, and the Clone Stamp tool duplicates them. You get the idea.

LESSON: PLAYING WITH PIXELS

The purpose of this next lesson is to show you that no matter what mysterious tricks we get into in the upcoming chapters, the underlying truth is always the same: Photoshop is just a playground for pixels. See Figure 3–9.

Lightening and Darkening Pixels

1. In Photoshop, choose File > Open. Open the file **chap3L1.psd** in the **chap03_lessons** folder.

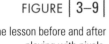

FIGURE | 3–9 |

The lesson before and after playing with pixels.

2. Save a copy of this file in your lessons folder: choose File > Save As and name your file **chap3L1_yourname.psd**.

3. From the menu bar, choose Image > Adjustments > Levels… , select Auto and click OK to have Photoshop automatically adjust the brightness and contrast (light- and dark-colored pixels) of the image. Ah, that's already much better.

Deleting and Transforming Pixels

1. With your **chap3L1_yourname.psd** file open, choose File > Open and open the file **tile.tif** located in the **chap03_lessons/assets** folder.

2. In the Application bar, click on the Arrange Documents icon and choose 2 Up. See Figure 3–10.

3. Select the Move tool in the toolbox. See Figure 3–11.

FIGURE | 3–10 |

Select the 2-up viewing option.

4. Click and drag the tile pattern on top of the **chap3L1_yourname.psd** file, and then let go of the mouse button. A copy of the image will appear on the file. See Figure 3–12. Right on!

5. Close the **tile.tif** file.

FIGURE | 3–11 |

Select the Move tool in the toolbox.

FIGURE | 3–12 |

With the Move tool, drag the selected tile pattern over the main image to copy the content of one file to another.

FIGURE | 3–13 |

Select the Magic Wand tool in the toolbox.

FIGURE | 3–14 |

Rename the layer.

6. Now, get rid of the white pixels around the tile pattern. Select the Magic Wand tool in the toolbox. See Figure 3–13.

7. With the Magic Wand tool, click on a white section of the tile pattern. All white areas of the image are selected. Press Delete or choose Edit > Clear. Ta-da! No more white pixels. The Magic Wand really is magic.

8. Choose Select > Deselect (Apple/Command-D on the Mac or Ctrl-D on Windows). The marching ants disappear.

9. Select Window > Layers to open the Layers panel (if it is not already open).

10. Double-click on the text **Layer 1** and rename it **tile pattern**. See Figure 3–14.

11. Be sure the tile pattern layer is highlighted. Choose Edit > Free Transform. In the Options bar below the menu bar, enter the following (see Figure 3–15):

> Note: *As an alternative to entering exact scaling and rotation numbers in the Options bar, you can scale and rotate the transform box that surrounds the selected image. See Figure 3–16 and Figure 3–17.*

▶ *Width (W):* 32.0%

▶ *Height (H):* 32.0%

▶ *Set rotation:* 55.0 degrees

FIGURE | 3–15 |

Scale and rotate pixels by entering exact increments in the Options bar for the Free Transform command.

FIGURE | 3–16 |

Scale interactively by clicking and dragging on a corner of the Free Transform box.

FIGURE | 3–17 |

Rotate interactively by clicking and dragging right above a corner of the Free Transform box. Note the rotation icon.

12. Select the Move tool in the toolbox. A dialog box will come up asking if you want to apply the transformation. Click Apply. (Double-clicking on the transformed image or hitting Return or Enter will work as well.)

FIGURE | 3–18 |

FIGURE | 3–18 |

Move the tile pattern over a tile in the photograph.

13. Move the tile pattern over one of the floor tiles in the photograph. See Figure 3–18.

14. Choose File > Save and save your work.

> Note: *If the Maximize Compatibility Options box appears, keep the default option selected.*

Altering, Blending, and Duplicating Pixels

1. In the Layers panel, be sure the **tile pattern** layer is highlighted.

2. Choose Filter > Texture > Craquelure from the menu bar.

3. Adjust the Crack Spacing to 10, Crack Depth to 2, and Crack Brightness to 10. See Figure 3–19.

4. Click OK to apply the effect on the tile pattern.

5. Ctrl-click (Mac) or right-click (Windows) on the **tile pattern** layer. Select Blending Options from the pop-up menu. See Figure 3–20.

6. In the Layer Style dialog box, check and then highlight (by selecting the name) the Bevel and Emboss style. The Bevel and Emboss options will appear to the right of the dialog box.

FIGURE | 3–19 |

Adjust options for the Craquelure texture.

FIGURE | 3–20 |

Select Blending Options.

7. Be sure the Preview option is checked so you can see the Bevel and Emboss options directly applied to the pixels of the tile pattern. See Figure 3–21.

FIGURE | 3–21 |

Select options for Bevel and Emboss.

For Structure:

► *Style:* Pillow Emboss

► *Technique:* Smooth

► *Depth:* 1

► *Size:* 3

► *Soften:* 10

For Shading:

► *Angle:* 120

► *Altitude:* 50

► *Highlight Mode, Opacity:* 75

► *Shadow Mode, Opacity:* 75

Leave the other settings at their default.

8. Click OK to apply the effect. To further blend the tile pattern into the photograph, be sure the **tile pattern** layer is highlighted. In the Layers panel, select Multiply for the blending mode and 60% Opacity. See Figure 3–22.

FIGURE | 3–22 |

Use a blending mode and opacity to further blend the tile pattern pixels with the photograph's pixels.

9. Select the Move tool in the toolbox.

10. Place the cursor over the tile pattern, hold down Option (Mac) or Alt (Windows), and then click and drag to make a duplicate of the pattern with all of its effects. Move the duplicate over another tile in the photograph.

11. Create several more duplicates and place them over other tiles in the photograph (Hint: go to View > Snap and check to be sure your snap option is turned off (no checkmark next to the command)). For reference, see the completed image in Figure 3–9.

> Note: *Each time you create a duplicate tile pattern, it creates a new layer for that tile object in the Layers panel. To move an individual tile pattern, select that tile pattern's layer in the Layers panel. To delete a tile pattern, highlight its layer and click on the Trash Can icon in the lower-right corner of the Layers panel. If you find yourself trying to move an element of your image and it is not cooperating, check the Layers panel and make sure the correct layer is selected. Even the pros come across this problem, so do not be embarrassed if this happens.*

12. Save the file with the new changes.

Hiding and Revealing Pixels

1. Let's open another file to add to your scene. Choose File > Open and open the file **ocean.tif** in the **chap03_lessons/assets** folder.

2. In the Application bar, click on the Arrange Documents icon and choose 2 Up.

3. Select the Move tool in the toolbox. Place the cursor over the ocean photo and drag a copy of it to your **chap3L1_yourname** file.

4. Close **ocean.tif**.

5. Position the photo in the top area of the file.

6. Choose Select > Load Selection from the menu bar.

7. In the Load Selection dialog box, select **Channel: arches** (See Figure 3–23). Click OK.

FIGURE | 3–23 |

Select a Channel in the Load Selections box.

8. A selection (marked by marching ants) is indicated on the file. This selection was premade and saved for this lesson. You will learn how to make your own saved selections in Chapter 8.

9. Choose Layer > Layer Mask > Reveal Selection in the menu bar. Amazing! The selection reveals the ocean scene, masking out all other pixels. The photo has taken on a whole new perspective—much more inviting, I think.

10. Save your file. You are done playing with pixels (at least temporarily).

SUMMARY

This chapter was heavy duty! It was a big bite into the nitty-gritty of bitmap and vector graphics, bit depth, resolution, and image formats, not to mention an opportunity to practice playing with pixels. Like studying the classics in any field, however, it was important to get this fundamental information out of the way, so you can more easily, productively, and creatively progress to the next level of Photoshop know-how.

▶ IN REVIEW

1. Briefly describe the differences between bitmap and vector graphics.

2. What are bits? Why is a black-and-white image considered a one-bit image?

3. How does resolution affect a bitmap image's dimensions?

4. Bitmap images are most common for what types of images? Why?

5. Text and logo treatments are created best as what type of graphic? Why?

6. What is an image file format?

7. What is the main ingredient in Photoshop? Name five ways you altered this ingredient in the lesson.

▶ EXPLORING ON YOUR OWN

1. In Photoshop, go to Help > Photoshop Help. Choose the topic "Opening and importing Images" and read the sections "Image essentials," "Image size and resolution," "Creating, opening and importing Images," and "Placing files."

2. Play with blending other tile patterns and background images in the **chap3L1.psd** file. Some sample patterns and background images for your use are located in the **chap03_lessons/samples** folder. You can also bring in your own tile patterns and background photos. For example, what would the image look like with an outer space or underwater scene revealed through the arches?

3. For more information on the mysteries of resolution, visit:

   ▶ The DPI dilemma (Resolution basics for beginners) at *http://desktoppub.about.com/od/ resolution/a/resolutiondots.htm*

   ▶ Jay Arraich's Photoshop Tips, Image Resolution: *http://www.garymgordon.com/misc/ tutorials/photoshop_tutorial/ref/resolution.htm*

   ▶ Monitor Resolution at The Scream Online: *http://www.thescreamonline.com/technology/ monitor/monitor_res.html*

Explorer PAGES

Darrel Anderson

"No matter what medium you work in . . . let the medium inform the process. Tap into that part of the brain that is able to recognize imagery. Don't preconceive too much, and allow the inspiration to occur to you and appear before you in the work."

 Learn more about this artist via an audio interview on the CD that accompanies this book.

About Darrel Anderson

Darrel Anderson has been creating and inventing professionally for over 30 years. His early love of science was diverted into the visual arts as a teenager. He originally pursued drawing as a means of visualizing ideas and inventions.

Digital Illustration: *leapLight*. © 2007 Darrel Anderson, Braid Media Arts

Darrel and several friends started their art careers straight out of high school. They were group-taught in the learn-as-you-go school and accepted any and all art jobs, relying on collaboration and determination. Underground Comics (under their own Everyman Studios label) and science fiction/fantasy illustration were their primary fields.

In the early 1980s an illustration job landed an Atari 800 on Darrel's desk. This inevitably lead to an intertwining of art and science in his creative pursuits. Since then he has traced the common thread of imaging through printmaking, tool building (software), animation, and illustration.

Darrel co-founded Braid Media Arts with Rick Berry. Braid is a group of creative collaborators with ongoing projects in the arts and sciences. Darrel designed and built their first Web site in 1995.

His diverse works include:

▷ Illustration of fiction by William Gibson, Arthur C. Clark, Ray Bradbury, and Stephen King

▷ Magazine illustration for *Antic, MacWorld, Computer Graphics World,* and *WIRED*

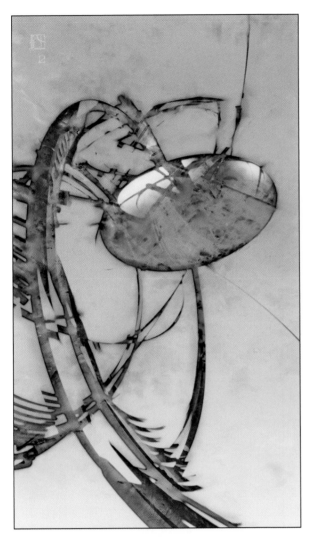

Digital Illustration: *winterWreathe*.
© 2007 Darrel Anderson, Braid Media Arts

▷ Online illustrations for the Syfy Channel; CGI for the TriStar/Sony film *Johnny Mnemonic*

▷ Creation of GroBoto, an intuitive, playful 3D graphics program built specifically for artists and designers who are not versed in the technical aspects of digital 3D

Darrel taught 3D graphics for the California State Universities' Summer Arts Program, and has been a guest speaker at Tufts University, the Digital Burgess Conference, and several Contact, Cultures of the Imagination Conferences.

About the Work of Darrel Anderson

Darrel's notes on the *winterWreathe* illustration:

"Although I use digital 3D tools extensively in my work, I have a bit of a love/hate relationship with them. I prefer work that is evocative rather than descriptive—and 3D usually has too much of the latter. Regardless of medium or tool, I use an exploratory approach—using the medium as a tool for seeing. The work is found in the process, rather than planned and executed. I find digital tools very well suited to this process, allowing infinite variety and flexibility. The ability to play with new combinations of techniques—often with no preconception of their end effect—gives unmatched creative freedom and breadth.

"Because of this approach, I rarely use the same set of techniques twice—and often don't quite remember how I arrived at the final result . . . but here are a few nuts and bolts I do remember about *winterWreathe*.

"For this image I started with a 3D model created in GroBoto. I created several Photoshop layers with shifted and/or distorted versions of the alpha channel (provided by the 3D rendering) as layer masks. This clipping and overlaying provided energy and abstraction, breaking away from the photoreal rendering. Another image (just something of mine chosen at random) was added as a color layer. Some Dodge & Burn (often utilizing layer masks) and a little blending work with a feathery brush and the Smudge Tool helped pull everything together and provide a painterly feel.

"It's nice to mix it up . . . that's what I would say about tools for success . . . And to be a good collaborator . . . it's one of the great ways to learn."

Explorer PAGES, *continued*

Digital Illustration: *clockSpring*.
© 2007 Darrel Anderson, Braid Media Arts

Digital Illustration: *copperVine*.
© 2007 Darrel Anderson, Braid Media Arts

Joel Hagen

Joel Hagen, computer graphics instructor and a collaborator with Darrel Anderson, has his own style of abstract creation using Photoshop.

Wetware by Joel Hagen. Compliments of Joel Hagen.

Ice Ram by Joel Hagen. Compliments of Joel Hagen.

| Selecting and Transforming |

4

charting your course

As you learned in Chapter 3, Photoshop knows pixels. And so will you, starting with this chapter. Using Photoshop's versatile and varied selection tools (such as the Marquee, Lasso, and Magic Wand) and transform commands (such as Scale, Rotate, and Skew), you will get up close and personal with selecting and transforming individual squares of color.

goals

In this chapter you will:

▶ *Get versatile with Photoshop's selection and transform tools*

▶ *Practice building a composite image*

ABOUT SELECTING AND TRANSFORMING

Selecting and transforming pixels work hand-in-hand. You select an area of your Photoshop image and then move, scale, or rotate it in some way (or add a fill or effect to it, which will be addressed in later chapters). Learning to select and transform pixels is a critical step in your study of Photoshop.

FIGURE | 4–1 |

A selection is indicated by a dashed line known as "marching ants."

FIGURE | 4–2 |

Each pixel has its own tone of color. Photoshop selects pixels based on their color range, or a tolerance.

HOW DO SELECTIONS WORK?

When you select something on your Photoshop document —that is, when the marching ants appear (see Figure 4–1) —what exactly are you selecting and how do you control these selections? When you examine pixels closely, you see that each pixel produced has its own shade of color. The computer can select pixels based on these shades or tones (see Figure 4–2). For example, the Magic Wand tool knows what pixels to grab by where you click it within an image and what you have chosen as its color tolerance. Tolerance defines how similar in color a pixel must be to be selected, ranging from 0 to 255 (you will learn more about the 0-to-255 range in Chapter 5). Feathering of selections is similar to tolerance; it determines how much transparency is created in each pixel.

The selection accuracy is also controlled by the frequency and/or proximity of pixels in a given area. For example, a Lasso tool controls what pixels it snaps onto not only by the contrast of colors from pixel to pixel (edge contrast) but also by the number of pixels within the tool's positioned area. The accuracy settings for the selection tools are always found in the Options bar of the selected tool. See Figure 4–3 on the next page.

All that being said, the concern here is not what feature of what tool does what (that comes next), but to get the big picture: Selections and their accuracy are determined by the color settings and location of pixels within a given area.

OVERVIEW OF SELECTION TOOLS

Before you start playing with selection tools in the next lesson, let me give you an idea of what each tool does and why one tool might be better suited for particular selections than another.

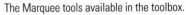

FIGURE | 4–3 |

Options available in the Magic Wand tool's Options bar.

Select Menu

The quick and easy way to select all items on a layer
is to choose the layer from the Layers panel and then,
from the menu bar, choose Select > All (Command-A
for Mac or Ctrl-A for Windows). From the Select
menu you can also choose to deselect all items on
a layer, reselect them, or invert the selection.

Marquee Tools

A marquee is a permanent canopy or bulletin board that
projects over the entrance of a building, like those seen over
Broadway theaters. They highlight, usually in bright
neon colors, the performance and performers of the
evening. In Photoshop, the Marquee tools are used to
highlight (select) an area as a shape, such as a rectangle,
ellipse, or row or column of pixels. See Figure 4–4. The
Marquee tools are the most convenient way to select
areas of an image. However, because the selections are
defined within a specific shape, the tools are not designed
to select more freeform areas of pixels. For instance, if
I wanted to select the eye of the giraffe in Figure 4–5
with minimal effort, I would use the Elliptical Marquee
tool. If I wanted to select an area of the giraffe's neck to
create a pattern or tile effect from it, we would use the
Rectangular Marquee tool. See Figure 4–6 on the next
page. If I wanted to select one of the irregular spots on the
giraffe, I would use another tool, such as a Lasso tool.

Three styles of selecting can be chosen in the Marquee
tool's Options bar:

FIGURE | 4–4 |

The Marquee tools available in the toolbox.

FIGURE | 4–5 |

Select circular areas with the Elliptical Marquee tool.

> ► *Normal:* In Normal style, you select the specific Marquee tool you want and
> then click and drag the tool over the area of the document you want to select.
> To constrain the shape proportionally, hold down Shift as you drag with the
> tool. When you let go of the tool, the marching ants appear, indicating the
> selection. See Figure 4–7 on the next page.

rectangular marquee (M)

FIGURE | 4–6 |

Select rectangular areas with the Rectangular Marquee tool.

FIGURE | 4–7 |

The Normal style Options bar.

FIGURE | 4–8 |

The Fixed Ratio style Options bar.

FIGURE | 4–9 |

The Fixed Size style Options bar.

▶ *Fixed Ratio:* In this style, you can define a selection with a fixed height-to-width ratio. An example would be an image compatible for the NTSC TV format, which requires a 4-by-3 aspect ratio. See Figure 4–8.

▶ *Fixed Size:* If you already know exactly what size you want a selected area to be, you can enter it in the Fixed Size style of the Marquee tool's Options bar. Keep in mind that the number of pixels needed to create a 1-inch selection depends on the resolution of the image (this concept is covered in Chapter 3). See Figure 4–9.

Magic Wand

If you recall, I revealed the secret of the Magic Wand tool to you at the beginning of this chapter. This tool selects pixels based on a color range or color tolerance, which is set in the tool's Options bar. See Figure 4–10 on the next page. Enter a low value to select the few colors very similar to the pixel you click, or enter a higher value to select a broader range of colors. The pixels can be selected conti-guously (sharing a boundary or touching one another) or noncontiguously.

For the giraffe on the left in Figure 4–11 on the next page, the Magic Wand tool's tolerance is set at 45 and is applied to the sky area around the giraffe. The range indicated is low enough that it selects the light pixels of the sky but not the darker pixels that define the giraffe. In the same figure, the giraffe on the right was selected with the Magic Wand tool with a tolerance set at 100. This increases the range of color possibilities that can be selected. The Magic Wand tool is great for selecting noncontiguous, free-form shapes of similar color in a photograph. See Figure 4–12 on the next page. To use the Magic Wand tool, choose the tool in the toolbox, set the Tolerance in the Options bar, and click on the area you want to sample for the selection.

FIGURE | 4–10 |

Select the Magic Wand tool in the toolbox to access its Tolerance settings in the Options bar.

Quick Selection Tool

If you are the type of person who loves to paint a selection, then the Quick Selection tool might be the tool for you. It lets you "paint" a selection that grows outward. The tool appears as a round-tip brush. As you click and drag it, it begins to create a selection around the areas you paint over.

FIGURE | 4–11 |

On the left, the color tolerance for the Magic Wand tool is set at 45 and is applied to the sky area of the image. On the right, the color tolerance is set at 100, expanding the selection area.

Lasso Tools

Unless you are a surgeon or you can thread a needle with a steady hand, the Lasso tools can be tricky to master. It takes practice, but it is worth the effort when you want

FIGURE | 4–12 |

You can use the Magic Wand tool to select areas of similar color, such as the patch on the hide of the giraffe.

FIGURE | 4–13 |

The Lasso tools in the toolbox.

FIGURE | 4–14 |

Use of the Lasso tool.

to select odd areas of an image, which might otherwise be impossible to do. There are three types of Lasso tools (see Figure 4–13):

▶ *Lasso:* This tool lets you draw selections with free-form or straight-edged segments. See Figure 4–14. To create freehand segments, click and drag around n area. To create straight segments, hold down Option/Alt, and click once at the beginning and once at the end. You can switch between free-form and straight-edged modes as you draw—cool! To close (define) the selection, make sure you are at the beginning of your selection, and let go of the mouse button.

▶ *Polygonal Lasso:* Like the Lasso tool, this tool lets you draw selections with free-form or straight-edged segments. To create freehand segments, hold down Option/Alt and drag over the area. To create straight segments, click once on the spot where the segment should begin and then click again where you want it to end. (Yes, the same commands do the opposite of the commands for the Lasso tool.) To close (define) the selection, double-click with the Polygonal Lasso pointer tool. See Figure 4–15 on the next page.

▶ *Magnetic Lasso:* Similar to the Magic Wand tool, the Magnetic Lasso tool is attracted to pixels based on color and their proximity to one another. As you move along the edge of an object you want to select, the tool attaches to pixels with fastening points. The more fastening points, the more precise the selection will be. If you draw free-form (click and then drag), the tool will automatically place fastening points based on the frequency you set in the Options bar. (To place fastening points wherever you want, simply click with the tool.) The higher the frequency number set in the Options bar, the more fastening points are created. This makes the selection border more precise. You can also determine something called edge contrast, which defines the lasso's sensitivity to edges (contrasts in color) in the image. A lower percentage detects lower-contrast edges (i.e., a white pixel next to a light-gray pixel); a higher percentage detects edges that contrast sharply with their surroundings (i.e., a dark-blue pixel next to a white pixel). Like the Polygonal Lasso tool, to close (define) the selection, double-click with the tool. See Figure 4–16.

FIGURE | 4–15 |

Use of the Polygonal Lasso tool.

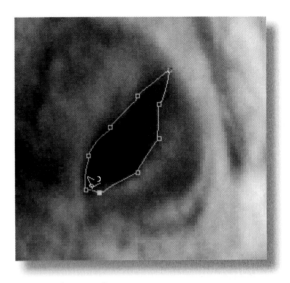

FIGURE | 4–16 |

The Magnetic Lasso tool deposits fastening points to define the selection border. In this example, the frequency of fastening points is set to 80, quickly and more precisely selecting the intended area.

Adding, Subtracting, and Refining Selection Areas

Inevitably your selections will not be perfect the first time. You might close and define the selection border and discover you missed some areas. You have two options here. You can redraw the selection, which is good practice but not always very efficient. Or, you can add to, subtract from, or intersect your selection area by choosing these options in the Selection tool's Options bar. See Figure 4–17.

FIGURE | 4–17 |

Add to, subtract from, or intersect your selection by choosing the option in the Options bar.

You can also add to a selection by using the Lasso, Quick Selection, Magic Wand, or Marquee tool and holding down Shift as you draw over the areas you want to add. To subtract, choose a selection tool and hold down Option/Alt as you draw over the areas you want to remove from the selection. See Figure 4–18. In addition to modifying a selection, the Refine Edge button in the Options bar gives you the ability to refine the edges of a selection. See Figure 4–19 on the next page. This is a great way to clean a selection's edge and preview how the selection looks against various backgrounds.

Selecting an Object on a Layer

When you begin to work with objects on multiple layers, often you will want to select items on a specific layer.

FIGURE | 4–18 |

Hold down Shift to add to a selection. Hold down Option/Alt to subtract from a selection. Note the plus or minus icon next to the selection tool's pointer, depending on your choice of action.

Refine Edge

View Mode

View: ☐ Show Radius
☐ Show Original (P)

Edge Detection

☐ Smart Radius

Radius: ━━━━━━━ 1.0 px

Adjust Edge

Smooth: ━━━━━━━ 3

Feather: ━━━━━━━ 1.0 px

Contrast: ━━━━━━━ 0 %

Shift Edge: ━━━━━━━ 0 %

Output

☐ Decontaminate Colors

Amount: ━━━━━━━ %

Output To: Selection

☐ Remember Settings

(Cancel)   (OK)

FIGURE | 4–19 |

The Refine Edge option in the Options bar further refines the edges of your selections.

FIGURE | 4–20 |

Get to Quick Mask Mode from the toolbox.

Edit in Quick Mask Mode (Q)

In the upcoming lessons, there will be plenty of opportunities to practice this selection method, but if you need to know right now, follow these three steps:

1. Choose Window > Layers to open the Layers panel (if not already open).

2. In the Layers panel, select the layer containing the item(s) you want to select. Be sure it is an active layer, not the Background layer.

Note: *To convert the Background layer to an active, editable layer, double-click on the Background layer thumbnail in the Layers panel and give it a new name.*

3. Roll the pointer over the selected layer, and Ctrl-click (Windows) or Command-click (Mac) the layer's thumbnail image. Note that the opaque items on that layer are selected in the document.

Quick Mask

Photoshop's Quick Mask selection feature can rock your world. It is complicated to get the gist of at first, but with time, it could become your favorite selection tool. See Figure 4–20. I will explain more about quick masks and let you practice masking in Chapter 8. For now, try to wrap your brain around the idea of making selections using a paintbrush (sized to your liking) and letting color differentiate what is fully and partially (semitransparently) selected.

▶DON'T GO THERE!

Once you have an area selected, whatever you do next in the program—move, add a filter, paint, etc.—will be applied to that area within the marching ants only. On occasion, you might select something inadvertently (or forget it was selected) and then attempt to do something else, like paint on another layer. When this happens, a warning circle comes up. See Figure 4–21. Do not freak out. Choose Select > Deselect from the menu bar to remove all selected areas (even those you cannot see), and then make sure the layer you want to modify is highlighted in the Layers panel.

FIGURE | 4–21 |

Warning: You cannot do that! Deselect all and check to be sure you are on the layer you want to modify.

HOW DOES TRANSFORMING WORK?

Once you select something in Photoshop, you might want to transform it. This means moving, scaling, rotating, or distorting it. You can transform numerically by entering exact numbers for the transformation in the Options bar. See Figure 4–22. Or, you can use the Free Transform command, which lets you interactively—and in one, continuous operation—transform (including rotate, scale and variations thereof, such as skew, distort, and set perspective) a selected item using selection handles and specific keyboard commands. See Figure 4–23.

FIGURE | 4–22 |

When an item is selected, you can numerically enter a transformation in the Options bar.

FIGURE | 4–23 |

The Free Transform command lets you transform an object interactively and with keyboard commands by adjusting the bounding box handles.

OVERVIEW OF TRANSFORM TOOLS

Briefly, let's go over the Transform tools:

- ▸ *Move:* Since moving (translating) things is so much a part of Photoshop, the Move tool is probably the most used tool in the program. See Figure 4–24.
- ▸ *Scale and Rotate:* To change the size of a selected object or to rotate it, choose Edit > Transform > Scale or Rotate. See Figure 4–25 and Figure 4–26.
- ▸ *Skew:* To slant an item vertically or horizontally, choose Edit > Transform > Skew.
- ▸ *Distort:* To stretch an item in all directions, choose Edit > Transform > Distort.
- ▸ *Perspective:* To apply perspective to an item (see Figure 4–27), choose Edit > Transform > Perspective.
- ▸ *Warp:* To stretch cross sections of an item, choose Edit > Transform > Warp.

FIGURE | 4–24 |

The Move tool in the toolbox.

> **N**ote: *When choosing Edit > Transform, you also have the option to rotate a selection 180 or 90 degrees clockwise or counter clockwise, or to flip it horizontally (from left to right) or vertically (from top to bottom).*

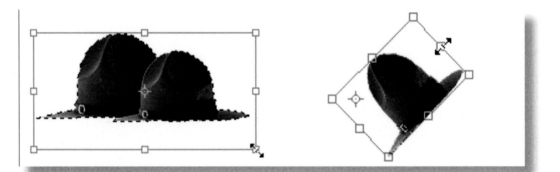

FIGURE | 4–25 |

Scale proportionally by holding down Shift while dragging the scale handles on the corner of the selection. To scale disproportionately, drag the selection handles on a corner or a side of the free transform bounding area without holding Shift. Note that the hat on the right is also being rotated.

FIGURE | 4–26 |

Position the pointer slightly outside a corner of the free transform bounding box to rotate the selection.

> **N**ote: *For quick ways to execute multiple transformations and adjust the reference point on an object, see item #3 of the Exploring on Your Own section at the end of this chapter.*

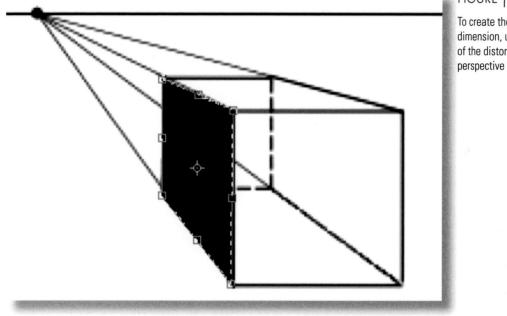

FIGURE | 4–27 |

To create the illusion of a dimension, use a combination of the distort, skew, and perspective transformations.

MORE OPTIONS FOR SELECTIONS

You can do more with selections than just transform them. You can also copy, paste, delete, duplicate, paint, draw, adjust, or add an effect or filter to the selection. Most of these operations will become second nature as you work with the program, but let me go over them briefly.

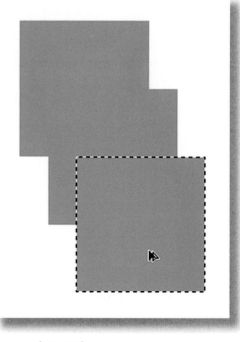

> ▶ *Copy, Paste, and Duplicate:* To copy and paste, first make your selection, then choose Edit > Copy, go where you want to paste it, and choose Edit > Paste. If you paste it into the same document, it will place the copy on a new layer, and perhaps directly over the original selection. Use your Move tool if you need to move one object away from another. Like most programs, shortcut keys for copy are Command-C (Mac) and Ctrl-C (Windows) and, for paste, Command-V (Mac) or Ctrl-V (Windows). To duplicate a selection on the same document, first make a selection, choose the Move tool, and, while rolling the pointer over the selection, hold down Option/Alt. A duplicate icon appears. See Figure 4–28. Click and drag to make the duplicate.

FIGURE | 4–28 |

To duplicate, make a selection, choose the Move tool, hold down Alt/Option, and click and drag to make the duplication.

▶ *Delete:* To delete contents within a selection, press Delete on your keyboard or choose Edit > Clear. To remove the selection and paste it somewhere else, choose Edit > Cut. See Figure 4–29.

FIGURE | 4–29 |

On the left is a duplicate of the giraffe's head. On the right the background has been selected and deleted.

▶ *Add Effect or Filter:* To adjust the color or add an effect or filter to a part of an image, select the layer and area you want to work on and then choose a filter from the Filter menu. Alternatively, you can invoke an image adjustment command (Image > Adjustments), such as Brightness/Contrast, Hue/Saturation, or Replace Color. You can also edit color fills and gradients. See Figure 4–30.

▶ *Paint, Draw, and Erase:* You can use the Brush, Pencil, and Erase tools within a selection—a convenient way to stay inside the lines.

FIGURE | 4–30 |

On the left the giraffe selection has been modified with the Plastic Wrap filter. On the right the background of the giraffe has been modified with a gradient and texture effect.

LESSON: DRESSING MAX

Finally, here is your chance to select and transform pixels. While dressing Max (see Figure 4–31 on the next page) for school (the Photoshop way), you'll learn how to use the Marquee, Magic Wand, and Lasso tools. You will also learn to move, scale, and rotate objects, and to transfer and organize selected pixels from one file to another.

Setting Up the File

1. In Photoshop, choose File > Open. Open the file **chap4L1.psd** in the **chap04_lessons** folder.

2. Save a copy of this file in your **lessons** folder. Choose File > Save As, and name your file **chap4L1_yourname.psd**.

> Note: *If you get a "Maximize compatibility" dialog box, keep the option checked and click OK.*

FIGURE | 4–31 |

Max before and after.

3. Choose View > Actual Pixels to see the document at 100% magnification. This is Max, a friend of mine.

4. Choose Image > Image Size. Note that the image is set at 72 pixels per inch (ppi)—a good resolution if you want to use this image on the Web or for screen display, or for experimenting with ideas, but not for documents that will be professionally printed. Close the dialog box.

5. Choose Window > Layers (if not already open) to view the three layers currently in the file. Each clothing item you bring into the file will have its own layer.

Selecting and Translating from One Document to Another

1. Choose File > Open and browse for **chap04_lessons/assets/hat.tif**. Click Open.

2. View the Layers panel. Note that the hat is located on a background layer. The Background layer is the default layer of any new Photoshop file. All other layers go above the Background layer, and you cannot change its stacking order, blending mode, or opacity. It is not necessary, however, to have a Background layer. Actually, I prefer to convert the Background layer into a regular layer, where I can create transparent content, move it anywhere in the Layers panel, and change its blending mode. To convert the Background layer of the hat image, double-click on the Background layer and enter a new layer name (such as hat) in the New Layer dialog box. See Figure 4–32.

3. Now, select the Magic Wand tool in the toolbox. See Figure 4–33. In the tool's Options bar, set the Tolerance to 10.

New Layer

Name: hat   OK

☐ Use Previous Layer to Create Clipping Mask   Cancel

Color: ☐ None

Mode: Normal   Opacity: 100 ▶ %

FIGURE | 4–32 |

Change the Background layer to an editable layer, so you have more options.

4. Click on the white background of the hat image to select it. Press Delete to remove the background pixels. The grid image you see behind the hat indicates that this area is transparent. The grid will not be saved when you convert the image into another format other than Photoshop (.psd) or when you print it. See Figure 4–34. You can change the grid size and colors in Preferences > Transparency & Gamut (Mac) or Edit > Preferences > Transparency & Gamut (Windows).

5. Choose Select > Inverse from the menu bar to select the hat area (the part you want!) rather than the background.

6. Position the **chap4L1_yourname** document (Max) and the **hat** document side by side on the screen by clicking on the Arrange Documents button in the Application bar and choosing the left 2-Up option. See Figure 4–35 and Figure 4–36. Select the **hat** document.

7. Select the Move tool in the toolbox. Move the pointer over the hat image and note that the pointer has a scissors icon next to it. The scissors indicate that you can move the hat by dragging it. Click and drag the hat to the **chap4L1_yourname** document (Max). Let go of the mouse to deposit a copy on the file—hey, that's sweet! See Figure 4–37 on the next page.

8. Close the **hat.tif** file. Do not save it; you are done with it.

FIGURE | 4–33 |

Select the Magic Wand tool in the toolbox. Then, in the Options bar, set the tool's tolerance to determine how many pixels within a certain color range the wand will select.

FIGURE | 4–34 |

The transparent areas of a layer are indicated by a grid pattern.

Photoshop   File   Edit   Image   Layer   Select   Filter   Analy

Tolerance: 32   ☑ Anti-alias   ☑ Arrange Documents   All Layers

FIGURE | 4–35 |

Select the Arrange Documents option on the Application bar.

FIGURE | 4–36 |

FIGURE | 4–36 |

Select the 2-Up option to view two open documents side by side.

Transforming the Hat

1. First, note in the Layers panel that the hat has been placed on a new layer at the top of the stack. Double-click on the layer title (**Layer 1**) and rename it **hat**. It is always good to keep your layers labeled intuitively. You never know when you are going to need to find something again.

2. On the **Max** document, it is obvious that the hat is too big to fit on his head. If you don't believe me, be sure that the **hat** layer is selected in the Layers panel, select the Move tool, and move the hat so it is positioned over Max's head—huge! See Figure 4–38.

3. With the **hat** layer selected, choose Edit > Free Transform. Click and drag inward on a corner of the transform bounding box to scale the hat to fit Max's head. To do this uniformly, hold down Shift as you drag. If you make a mistake, don't worry: choose Edit > Undo, or reverse your steps in the History panel.

FIGURE | 4–37 |

With the Move tool, drag the selection from one file to another to make a copy of it.

4. To position the hat, click within the selected portion of the image, but not right on center, because that would move the object's registration point, and drag the hat to the desired location. If the hat seems to be jumping around his head, go to View > Snap on the menu bar and make sure it is unchecked.

5. To rotate the hat, position the pointer slightly outside a corner of the free transform bounding box. An icon with two curved arrows will appear. Click and drag to execute the rotation. See Figure 4–39.

6. To complete the transformation, do one of the following: click on the check-mark button in the Options bar, hit Return or Enter, or double-click on the hat. If you do not want to commit to the transformation, choose the warning circle button in the Options bar or hit Esc. See Figure 4–40.

7. Save your file.

FIGURE | 4–38 |

The huge hat!

FIGURE | 4–39 |

Three transformations occur to fit the hat on Max's head: scale, move, and rotate.

FIGURE | 4–40 |

Complete the transformation by clicking the check mark on the Options bar.

Note: *For fun, play with the Warp option. Be sure the hat layer is highlighted in the Layers panel. Choose Edit > Free Transform. Select the Warp feature in the options bar. See Figure 4–41. Click and drag one of the nodes of the Warp mesh and move it to make a crazy version of the hat. Hit Esc on the keyboard to cancel the transformation and revert to the original version of the hat.*

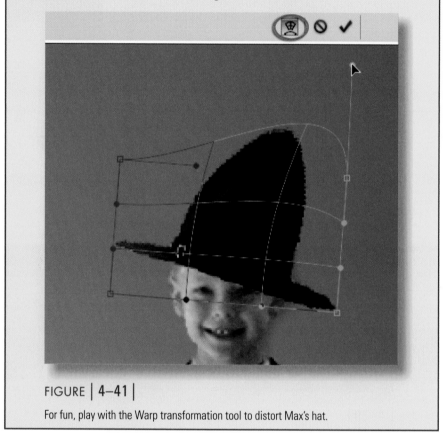

FIGURE | 4–41 |

For fun, play with the Warp transformation tool to distort Max's hat.

Adding Another Clothing Item

1. Choose **chap04_lessons/assets**. Open the **pants.tif** file.

2. Select the white background pixels with the Magic Wand tool.

3. Hit Delete to remove the pixels.

4. Choose Select > Inverse to get just the pants.

5. Click on the Arrange Documents button in the Application bar and choose the left 2-Up option, so you can see both images side by side. Refer to Figure 4–35 and Figure 4–36 again.

6. With the Move tool, click on the pants and drag a copy of them to the **Max** document.

7. Close the **pants** file. No need to save changes.

8. On the **Max** file, rename **Layer 1** to **pants**.

9. Select the pants layer and choose Edit > Transform > Scale. In the Options bar resize the pants numerically and proportionally. First, click on the chain icon between the Width (W) and Height (H) fields in the Options bar to maintain the aspect ratio of the selection. Then, type the number 65 in the Width field and hit Enter; automatically the Height field will adjust to the same scale amount. See Figure 4–42.

10. Position the pants to fit on Max. Double-click on the selection to execute the transformation.

FIGURE | 4–42 |

Resize the pants numerically. Note the chain icon between the width and height fields. When the chain is linked it indicates that the width and height will size proportionally to each other.

> Note: *If there are stray white pixels around the edge of the pants, you can clean them up. Select the pants layer, choose Layer > Matting > Defringe. For the Defringe Width, enter 4 (pixels). Click OK. Ahh, much nicer.*

11. Save your file.

Adding to and Marqueeing a Selection

1. Choose File > Open and open the file **boots.tif** in **chap04_lessons/assets**.

2. In the Layers panel, double-click on the Background layer to change it to a regular layer. Name it **boots**.

3. On the document, select the white background pixels with the Magic Wand tool.

4. Hit Delete to remove the pixels. Look closely. There are still some white areas that need to be removed within the loops of the boots. These white areas are enclosed by the red pixels of the boot and therefore were not detected by the Magic Wand tool.

5. Zoom in on the boot's loop on the far left-hand side of the document. See Figure 4–43. Select the Zoom tool from the toolbar or the Application bar.

6. Select the Lasso tool and draw around the white pixels in the center of the boot's loops. See Figure 4–44 and Figure 4–45. Close the circle shape and let go of the mouse to see the marching ants selection. This takes a steady hand, so if you find yourself selecting more than the white pixels, choose Edit > Undo Lasso and try again.

7. OK, let's add to this selection. It will take some coordination on your part, so be patient. Select the Hand tool and move the document to the left until you see the next boot loop. Or, alternatively, use the Navigation panel (Window > Navigator).

8. Select the Lasso tool and position the pointer over the white pixels in the center of the boot's loop. Hold down Shift and note that a plus (+) icon appears next to the Lasso pointer. Keep holding down Shift and draw around the white pixels within the boot loop. See Figure 4–46. Close

FIGURE | 4–43 |

With the Zoom tool, marquee the area you want to see close-up.

FIGURE | 4–44 |

Select the Lasso tool.

FIGURE | 4–45 |

With the Lasso tool, draw around the white pixels within the boot loop.

the shape, then let go of the mouse to see the marching ants selection. See Figure 4–47.

9. Keep adding to the selection. Hold down the spacebar to toggle to the Hand tool. Keep the spacebar pressed as you move the document window to the left until you see the last boot loop on the right.

10. Release the spacebar to toggle back to the Lasso tool. Position your pointer over the white pixels in the center of the boot's loop. Hold down Shift and draw around the white pixels within the boot loop. Close the shape.

11. The white areas within each boot loop are selected. Hit Delete to remove the unwanted pixels.

12. Choose View > Actual Pixels to view the boots at 100% magnification.

13. To move the boots to Max's feet, position the **boot** document and **Max** document side by side on the screen by clicking on the Arrange Documents button in the Application bar and choosing the 2-Up option. Select the Rectangular Marquee tool in the toolbox. See Figure 4–48.

14. In the Options bar, verify that Normal is selected in the Style box. Marquee around the boot on the left. See Figure 4–49. With the Move tool, click and drag a copy of the boot to the **Max** document. Position the boot over his right foot.

FIGURE | 4–46 |

Hold down Shift to add to a selection.

FIGURE | 4–47 |

Close the shape to define the selection.

FIGURE | 4–48 |

Select the Rectangular Marquee tool.

FIGURE | 4–49 |

Marquee around a boot and move it to another document.

15. Select the other boot, and move a copy of it to Max's left foot.

16. Close **boots.tif** without saving it; you will not need it again.

17. In the Layers panel, rename **Layer 1 to right_boot**, and **Layer 2 to left_boot**.

18. Select the **right_boot** layer, and then choose Layer > Matting > Defringe. Type in 4 (pixels). Do the same thing for the **left_boot** layer.

> Note: *What does "Defringe" do? When you move or paste a selection, some of the pixels surrounding the selection border are included with the selection. This can result in a fringe or halo around the edges of the pasted selection. Defringe replaces the color of any fringe pixels with the color of pixels farther in from the edge of the selection that don't contain the background color, thereby reducing the halo effect and creating a cleaner-looking edge.*

19. Move the **pants** layer above the **boot** layers. See Figure 4–50 on the next page. Position the boots, if necessary, to appear behind the pants.

20. Save the file.

FIGURE | 4–50 |

Rearrange the stacking order of
layers by clicking and dragging
a layer between two others.

Selecting a Textured Background

1. Open **shirt_blazer.tif** in the **chap04_lessons/assets** folder.

2. With the Lasso tool, draw a cursory selection around the blazer. Be sure to include the shirt and tie in the selection. See Figure 4–51.

FIGURE | 4–51 |

Cursorily select the blazer with the Lasso tool.

3. Place the **shirt_blazer.tif** and **Max** file side by side on the screen by clicking on the Arrange Documents button in the Application bar and choosing the 2-Up option.

4. With the Move tool, click and drag a copy of the blazer selection to the **Max** file.

5. In the Layers panel, rename the new layer **blazer** and move it above the other layers.

6. With the **blazer** layer selected, choose the Magic Wand tool.

7. In the Options bar for the Magic Wand tool, enter 40 for the Tolerance. Then click the green textured area to select it. Note that not all parts of the textured background have been selected.

8. Change the Magic Wand tool's Tolerance to 65 and reselect the textured background. Do you get more or all of the background pixels? Play with the tolerance until all the green pixels are selected. You might also need to add or subtract from your selection if some of the green pixels are not contiguous, or try selecting an area with the Contiguous option deselected in the Magic Wand tool's Options bar.

9. Press Delete on the keyboard to remove the selected background pixels.

10. Position and/or transform the blazer to fit Max. See Figure 4–52.

11. If you'd like more practice, add the flowered red shirt image to fit Max. (To see what you're doing more easily, turn off the visibility of the blazer by clicking the eye icon to the left of the layer.)

12. Save the file. Max is dressed and ready to head off to school.

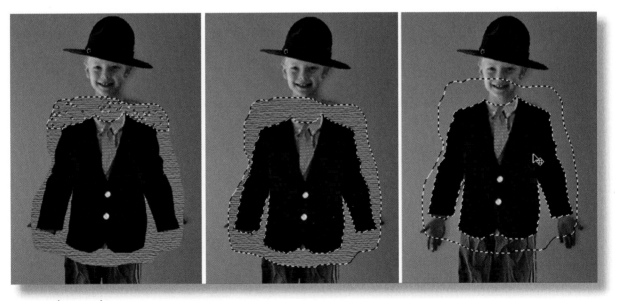

FIGURE | 4–52 |

The stages of selecting a blazer for Max (steps 6 through 9).

SUMMARY

As you have learned, selecting and transforming objects is the most fundamental procedure in Photoshop. Identifying the best tools for the task makes these actions easier and more efficient to execute, letting you move on to more miraculous creations in the program.

▶ IN REVIEW

1. Describe how the Magic Wand Tolerance setting works.

2. Name at least two ways to get better selection accuracy.

3. What selection tool is the least efficient in selecting irregular areas of an image?

4. What does the Contiguous option do when you are using the Magic Wand tool?

5. What shortcut key command lets you make straight-edged segment selections with the Lasso tool and freehand segments with the Polygonal Lasso tool?

6. Using any selection tool, what shortcut key command lets you add to a selection? Subtract from a selection?

7. Photoshop allows you to transform objects numerically, but that's not your only option. Describe the other transforming method.

8. Describe the Background layer. How is it different from a regular layer?

▶ EXPLORING ON YOUR OWN

1. In Photoshop, go to Help > Photoshop Help. Read the sections "Selecting and masking" and "Retouching and transforming" (no need to get into the retouching part of this section, which is covered in Chapter 6). Also, refer to the section on Keyboard shortcuts > Default keyboard shortcuts > Keys for selecting and moving objects.

2. To complement Max, select and bring a copy of Mina the kitty (**chap04_lessons/assets/mina.tif**) into the **chap4L1 file** you created. For an example, see the "after" picture of Max (Figure 4–31) or **chap4L1_final. psd** in the **chap04_lessons** folder to see how I placed Mina. I removed the unwanted background pixels, scaled her, flipped her horizontally (Edit > Transform > Flip Horizontal), rotated her, "defringed" her (Layer > Matting > Defringe), and added a drop shadow (Layer > Layer Style > Drop Shadow).

3. There is a quick way to execute transforms on an object without having to individually choose the Edit > Transform options. Select a layer with an object on it (like the **hat** layer on the Max file you just completed). Choose Edit > Free Transform (one of my favorite tools) or Command-T (Mac), Ctrl-T (Windows) and apply transforms with the following methods. See also Figure 4–53.

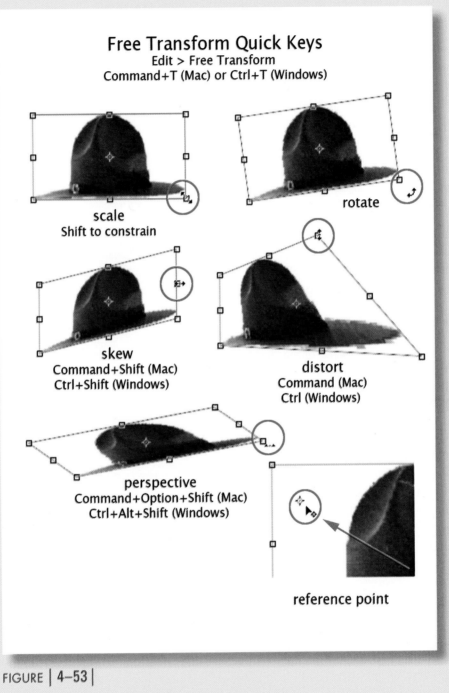

FIGURE | 4–53 |

Quick commands to execute transformations on a selected object.

Scale

To scale, drag a handle on the transform bounding box. Press Shift as you drag a corner handle to scale proportionately. To scale numerically, enter percentages in the Width and Height text boxes in the options bar. Click the Link icon to maintain the aspect ratio.

Rotate

To rotate, move the pointer outside the bounding border (it becomes a curved, two sided arrow), and then drag. Press Shift to constrain the rotation to 15° increments. To rotate numerically, enter degrees in the rotation text box in the Options bar.

Distort

To distort freely, press Command (Mac) or Ctrl (Windows), and drag a handle. To distort relative to the center point of the bounding border, press Option (Mac) or Alt (Windows) and drag a handle.

Skew

To skew, press Command+Shift (Mac) or Ctrl+Shift (Windows), and drag a side handle. When positioned over a side handle, the pointer becomes a white arrowhead with a small double arrow. To skew numerically, enter degrees in the H (horizontal skew) and V (vertical skew) text boxes in the Options bar.

Perspective

To apply perspective, press Command+Option+Shift (Mac) or Ctrl+Alt+Shift (Windows) and drag a corner handle. When positioned over a corner handle, the pointer becomes a gray arrowhead.

Reference Point Adjustment

All transformations are performed around a fixed point called the *reference point*. By default, this point is at the center of the item you are transforming. However, you can change the reference point or move the center point to a different location. This is useful if, for example, you want to rotate an arm of a character and you want the rotation to originate at the shoulder and not the center. See Figure 4–54. To do this click a square on the reference point locator in the Options bar. See Figure 4–55. You can also click and drag the reference point within the selected area if you need a more precise placement. To move an item based on its reference point, enter values for the new location of the reference in the X (horizontal position) and Y (vertical position) text boxes in the Options bar, or click on the X or Y icon and drag left and/or right (very swift!). See Figure 4–56.

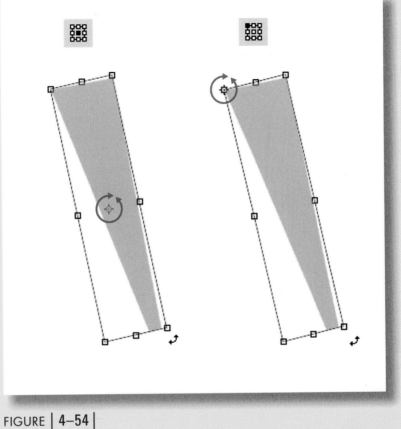

FIGURE | 4–54 |

Adjust the reference point of an object to alter the origin from which a transformation occurs.

FIGURE | 4–55 |

Adjust the reference point location in the Option bar for the Free Transform tool.

FIGURE | 4–56 |

Quickly move an item by dragging left and/or right near the X and Y position text boxes in the Options bar.

Explorer PAGES

Tim Warnock

Sunset Boulevard. Tim Warnock, Matte Painter/Concept Artist

Farewell. Tim Warnock, Matte Painter/Concept Artist

About Tim Warnock

Tim Warnock has been working as an artist for 12 years. In that time he has done a number of different things, but digital tools, specifically Photoshop, have always been central to what he does. Working as a matte painter and concept artist, he had the opportunity to be a part of films such as Silent Hill, Babel, and The Number 23.

Tim's post-secondary education began in the Graphic Design program at St. Lawrence College in Cornwall, Ontario. After completing his studies there he went on to the Illustration program at Dawson College in Montreal, Quebec. In addition to his college education he has taken 3D and matte painting training at the NAD Center in Montreal. To see more of his work, visit *http://www.thenextside.com.*

"Focus on fundamentals, perspective, color, lighting, scale, and all of those things. What you see as a mistake with a lot of young artists is they neglect those things. They might have really good 3D skills with texture and lighting, but the composition is terrible. Study the masters and even current artists who are highly regarded. When you master the fundamentals it's just a matter of learning the tools. You can then be given anything and create something that's solid."

Learn more about this artist via an audio interview in the back of the book CD.

About the Work of Tim Warnock

Tim shares his work process: "Whenever I sit down to create a painting, research is always the first thing that I do. This could involve searching for images online or going out and shooting reference material. I have a Canon Rebel XTi that takes 10MP images. As much as I can, I like to use my own images because the resolution and color depth is greater than most of what I can find online.

"Once I'm satisfied with the research material I've gathered I set to working out my composition. This is accomplished with loose sketches in Photoshop. During this stage I will often begin playing with different photos to see what might work. This 'blocking in' stage is where the perspective, color palette and composition get worked out.

"From this point I make decisions about how the detail is to be achieved. Some things can be painted. Some things will require photographic material. Some things will require 3D elements. For Desert Ruin I had done a lot of research on Egypt for another project. I had come across so many interesting things that I was inspired to do this piece. Following the process above I combine many images to create one seamless image. This is where an understanding of perspective and color is critical. Special care is given to color values to create depth and ensure that everything is sitting in the same space. These color changes are made by using QuickMask to isolate sections of the image and then color correcting with tools like Curves or ColorBalance. I like to choose one image to be my main reference for lighting and values and refer to it often to ensure I'm headed in the right direction. Paint work is mainly done with standard Photoshop brushes, but I do occasionally create custom brushes for things like leaves and grass.

"The final application of the painting is a 2.5D matte painting incorporating a crane camera move that starts fairly low to the ground and finishes with this composition. To do this the painting is constructed on layers in Photoshop and then mapped onto rudimentary geometry in XSI (3D software) using camera projections. The end result is fairly realistic parallax and perspective shifts that couldn't be easily accomplished with a 2D compositing approach."

Desert Ruin. Tim Warnock, Matte Painter/Concept Artist

| Working with Color |

charting your course

In Chapter 4 you selected and transformed pixels. Now you get to change the color of pixels. This chapter covers some fundamental concepts of color, such as how color is reproduced, color modes, and a hands-on study with color models that will pique your interest as a designer. I will also get into some important aspects of color specifically related to Photoshop, such as tips for managing color, dealing with channels, and using the color application tools.

goals

In this chapter you will:

▶ *Understand the concept of a color gamut*

▶ *Get acquainted with color models*

▶ *Know what color mode to use*

▶ *Apply color to pixels*

▶ *Explore the color features and tools*

▶ *Make gradients*

▶ *Study, hands-on, the use of color models and tonal value*

OPTICAL MIXING

Step away from your computer for a moment and find a painting somewhere. Look very closely at the painting. Examine how the brush strokes blend and how the mixing of pigment produces varied effects and transitions of color. When a color is blended with white, it produces a lighter version (tint) of the color, and, when blended with black, it produces a darker version (shade) of the color. This method of blending—mixing paint to produce colors—is different from how a computer produces color. In digital image-making, each individual color produced is contained in its own pixel area. See Figure 5–1. The effect of color blending, as occurs in a traditional painting, is only an illusion manifested by our eyes, often referred to as optical mixing.

FIGURE | 5–1 |

The image looks like a smooth gradient of color, but when we zoom in close to a selection, we see that each pixel contains its own shade of color.

Optical mixing is found in traditional painting and drawing and is often known as pointillism. Pointillism is a method of painting or illustration in which tiny dots (or shapes) of color are combined with such precision that, when viewed from a certain distance, the pattern forms a complete picture. Post-impressionist painter Georges Seurat (1859–1891) codified the technique of pointillism. Whereas other artists were blending paint colors on their canvases, he was creating the same effect by applying pigment in small dabs or points of color.

From *Understanding Art* (Seventh Edition), by Lois Fichner-Rathus, "Upon close inspection, the painting (Seurat's) appears to be a collection of dots of vibrant hues—complementary colors abutting one another, primary colors placed side by side. These hues intensify or blend to form yet another color in the eye of the viewer who beholds the canvas from a distance."

FIGURE | 5–2 |

A Sunday Afternoon on the Island of La Grande Jatte, by Georges Seurat. Using a technique called pointillism, Seurat painted this picture with hundreds of thousands of dots of color.

Chuck Close, a modern painter and photographer, uses this type of illusionary picture-making. He combines detailed pattern shapes into famous portraits. The method of creating patterns by sewing colored patches together in quilting is also a form of optical mixing. In what other ways might you think images are formed optically? See Figure 5–2.

When we look closely at a digital image, each pixel is a single color. When we view multiple pixels from a distance, they appear to be a completely blended image. Digital images produce form through optical mixing. One technique that facilitates this illusion is antialiasing. Antialiasing smoothes the jagged edges of a digital image by softening the color transition—with gradations of color or shades of gray—between edge pixels and background pixels. In other words, it makes an object that is composed of square pixels appear rounded, smoothed, or curved, not "pixelated." See Figure 5–3.

FIGURE | 5–3 |

Image with and without antialiasing. The top circle has antialiasing applied and appears smoother. The bottom circle does not have antialiasing and appears "pixelated."

SPECTRAL ILLUSION

OK, we learned our eyes have an uncanny way of optically mixing colors to form recognizable images. Now, discover that our eyes view different colors depending on where we are and the conditions under which we are looking. Every device that has the capability to reproduce color, such as a computer screen, a printer, or a TV, has its own color range (or limit), which is defined as its color space or *gamut*. For example, although today's monitors can reproduce millions of colors, what we see on a computer screen is not all the colors available in our universe. In fact, our human color device—our eyes—can perceive many more colors than any type of digitized screen or printer device can reproduce.

Take a good look at Figure 5–4. The chart indicates the visual (human), computer screen (RGB), and print (CMYK) color gamuts. (You will learn about RGB and CMYK in the next section.) Notice the marked areas indicating the gamuts. All of the gamuts overlap; each is able to view some similar color shades. However, the print (CMYK) gamut, indicated by the smallest gamut area, has the least amount of viewable color possibilities.

visual gamut

RGB gamut (screen)

CMYK gamut (print)

FIGURE | 5–4 |

The visual, screen, and print gamuts.

So, when you pick a color for your digital image in Photoshop—which, by default, uses the RGB screen gamut—and print it, you might find that color to be different from the one you picked. Most likely, the color you picked in Photoshop is not available in the printer's gamut. It gets even more particular. For example, a CRT monitor and an LCD monitor will show the same color blue differently, as will a PC monitor versus a Macintosh monitor. No doubt this can be very frustrating, but once you understand why it happens there are many ways to achieve the result you want (this is what is referred to as "Keeping colors consistent" in the

Photoshop Help file—Help > Photoshop Help > Contents). In fact, this is just another of Photoshop's many features: the ability to simulate for users what colors will eventually look like when they are reproduced on different devices. We cannot cover all the ways in this chapter, but we will get you started with some explanation of color models and modes and provide you with some additional reading in the Exploring on Your Own section.

CHOOSING A COLOR MODEL

A color model is a system for describing color. You use color models when choosing, creating, and controlling colors in your digital images. All color models use numeric values to represent the visible spectrum of color. For instance, the truest red color on a screen is indicated as 255 Red, 0 Green, 0 Blue (or 255,0,0). There are many different color models, but in computer graphics and specifically in Photoshop, we will look at the following: Grayscale, RGB, HSB, CMYK, and Lab.

GRAYSCALE

The Grayscale color model is used to select tints of black ranging in brightness from 0% (white) to 100% (black). When you convert color images into grayscale in Photoshop the luminosity (tonal level) of each color in the artwork becomes a representation of a shade of gray (you will get a taste of this in the upcoming lesson). To select colors in grayscale, choose Window > Color (if not already open) and, from the panel's Options menu, choose the Grayscale Slider. See Figure 5–5.

FIGURE | 5–5 |

The Color panel with the Grayscale model selected.

FIGURE | 5–6 |

The RGB color model.

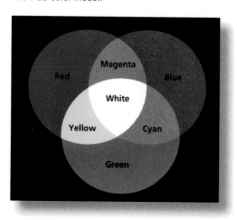

RGB

The RGB model represents the primary colors of visible light: red, green, and blue (RGB). The mixing of red, green, and blue light in various proportions and intensities produces a wide range of colors in our visual spectrum. RGB color is also referred to as additive color. When R, G, and B lights are combined equally they create white, which is what you see when all light is reflected back to the eye. (The absence of colored light is black—what you get when you wander down a cave without a flashlight.) When R, G, and B overlap, they create cyan, magenta, and yellow. See Figure 5–6. Devices that reproduce color with light are using the RGB color model. Examples are your TV, the miniscule screen on your PDA, and, of course, your computer monitor.

Each component (red, green, or blue) in the RGB color model is given a value ranging from 0 to 255. This means you can have a total of 256 shades of red, 256 shades of green, and 256 shades of blue, and any combination thereof (a lot of colors!). For example, the most intense red color is represented as 255 (R), 0 (G), 0 (B), and a shade of deep purple is represented as 137 (R), 95 (G), 137 (B). See Figure 5–7.

Photoshop also includes the Web Color model, a modified RGB model that indicates a spectrum of colors most appropriate for use on the Web. The color components in the Web Color space are measured using hexadecimal, a number/letter system used to represent colors. For example, the same shade of deep purple from Figure 5–7 in hexadecimal is indicated as #895F89. See Figure 5–8.

FIGURE | 5–7 |

The Color panel with the RGB model selected.

FIGURE | 5–8 |

The deep purple shade from Figure 5–7 in hexadecimal is indicated as #895F89.

FIGURE | 5–9 |

The HSB color model in the Color panel.

HSB

Color can also be defined as levels of HSB—hue, saturation, and brightness. Hue identifies a main color property or name, such as "blue" or "orange." It is measured by a percentage from 0 to 360 degrees, as if picking colors from a standard color wheel. (See the Exploring on Your Own section of this chapter for color wheel examples.) Saturation is the strength or purity of color. It is measured as an amount of gray in proportion to the hue, ranging from 0% (gray) to 100% (fully saturated). Brightness is the relative lightness or darkness of a hue, measured as a percentage from 0% (black) to 100% (white). See Figure 5–9.

CMYK

In contrast to the RGB color model, which reproduces color based on light, the CMYK model reproduces color based on pigment or ink. The colors of CMYK—cyan (C), magenta (M), yellow (Y), and black (K, or key)—are called subtractive, because when you add these pigments to a white page or canvas, they subtract or absorb some of the light, leaving what is left over to reflect back to your eyes. When the colors overlap, interestingly, they produce red, green, and blue (RGB). See Figure 5–10.

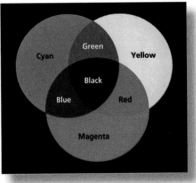

FIGURE | 5–10 |

The CMYK color model.

The "black" part of the CMYK color model is a bit elusive. To print a true black color on white, a higher percentage of cyan is mixed with magenta and yellow; it is not really an equal amount of each color as Figure 5–10 might lead you to believe. An equal mix of cyan, magenta, and yellow would actually result in muddy brown, not black, because of the absorption that occurs when ink hits paper. This is why black ink is used in addition to the subtractive primaries cyan, magenta, and yellow in four-color printing.

FIGURE | 5–11 |

The CMYK color model selected in the Color panel.

Each color component of the CMYK model is represented by a percentage ranging from 0% to 100%. To produce a shade of mauve-colored paint, for example, you mix 51% cyan, 70% magenta, 24% yellow, and 3% black. See Figure 5–11. In the print industry, this combining of the CMYK colors is called four-color process (or full-color printing). The individual colors produced by the mixing of any of these four colors are appropriately identified as process colors. In addition to process colors, another color type used in printing is spot colors. These are special colors composed of premixed inks that require their own printing plate other than the ones used for four-color processing. You will run into process and spot color types as you work with colors in Photoshop, but don't worry about them right now. Preparing an image for a professional print job can easily become an advanced topic beyond the scope of this book. A good start is to know that if your Photoshop graphic is going to go to print, you should choose colors in the CMYK model. If the project is destined for the WEB, using the RGB model is more appropriate.

LAB

In Photoshop, color can also be defined as Lab, based on the human perception of color—the colors seen by a person with normal vision. The primary color components of Lab include lightness (or L) and two chromatic components: "a" for green and red and "b" for blue and yellow. See Figure 5–12. Interestingly, Lab color is not often used by the average Photoshop user. However, it plays a vital role behind the scenes. Lab describes color by how it looks to the human eye rather than through the lens (limited color range) of a particular device (a monitor, digital camera, or desktop printer). That is why Lab is considered a device-independent color model, which makes it a great color mode for Photoshop to use when it needs to convert colors based on a user's specified color management system. You could think of it as the color system used to adjust colors between color systems. If we just lost you there, don't worry. It is good to know Lab exists, but it's not necessary to completely comprehend it in the initial stages of your Photoshop study.

FIGURE | 5–12 |

The Lab color model.

GETTING IN THE MODE

Although you can select colors from various color models, ultimately you will want to set up your Photoshop image to a specific color mode or working space depending on the artwork's intended purpose. A color mode determines how your artwork will be output, either for display on the screen (RGB) or for print (CMYK). When you create a new document in Photoshop, you must specify the color mode. You can do this when you first create the document or by switching modes while working on the document. See Figure 5–13. The main color modes are Bitmap, Grayscale, RGB Color, CMYK Color, and Lab Color.

FIGURE | 5–13 |

Set the color mode of a document.

Photoshop also includes specialized modes (such as Duotone, Multichannel, and Indexed Color) that you can delve into on your own. You can change between the CMYK and RGB Color modes at any time by choosing Image > Mode on the menu bar. There are a couple of reasons you might want to change color mode: you want to use one of Photoshop's tools or filters, which can only be applied when the document is in RGB Color mode, or you change your mind about where you want to output your artwork. Be aware that moving between modes can cause significant shifts in the colors you see on the screen, and it can degrade the color accuracy of the image if you switch modes too many times.

Why all this color mode business? Well, remember, when it comes to color reproduction, what you see is not necessarily what you will get from print to screen and screen to print, but it doesn't hurt to try every means possible to come close. Setting the proper color mode is one of those means; you specify the mode when you first make the document (File > New) or while working on the document (Image > Mode).

APPLYING COLOR

Applying color in Photoshop starts out easily enough. First choose the color you want, and then apply it to a selected area with a command or tool. The hard part comes in trying to decide what color you want. There are, of course, numerous "theoretical ways" in which to pick colors that work well together. One suggestion is to use a standard color wheel to identify complementary colors; colors that are opposite each other on the color wheel, such as blue and orange. (For examples and more information on color wheels, see the Exploring on Your Own section at the end of this chapter.) The use of color models or wheels to mix and choose a color

FIGURE | 5–14 |

The upper image indicates options for the foreground and background selection area of the toolbox. The lower image shows how erasing an image reveals the background color (white).

FIGURE | 5–15 |

Select the Paint Bucket tool to fill in selections.

FIGURE | 5–16 |

Select the Eyedropper tool and take a sample of color from an image.

can help to identify color based on a numeric system, but for the inquisitive artist, it might be just as well to play with colors until you see something you like. Just remember that the color you see on the screen might not visually reproduce exactly as the same color in another medium, such as on paper.

In Photoshop, you choose colors for either a foreground or background. The foreground color is used to paint, fill, and stroke selections, while the background color is used to make gradient fills and fill in the erased areas of an image. See Figure 5–14.

Color is applied using the Paint Bucket tool or a drawing or brush tool, or by choosing Edit > Fill or Stroke. See Figure 5–15. You can also take a sample of an existing color within an image with the Eyedropper tool. See Figure 5–16.

You can choose colors in the Color panel, the Color Picker (accessed by clicking the foreground or background color selection box in the toolbox), or the Swatches panel. You can also create graduated blends of color using the Gradient tool. Each of these color selection options is described in the sections that follow.

THE COLOR PANEL

The Color panel (see Figure 5–17) allows you to choose various color models and to switch between choosing and adjusting colors on either the foreground or background of a selected object.

THE COLOR PICKER AND COLOR LIBRARIES

The Color Picker (see Figure 5–18) is a sophisticated version of the Color panel, offering the option to view, select, and adjust colors from a number of color models in one window. It can be a little overwhelming, so we will break it down for you in the following figures.

At the top of the window, the Color Picker title appears followed by the words Foreground Color or Background Color to make you aware of the color being changed (refer to Figure 5–18). You choose colors on the left side of the Color Picker. See Figure 5–19. The spectrum bar on the right is where you pick the hue, such as red, blue, or green. The large box to the left allows you to adjust the hue's saturation (moving horizontally) and brightness (moving vertically).

FIGURE | 5–17 |

Go to Window > Color (if not already open) to open the Color panel.

The area shown in Figure 5–20 is where you preview the colors you are selecting in the Color Picker. Your current color selections are updated automatically in the top area of the box, while the lower part indicates the original color of the current foreground color. Gamut warnings appear next to the color indicator if you have chosen a color that is outside either the Web-safe (the 3D box icon) or the CMYK

FIGURE | 5–18 |

Full view of the Color Picker.

FIGURE | 5–19 |

The left side of the Color Picker is for choosing colors.

(alert triangle icon) gamut. When you click on the 3D box icon, the color shifts to the closest Web-safe color. Similarly, when you click on the alert triangle, the color shifts to the closest CMYK (print) color. This is a really handy feature!

On the right side of the Color Picker (see Figure 5–21 on the next page) you can adjust colors numerically in any of the four color models: HSB, RGB, CMYK, and Lab. The hexadecimal color code (#) for selected colors is provided for artwork intended for Web pages.

By choosing the Color Libraries button at the top right of the Color Picker (refer to Figure 5–18), a whole new

FIGURE | 5–20 |

In the Color Picker, there is an area to preview a color you have chosen above the original color of the current foreground color.

FIGURE | 5–21 |

Adjust colors numerically on the right side of the Color Picker.

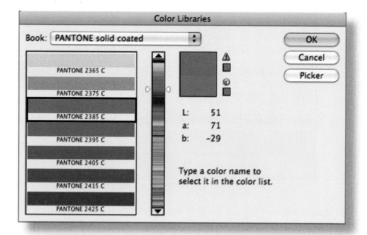

FIGURE | 5–22 |

Color Libraries area of the Color Picker.

FIGURE | 5–23 |

The Swatches panel.

FIGURE | 5–24 |

Click on a swatch to use that color in your image.

world of color possibilities emerges. This area (see Figure 5–22) lets you choose predefined color libraries, equivalent to those in printed swatch books, such as PANTONE or TRUMATCH.

THE SWATCHES PANEL

After you spend long hours picking your favorite colors, it is good to know you can save them in the Swatches panel. See Figure 5–23. To apply your saved colors to selected objects, click on your saved swatches in the Swatches panel window. See Figure 5–24. You can make swatch libraries to reuse in other documents or use one of the many already provided for you. The Swatches panel will not only save and load your specific color selections, but also will load other custom color libraries.

THE GRADIENT TOOL AND GRADIENT PANEL

Gradients are graduated color blends. They are used to create smooth transitions of color within an object or across multiple objects, giving them a more dimensional look. Gradients come in several varieties, including linear, radial, angle, reflected, and

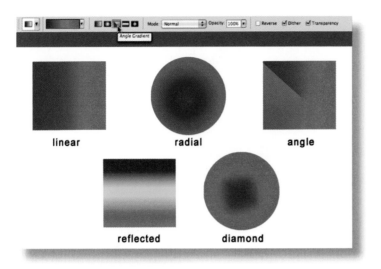

FIGURE | 5–25 |

Gradient Options bar and examples of the different gradient blends.

diamond, any of which you can choose from the Gradient tools Options bar. See Figure 5–25. Gradients are created in the Gradient Editor (see Figure 5–26) and then applied with the Gradient tool (see Figure 5–27) in the toolbox. To get to the Editor, select the Gradient tool in the toolbox, and then click inside the gradient sample area in the Options bar to open the Editor and edit the gradient (refer to Figure 5–26 for steps).

FIGURE | 5–26 |

To modify or create new gradients, use the Gradient Editor.

FIGURE | 5–27 |

Gradient tool.

Solid gradients are the most common Gradient Type to choose in the Gradient Editor, but you can also have fun with Noise gradients, a more random blending of color with variable roughness, and create gradients from opaque color to varying levels of transparency. Expect to spend a lot of time in the Editor making and saving new gradients. You will get some practice in the next lesson.

ADJUSTING COLOR

A big part of dealing with color in Photoshop is adjusting colors that are already in an image. There are a multitude of image adjustment options (Image > Adjustments) that can absorb your time and creativity, including options to change the tonal quality of a photograph (highlights, shadows, and midtones) and a photograph's hue and saturation levels. You will get into adjusting color extensively in Chapter 6. But first, let me explain two important concepts related to color adjustment: channels and bit depth.

ABOUT CHANNELS AND BIT DEPTH

We cannot skip the concept of channels and the effect of bit depth when working with color in Photoshop. Inevitably, you will run into both. When you really start getting into the intricacies of color correction and manipulation, channels will provide the necessary clues to attain the result you want. Channels are grayscale images that store information about each primary color of a color model. For example, the RGB model contains a red channel, a green channel, a blue channel, and a composite channel (which is all three channels combined and what you normally see when you view the image). To view the channels available in any document, choose Window > Channels, if not already open. See Figure 5–28.

Each channel can be edited separately, giving you full control over specific ranges of color in the image. For example, if your photograph is too red, you can lessen the amount of red in the image with the Channel Mixer (Image > Adjustments > Channel Mixer). See Figure 5–29. You can also create additional channels, such as a spot color to be used in the printing process or an alpha channel, which stores a specific selection or mask (these will be covered in Chapter 8).

The more channels in an image, the larger the image file size, which is where bit depth comes in again. Remember, in Chapter 3, we mentioned that the larger an image's bit depth (accumulation of zeros and ones), the more variations of color an image can contain. Moreover, the more variations, the larger the image file size. All of this bit depth information is stored in channels. A black-and-white image, also called a one-bit image or bitmap, has one channel and a bit depth of 1, with the possibility of holding only two colors: black and white. See Figure 5–30. The same image saved in CMYK color, which has four channels and more room to store colors, has a file size of 351.1K as compared to only 11K for the black and white—heavy! See Figure 5–31.

There actually is method to this madness, but at this point all you need to understand is that bit depth, channels, and color models are all interrelated:

> ▶ Bitmap images have one channel and contain 1 bit of color (black and white).

FIGURE | 5–28 |

The Channels panel.

FIGURE | 5–29 |

Adjust the red pixels in the image using the Channel Mixer.

FIGURE | 5–30 |

A one-bit image (or bitmap) has one channel, which supports a bit depth of two colors, black and white. The file size of this image is 11K.

FIGURE | 5–31 |

An image saved in the CMYK Color mode has four channels and more room to store colors. The file size of this image is 351.1K.

- Grayscale images have one channel that contains 8 bits of color, which produce 256 different shades of gray.
- RGB images have three channels of color that contain 8 bits of color per channel, which can produce 256 shades for each of the colors red, green, and blue. Remember that each bit contains two possible values: 0 or 1. To calculate the total possible number of shades within a single color, take 2 to the 8th power (8 bits): $2 \times 2 \times 2 \times 2 \times 2 \times 2 \times 2 \times 2 = 256$ shades. To calculate the total number of colors in an entire RGB image, take 256 shades to the 3rd power (red, green, and blue): $256 \times 256 \times 256 = 16.7$ million colors.
- CMYK images have four channels of color that contain 8 bits of color per channel, which can produce 256 shades of each of the colors cyan, magenta, yellow, and black. You do the math!

Note: *Catering to the "more is better" world that we seem to live in, Photoshop also offers the capability of creating images containing 16 bits (65 thousand shades) or 32 bits (four billion shades) of color per channel, expanding the amount of color variations that can be stored in the image. Why so many? The need is specific depending on the area of computer graphics. For instance, in the realm of digital photography, photographers use HDR, or high-dynamic range, to pull out details and nuances in their photos that may be invisible to the naked eye. HDR is a term often associated with 32-bit images. In contrast, 8-bit and 16-bit images are considered LDR, or low-dynamic range. (Note that there are many fine details that differentiate an HDR from an LDR image that go well beyond the scope of this book.)*

LESSON: PLAYING WITH COLOR MODELS

In this lesson, you'll play with pairing complementary colors, blending them with gradients, and switching to grayscale. Refer to Figure 5–32.

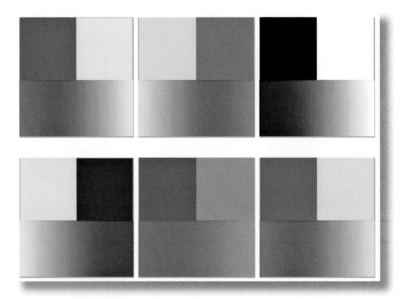

FIGURE | 5–32 |

Lesson example shown in grayscale.

Setting Up the File

1. In Photoshop, choose File > Open. Open the file **chap5L1.psd** in the **chap05_ lessons** folder.

2. Save a copy of this file in your lessons folder: choose File > Save As and name your file **chap5L1_yourname.psd**. This file contains a template and guides for you to build the color models lesson. Be sure to chose Reset > Essentials at the top right of the Application bar to reset your workspace to the default setting. Refer to figure 5–33.

> **Note:** *If you do not see the guidelines, choose View > Show > Guides. Also, make sure Snap is checked under View > Snap.*

3. Open the Layers panel, if it is not already open (Window > Layers). Select **Layer 1** and name it **red**.

FIGURE | 5–33 |

To reset to the Essentials workspace, choose Reset Essentials from the Workspace options found on the Application bar.

Creating True Opposites

1. Click on the foreground color swatch in the toolbox to open the Color Picker.

2. In the RGB model settings fields, enter 255 for red, 0 for green, and 0 for blue. Red 255 is the truest red color you can create on the screen. Click OK. See Figure 5–34.

3. Select the Rectangle tool in the toolbox. See Figure 5–35.

FIGURE | 5–34 |

Select a true red in the Color Picker.

FIGURE | 5–35 |

Select the Rectangle tool.

FIGURE | 5–36 |

Select the Fill pixels option in the Rectangle tool's Options bar.

4. In the Options bar, select the Fill pixels option. See Figure 5–36.

5. In the Options bar, select the Geometry options pop-up to display the options for the Rectangle tool (the second down-pointing arrow from the left of the Options bar). In the Rectangle Options box, choose Fixed Size. For W, enter **.62 in.** and for H, enter **.66 in.** See Figure 5–37.

> Note: *As an alternative to setting a fixed size for the rectangle, you can choose Unconstrained and draw the rectangle free-form using the guides and template as positioning markers.*

6. Click on the down-pointing arrow of the Geometry options pop-up again to close it.

7. Place your cursor in the upper-left corner of the first rectangle or shape indicated in the file. Then, click once to place the fixed-size rectangle—or click and drag down if you are creating an unconstrained rectangle. See Figure 5–38.

FIGURE | 5–37 |

Set a fixed size for the rectangle in its Options bar.

FIGURE | 5–38 |

Place the rectangle on the document.

8. Select the Move tool, and place the pointer over the red rectangle you just created.

9. Hold down Option/Alt, and then click and drag to the right to make a copy of the rectangle. Place it right next to the first rectangle. Now you have what appears to be a red rectangle.

> Note: *As you drag the duplicate, also hold down Shift to constrain its horizontal positioning.*

10. Note that when you make a duplicate it creates a new layer in the Layers panel (red copy). Rename this layer **cyan**.

11. With the **cyan** layer selected, choose Image > Adjustments > Invert to create the complement (invert or dyad) of the red color, which is cyan.

> Note: *In the Exploring on Your Own section of this chapter, study the color wheels. Identify the red section in the wheel, and note the cyan section directly opposite it. Interestingly, the RGB and CMYK color models overlap in the color wheel to create a full spectrum of colors.*

12. Create a new layer (Layer > New > Layer) and name it **green**.

13. Click on the foreground color box in the toolbox to open the Color Picker.

14. In the RGB model settings fields, enter **0** for red, **255** for green, and **0** for blue.

> Note: *You can also set this color using the Color panel (Window > Color). In the Color panel, if not already selected, choose the RGB Sliders option from the panel's options menu.*

15. Select the Rectangle tool in the toolbox.

16. Click on the upper-left corner of the boxed area next to the cyan rectangle to create a green rectangle, or drag a box approximately the same size as the others. See Figure 5–39.

17. Select the Move tool, hold down Alt/Option, and create a duplicate of the green box right next to itself.

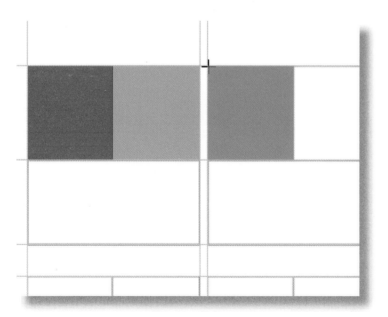

FIGURE | 5–39 |

Create another colored rectangle on a new layer.

18. Rename the duplicate layer **magenta**, the complement (invert or dyad) of green.

19. Choose Image > Adjustments > Invert—or press Command-I (Mac) or Ctrl-I (Windows)—to convert the color to magenta.

20. Click on the foreground color box in the toolbox to open the Color Picker one more time.

21. In the RGB model settings area, enter **0** for red, **0** for green, and **255** for blue.

22. Create a new Layer and name it **blue**.

23. Create a blue rectangle in the boxed area next to the magenta rectangle.

24. Duplicate the rectangle using the Move tool.

25. Rename the duplicate layer **yellow**.

26. Invert the color. See Figure 5–40.

27. Save your file.

FIGURE | **5–40** |

Lesson with inverted colors.

Creating a Gradient Between Two Complements

1. Select the Gradient tool in the toolbox. See Figure 5–41.

2. Click inside the gradient sample in the Options bar to open the Gradient Editor. See Figure 5–42.

3. Let's create a custom gradient using the red and cyan complements. This will blend the hues between the two, including chromatic gray in the center. Reposition the Gradient Editor by dragging from its toolbar, so you can see the red and cyan rectangles on the document.

FIGURE | **5–41** |

Select the Gradient tool.

FIGURE | **5–42** |

To open the Gradient Editor, click inside the gradient sample in the Options bar.

▶ DON'T GO THERE

Be sure to click inside the gradient sample area, not on the down-pointing arrow next to it. The options under the down-pointing arrow only give you the currently saved gradients, not the full Gradient Editor window.

4. In the Gradient Editor, select the color stop in the left-hand bottom corner of the gradient ramp (it will highlight in black). See Figure 5–43.

5. Position the pointer over the red rectangle in your document and note that the pointer changes into an Eyedropper tool. Click on the red to take a sample of the color. The sample is automatically placed into the selected color stop of the gradient ramp. See Figure 5–44.

6. Select the color stop on the right-hand bottom side of the gradient ramp.

7. Take a sample of the cyan-colored rectangle in the document. The gradient between the two colors is created.

FIGURE | 5–43 |

Select a color stop to apply a color to the gradient.

FIGURE | 5–44 |

Take a sample of color to apply to the selected color stop.

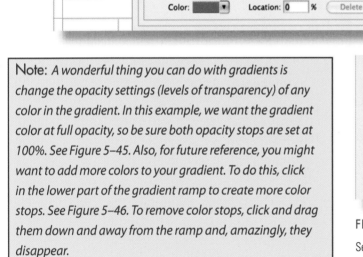

Note: *A wonderful thing you can do with gradients is change the opacity settings (levels of transparency) of any color in the gradient. In this example, we want the gradient color at full opacity, so be sure both opacity stops are set at 100%. See Figure 5–45. Also, for future reference, you might want to add more colors to your gradient. To do this, click in the lower part of the gradient ramp to create more color stops. See Figure 5–46. To remove color stops, click and drag them down and away from the ramp and, amazingly, they disappear.*

FIGURE | 5–45 |

Set the opacity stops at 100%.

8. Select New to define (save) the gradient in the gradient sample area. Click OK to close the Gradient Editor.

9. OK, you have made the gradient, now let's apply it to the document. Create a new layer and name it **gradient1**.

10. Select the Rectangular Marquee tool in the toolbox—be sure it is the Add this as step #11, and rename steps after Marquee tool, not the Rectangle tool.

FIGURE | 5–46 |

Add color stops to create more color blends.

FIGURE | 5–47 |

Select the Linear Gradient option in the Gradient tool Options bar.

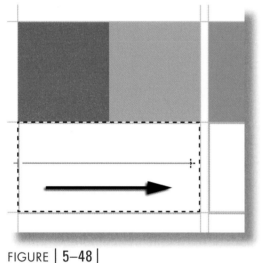

FIGURE | 5–48 |

Apply the gradient. Click and drag with the tool from left to right.

11. Choose View > Snap To > Guides, so that the selection will snap nicely to the guides in the next step.

12. Select the rectangle area below the red and cyan boxed areas. Marching ants should appear, indicating the selection.

13. Select the Gradient tool in the toolbox. Verify that the Linear Gradient effect is selected in the Gradient tool options bar. See Figure 5–47.

14. Hold down Shift, click and drag the tool from left to right in the selected area, and then let go to apply the gradient. See Figure 5–48.

15. Create a new layer and name it **gradient2**.

16. Follow steps 1–15 to create and apply another new gradient using green and magenta under the green and magenta boxed areas.

17. Ditto for the blue and yellow area. See Figure 5–49.

18. Save your file.

Exploring Complementary Hues

1. Let's do a little experiment. First, choose View > Show > Guides to turn off the guides in the document and get a better look at what you are doing.

2. In the Layers panel, select the top layer (**gradient3**), hold down Shift, and then click on the lower layer (**red**). This action selects all the layers between **gradient3** and **red**. See Figure 5–50. Do not select the template layer set and/or Background layer.

3. In the Layers panel, click on the down arrow with four bars in the upper-right corner of the panel to access more layer options. Choose

FIGURE | 5–49 |

The lesson with gradients applied.

FIGURE | 5–50 |

Merge linked layers.

FIGURE | 5–51 |

All the layers are merged and renamed.

Merge Down to combine the selected layers. See Figure 5–50. Rename the layer **top_color_set**. See Figure 5–51.

4. It's not a bad idea to save your file with a new name, preserving the original file with all layers intact; you never know when you might need to access those layers again. Choose File > Save As and save the file in your lessons **folder as chap5L1_yourname_merge.psd**.

FIGURE | 5–52 |

Duplicate the color set layer.

5. Make a duplicate of the top color set using the Option/ Alt key and the Move tool. Drag this duplicate below the top color set on the document. See Figure 5–52.

6. In the Layers panel, rename the copied layer **bottom_ color_set**.

7. Select the **top_color_set** layer and then choose Window > Adjustments to open the panel. Next, click on the Hue/Saturation option in the Adjustments panel. See Figure 5–53. Slowly drag the Hue slider all the way to the right and watch how the colors change through all the complementary hues. Move the Hue slider all the way to the left and you get the same result. Set the Hue slider to around 40 to see the intermediate complementary colors within the spectrum. See Figure 5–54 and Figure 5–55. These sets of colors are good starting points for creating colors that go well together.

8. While you are in the Hue/Saturation dialog, play with the Saturation and Lightness settings. Saturation increases or decreases the intensity (vibrancy) of the colors. Lightness lightens and darkens the colors. Click OK.

9. Save the file.

FIGURE | 5–53 |

Select the Hue/Saturation option in the Adjustments panel.

FIGURE | 5–54 |

Adjust the Hue slider to see the shift of complementary colors.

FIGURE | 5–55 |

Example of lesson with shifted, complementary hues.

Go Grayscale

1. Every color in the spectrum has an equivalent gray tone. To identify the gray tones in the image, choose Image > Mode > Grayscale. Choose OK (or the Don't Flatten option) to preserve the layers in the document. If the window pops up, click on the Discard button to discard the color in the image.

> Note: *Once a file is converted to grayscale, it completely discards all color information. Notice the variations of shades in the grayscale image. You can go back to RGB or CMYK mode at any time to add more color, but the parts originally converted to grayscale will remain that way. With this in mind, it is a good idea to keep a saved version of your file in full color before converting to grayscale.*

2. Choose File > Save As and save a copy of this file as **chap5L1_yourname_gray.psd**. That's all for now.

SUMMARY

Now that you know how color performs in Photoshop—optical mixing, digital style—and how to apply it, hopefully your world is coming up rainbows (or spinning color wheels and spectrum arrays, at least). There is a definite correlation between where color is reproduced and how it appears to us visually. Lucky for us, Photoshop has the distinctive capability to translate different modes of color, preparing our artwork for all types of output.

▶ IN REVIEW

1. Describe how optical mixing works.

2. What is antialiasing in digital imaging?

3. Define color space, or gamut. Name some devices that use gamuts.

4. What is the distinction between a color model and a color mode?

5. RGB is considered an additive color model; CMYK is subtractive. Why?

6. Why is the Lab color model considered device-independent?

7. What are gamut warnings in Photoshop and where do you find them?

8. What kind of information is stored in channels?

9. What is a complementary color?

10. Where do you find and use color stops in Photoshop?

▶ EXPLORING ON YOUR OWN

1. Using a color wheel to choose colors that visually work well together can be very useful. See examples of color wheels in Figure 5–56 and Figure 5–57. To learn more about color wheels and color theory:

   ▶ Color Matters: *http://www.colormatters.com/colortheory.html*
   ▶ Download some color wheels from Tigercolor: *http://www.tigercolor.com/color-lab/color-wheel/color-wheels.htm*

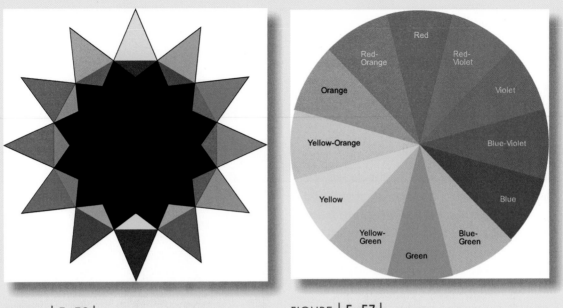

FIGURE | 5–56 |

An example of a color wheel.

FIGURE | 5–57 |

Another type of color wheel.

▶ Use the Color Schemes Generator from colorschemedesigner.com to pick colors quickly: *http://colorschemedesigner.com/*

▶ Create your own color wheel using Photoshop: http://homepage.ntlworld.com/tim.ross/ColourWheel/

2. Go to Photoshop Help (Help > Photoshop Help > Contents) and look up the topics "Color" and "Color management." You will find a lot of interesting information about how to best set up your work area and document, so you achieve consistency of color when you reproduce the image on different devices and platforms. You might find yourself ready to absorb some of it. You might wait to read other parts once you start feeling more comfortable with using the program.

3. Practice saving and loading a swatch library. The commands to do this are located in the Swatches panel drop-down options menu.

4. Create a Georges Seurat Pointillism effect in Photoshop. Open any photograph and choose Filter > Pixelate > Pointillize.

5. Create and publish your own color schemes using Adobe Labs dynamic color selector program at Window > Extensions > Kuler from Photoshop's main menu bar or at http://kuler.adobe.com/

Explorer PAGES

Natascha Roeoesli

About Natascha Roeoesli

Besides the fact that her parents are photographers, Natascha has not had any specific art education. She did consider attending art school in Switzerland but felt it was not good enough, even though she did pass the acceptance test. Most of her knowledge comes from observing her surroundings. She loves to try to figure out why something works the way it does. Physics is an important part of understanding how colors work, how we see shapes, and much more. Being self-educated is, in her opinion, a great advantage because it forces you to really understand what you are painting instead of learning theory. "However, there are books," Natascha notes, "… like *Exploring Photoshop CS5* or theory books, that help you fill in the gaps you might not have elsewhere."

Natascha has worked for over two years for the game industry, several fantasy authors, and private clients.

In the tutorials section of her Web site (*http://www.tascha. ch/*), Natascha shares her techniques for creating such effects as the silky fabric on the female character in *Wax Dragon*.

To view more of her work, visit *http://www.tascha.ch/*.

About the Work of Natascha Roeoesli

In her own words, Natascha shares her artistic process in the creation of Can't Stand the Light:

"*Can't Stand the Light* started as normal pencil sketch where I brainstormed a few compositions and character tryouts."

"Once I had the general idea, I used Adobe Photoshop and my Wacom tablet to rough in some guidelines to work

Wax Dragon. Compliments of Natascha Roeoesli.
In the tutorials section of her website (*http://www.tascha.ch/*),
Natascha shares her techniques for creating such effects as the
silky fabric on the female character in *Wax Dragon*.

from using a hard-edged brush, which imitates a ball pen or ink pen."

"I am much more of a painter than a drawer and think more in shapes than lines. This is the reason I am normally not taking much time for sketches. The lines, however, help me to not make big anatomical mistakes and stay somewhat true to my initial idea.

"Once I do have the rough layout, I copy this layer and hide it as a backup and create a new background layer, which I fill with the color I want to use for my ambient light (green for forest, blue for sky, and so on). The original sketch layer now gets painted on, starting with roughing in color using a brush with special settings, like 80% flow. This helps with not painting full opacity and lets the background color get mixed into everything I paint (most important: skin color). Switching the brushes during painting is also quite important."

"My paintings develop a lot while I work. They constantly change as I am trying out different hairdos or clothing combinations for my characters. Even the color scheme for this changed drastically during the process. Using Photoshop's amazing color adjustment tools, I shifted the colors of the almost-finished painting and then worked some more with the changed color scheme."

Summer. Compliments of Natascha Roeoesli.

"Using the Color Picker is something I do almost without a break. Picking colors from my background and mixing them ever so slightly with the main objects (or the other way around) helps to unify the painting."

"I also use a lot of layers, mainly to keep the background, foreground, and main objects separated from each other. In this case I was able to correct a compositional error and move the character slightly more to the right from where she started out. I did this to give more focus to the hand and more space to the left."

Can't Stand the Light.
Compliments of Natascha Roeoesli.

| Image Correction |

6

charting your course

It is no surprise that Photoshop is used widely for correcting photographs. After all, it was the fascination of brothers John and Thomas Knoll with darkroom photography and computer programming that brought Photoshop into existence and into the hands of consumers in 1990. Like any great inventor, John kept asking questions: how can the personal computer save photographs into other formats or adjust the contrast (lights and darks) in a photographic image? In all their simplicity—or complexity, depending on how you look at it—the answers are now at your fingertips in the form of Photoshop CS5.

This chapter presents fundamental techniques in the image-correction process. A photograph's tonal and color quality, not to mention its subject matter, is unique, and in so many ways is subject to the judgment of the artist. However, there are some general steps we can use as a springboard for understanding the image-correction process. Let's take a look at them.

goals

In this chapter you will:

▶ *Discover six basic steps for image correction*
▶ *Learn how to use Levels to affect brightness and contrast in an image*
▶ *Explore the use of adjustment layers*
▶ *Get familiar with the image retouching tools, such as Clone Stamp, Smudge, Dodge, and Sharpen*
▶ *Add an effect to a photograph*

SIX STEPS OF EN"LIGHT"ENMENT

So, you have a photograph and it needs correction. It is too dark, too light, the color is off, something is missing, or something has to go. It's all so overwhelming that you wonder where to begin. When I teach students Photoshop's capabilities for image correction for the first time, I start with six basic steps: import, resize, enhance, retouch, effect, and save. Depending on the photograph, you might choose to use some or all of them. Let's review the steps and then you can explore them in the lesson.

IMPORT

To get your photographic image into Photoshop, it must be in a digital format. You can get the image from a digital camera, or cellphone, scan it, copy it from a CD, or download it from the Internet. Try to get the highest-resolution image possible. It is better to have more pixels to work with than fewer, which is why downloading images from the Internet should be your last option; those images are small and of low resolution. You could also obtain images from a stock image distributor, such as Corbis, Comstock, or PictureQuest, but those kinds of images are usually already corrected and will not need much tonal adjustment. To import an image into Photoshop, choose File > Open and browse for the image on your system.

RESIZE

It is unlikely your image will be the exact size and/or orientation you desire for its final output. You might need to change its dimensions and resolution, add more or less area to the overall canvas, or crop out unnecessary parts. Whatever you do, save a copy of the original image in case you want to use it again.

Image Dimensions, Resolution, and Mode

First you will want to check the image's resolution and size to be sure it contains enough pixels to complete the task you have chosen. For example, if you want the image to be printed on a fine magazine cover, you will want the resolution to be about 300 pixels per inch (ppi). If it is going to be printed in a newspaper, 150 ppi will suffice. For the Web or another digital environment, 72 ppi will work. (If you need to review the section on the relationship between resolution and the size of an image, see Chapter 3.) To adjust the size and resolution of an image, go to Image > Image Size. Remember you can sample down (reduce) the resolution of an image without losing detail in the image, while sampling it up will degrade the image's quality.

You should check what color mode the image is in (Grayscale, RGB, CMYK) and set it to the mode you would like to work in (review color modes in Chapter 5). Be aware that you can do certain things in some modes and not in others. For example, if you change to Grayscale mode, all color will be discarded from the image and cannot be restored. If you choose RGB, you can work with the many effects and filters in the program that are unavailable in other modes. Remember, when your image is almost complete, it is important to set the mode for its intended output. In general, use RGB for screen display and CMYK for print.

Canvas

You may want to add some more blank canvas area around the image, perhaps to include some text, a border, or other elements. To adjust the canvas size, choose Image > Canvas Size. See Figure 6–1 and Figure 6–2.

FIGURE | 6–1 |

The Canvas Size dialog box. You can use several types of measurements (such as pixels, inches, and percentages) to determine the size.

FIGURE | 6–2 |

The canvas of an image resized by 20 pixels all the way around.

Cropping

When the composition of your photograph is not right or it was not aligned properly during the scanning process, it is time to bring out the Crop tool. Reminiscent

FIGURE | 6–3 |

Specify and adjust a crop selection.

of a bout of spring cleaning, the Crop tool can put everything in its place and remove unwanted or unusable areas. To crop an image, select the Crop tool and click and drag over the area of the image you want to keep. Once the area is defined you can readjust or rotate the Crop selection more precisely before committing to the crop action. See Figure 6–3.

ENHANCE

Enhancing is where you begin to get into the heart of image correction, which includes adjustments to an image's tonal levels (brightness and contrast) and color balance. Under Image > Adjustments in the main menu, you will find many commands that relate to tonal and color balance editing. See Figure 6–4. Photoshop features auto-correction commands for quick fixes to photographs (Auto Tone, Auto Contrast, Auto Color). However, if you want to apply more precise correction to specific pixels and their tonal quality, experiment with the Levels, Curves, and Channel Mixer options. See Figure 6–5 and Figure 6–6.

Image	Layer	Select	Filter	Analysis	3D	View	Win

Mode	▶
Adjustments	▶

	Brightness/Contrast...
	Levels... ⌘L
Auto Tone ⇧⌘L	Curves... ⌘M
Auto Contrast ⌥⇧⌘L	Exposure...
Auto Color ⇧⌘B	
	Vibrance...
Image Size... ⌥⌘I	Hue/Saturation... ⌘U
Canvas Size... ⌥⌘C	Color Balance... ⌘B
Image Rotation ▶	Black & White... ⌥⇧⌘B
Crop	Photo Filter...
Trim...	Channel Mixer...
Reveal All	
	Invert ⌘I
Duplicate...	Posterize...
Apply Image...	Threshold...
Calculations...	Gradient Map...
	Selective Color...
Variables ▶	
Apply Data Set...	Shadows/Highlights...
	HDR Toning...
Trap...	Variations...
	Desaturate ⇧⌘U
	Match Color...
	Replace Color...
	Equalize

FIGURE | 6–4 |

Options available for image enhancements.

FIGURE | 6–5 |

An image before adjustments to its tonal range.

FIGURE | 6–6 |

An image after adjustments to its tonal range. For more precise control over the shadows, mid-tones, and highlights of an image, adjust the histogram (graph of the total distribution of colored pixels in an image).

Note: *Alternatively, you can find similar adjustment options under Layer > New Adjustment Layer in the main menu or the Adjustments panel (Window > Adjustments). What's the difference between applying an adjustment from the Image > Adjustments list versus Layer > New Adjustment Layer's list or Adjustments panel? From the Photoshop Help files: "An adjustment layer applies color and tonal adjustments to your image without permanently changing pixel values. For example, rather than making a Levels or Curves adjustment directly to your image, you can create a Levels or Curves adjustment layer. The color and tone adjustments are stored in the adjustment layer and apply to all the layers below it. "See Figure 6-7. You can discard your changes and restore the original image at any time. You will explore working with adjustment layers in the "Correcting the Mike Photo" lesson. See also the Exploring on Your Own section at the end of this chapter.*

FIGURE | 6–7 |

A Levels adjustment layer is located above the layer(s) it affects. To edit the levels, double-click on the histogram thumbnail in the adjustment layer.

RETOUCH

It can be a full-time job retouching photographs—fixing the very large or very minute blemishes. There definitely is an art to retouching so it looks invisible to the viewer, but Photoshop makes it easier—quite painless, really—with such tools as the Clone Stamp, Healing Brush, Spot Healing Brush, Pattern Stamp, Patches, Red Eye, Smudge, Blur, and Sharpen. See Figure 6–8 and Figure 6–9 (on the next page).

EFFECT

Once the photograph is adjusted to your liking, you can consider adding something more, such as an effect, a text element, a frame or border, or a filter or color enhancement. See Figure 6–10 (on the next page).

FIGURE | 6–8 |

Use the Clone Stamp tool to take sampled areas of an image to use in place of unwanted areas.

SAVE

Hopefully, you save your document frequently as you work on image correction, but consideration should be given to output and creating copies of the work for its intended purpose. This might include saving the image in a compressed JPEG format for Web publication or in TIFF format to send to the printer or page layout program.

FIGURE | 6–9 |

The Dodge tool quickly lightens areas of an image.

FIGURE | 6–10 |

Using feathering, a soft effect is added around the image.

FIGURE | 6–11 |

The lesson before and after. Original photo compliments of Bruce and Linda Lord.

LESSON: CORRECTING THE MIKE PHOTO

In this lesson you will follow the six basic steps of image correction, and then you will be on your way to correcting and enhancing your own photographs. See Figure 6–11.

Import

1. In Photoshop, choose File > Open. Open the file **chap6L1.psd** in the **chap06_lessons** folder. Be sure the Essentials workspace is selected.

2. Save a copy of this file in your **lessons** folder. Choose File > Save As and name it **chap6L1_yourname.psd**.

3. Choose View > Actual Pixels to see the document at 100% magnification. This is a photograph taken of my friend's brother, Mike, during the Vietnam War. You can see the photo is faded and worn. Let's take it through the six image-correction steps. The first step, import, has already been completed.

Resize

1. The photograph is in RGB Color mode, but for simplicity—in this lesson—change it to Grayscale. Choose Image > Mode > Grayscale. A dialog box asks if you would like to discard all color information in the photo. Choose Discard, and rest assured that you have a backup copy of the color version on the lessons CD.

> Note: *Another option for making more precise adjustments to the blacks, whites, and grays of an image is Image > Adjustments > Black & White. This adjustment leaves the image in RGB Color mode, yet it offers different photographic filters and color channel adjustment options to adjust the grayscale image. See Figure 6–12. For a review of channels, see the section on "Adjusting Color" in Chapter 5. For further study of color balance, you can explore the color version of the photo in the Exploring on Your Own section of this chapter.*

2. Choose Image > Image Size. The photo's resolution is currently set to 300 ppi. At this resolution, if the photo goes to print it will be approximately 2.7 by 2.3 inches. Uncheck the Resample Image option if it is checked (see Figure 6–13) and enter **150** ppi for the Resolution. The overall print dimensions increase. For most print jobs 150 ppi is a good resolution; a higher resolution is needed for high-quality magazine covers and similar media, which you will learn about in Chapter 10. Click OK.

3. Choose View > Print Size to see the exact dimensions of the photograph if it were to be printed. Choose View > Actual Pixels to see the size of the image on screen—almost twice

FIGURE | 6–12 |

Make subtle adjustments to a grayscale image using the Black and White adjustment feature.

FIGURE | 6–13 |

To know what you are working with, always check the image size of your document. Uncheck Resample Image if you want to change the resolution and keep the highest visual quality of the image.

as big because the screen views at about 72 ppi. (If I just lost you here, review the section on resolution in Chapter 3.)

4. OK, you have set the image size, but as you can see the image is crooked on the canvas, which can happen in the scanning process when the image is not properly aligned on the scanning bed. Select the Crop tool in the toolbox (fifth tool down). Click and drag an area around the photograph inside the tattered black border that approximates the dimensions of the photograph. (It won't be exact; we will fix that next.) Use the Crop tool and the selection handles to scale and rotate the photograph, just as you would using Edit > Transform (see Figure 6–14), and then execute the crop (see Figure 6–15).

5. Choose File > Save As. Name your new file and click Save.

FIGURE | 6–14 |

Using the transform handles, adjust the crop selection around the image.

FIGURE | 6–15 |

Choose the check mark on the Options bar to execute the crop.

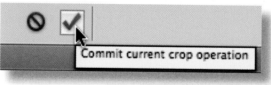

Commit current crop operation

Enhance

1. Now for the fun stuff. Choose Image > Adjustments > Levels. In the Levels dialog box be sure the Preview option is checked, then choose the Auto option. Note the automatic tonal correction made to the image. See Figure 6–16. It is looking better already. Choose Cancel to go back to the uncorrected image. Let's try a different method—something with more control and using an adjustment layer to make the corrections instead

FIGURE | 6–16 |

Select the Auto option to quickly correct the levels of an image.

FIGURE | 6–17 |

Adjust the levels by moving the shadow, mid-tone, and highlight markers. Be sure to preview the document as you make changes.

of altering the actual photo. (If you're wondering, "What's an adjustment layer?," review the Enhance section of this chapter).

2. In the menu bar choose Layer > New Adjustment Layer > Levels. Keep the **Levels 1** layer name and click OK. A histogram comes up in the Adjustments panel. This is a graph that shows the distribution of shadows, mid-tones, and highlights in an image. The far-left marker at the bottom of the graph indicates the end range for the darkest (shadow) pixels in the image. The far-right marker indicates the end range for the lightest (highlight) pixels in the image. The marker in the middle adjusts all chromatic gray pixels in between. The higher the graph in a particular area, the more instances of that particular shade in the image. See Figure 6–17.

3. A quick way to find a good tonal balance in the image is to move the black (shadow) marker on the histogram inward until it aligns with the first vertical stretch of pixels in the histogram. Do the same with the white (highlight) marker. Note the changes occurring directly on the document. Adjust the mid-tones marker to the right or left to see how much control you have over the photo's brightness and contrast. Refer to Figure 6–17.

4. Open the Layers panel. Notice that the adjustment layer you created in step #1 is automatically created above the **mike_photo** layer.

5. OK, let's add some color back into the image—a sepia tone. First change the image mode back to RGB via Image > Mode > RGB Color. Select the Don't Merge option.

FIGURE | 6–18 |

Colorize the photograph with a photo filter.

6. Be sure the **mike_photo** layer is highlighted in the Layers panel, and then choose Layer > New Adjustment Layer > Photo Filter. Name the new layer Sepia, and choose OK. The options for the photo filter open in the Adjustments panel. Select the Sepia filter from the drop-down menu. Try a Density setting of about 75%. Click OK. What do you think? Feel free to try the other filters if sepia is not your color. See Figure 6–18.

7. Let's work with the Sharpen feature. This next enhancement is optional, but it is sometimes necessary on images that have gone through a scanning process, which tends to blur some images. Sharpening is also a good idea when you want to bump up the readability of text in a photo. Select the **mike_photo** layer, and then choose Filter > Sharpen > Sharpen and note the subtle clarity in the image. (If you did not catch this the first time, choose Edit > Undo Sharpen, zoom in closer to the image, redo the step to see the shift in image detail, and then zoom out to see that it is, indeed, an improvement.)

8. Save your work.

> Note: *Unsharp Mask and Smart Sharpen are also available in the Sharpen filters. They work like the Sharpen feature but give you more control over the effect. Give it a try, if you like. You can always undo the effect in the History panel: use Edit > Step Backward a few times, or File > Revert to go back to your last saved version.*

Retouch

1. OK, on to some real magic. The Mike photo is well-worn. Note the stains and scratches on the photo, particularly those on the left-hand side. See Figure 6–19.

FIGURE | 6–19 |

The circled areas indicate scratches and stains in the photo.

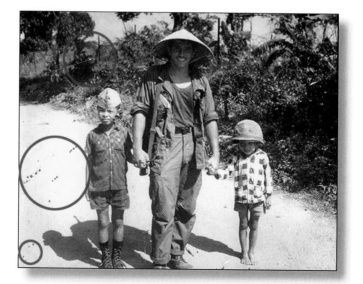

2. Change the tool icons to look more like brushes and work more accurately: choose Photoshop > Preferences > Cursors (Mac) or Edit > Preferences > Cursors (Windows). Under Painting Cursors, choose Normal Brush Tip (if it is not already selected). Click OK.

3. Select the Clone Stamp tool in the toolbox. See Figure 6–20.

4. In the Options bar, click on the brush thumbnail to open the brush options. Click on the arrow inside a circle in the upper right corner of the drop-down menu to open further options. Choose to view the brushes with Small Thumbnails. See Figure 6–21. The Clone Stamp tool takes a picture of an area of an image that can then be duplicated elsewhere on the image. The brush size determines the size of the picture area. Choose the Soft Round Pressure Size brush and set its size to 27 pixels. See Figure 6–22 (on the next page). Click the down arrow in the Brush options to close the panel, or hit Enter (Mac) or Return (Windows) on the keyboard.

5. Place the Clone Stamp tool over an unstained, lighter area on the left-hand side of the image. See Figure 6–23 (on the next page). Hold down Alt/Option and click to take a picture (sample) of that pixel area (zoom in if necessary).

FIGURE | 6–20 |

The Clone Stamp tool.

FIGURE | 6–21 |

Select to view the brushes in small thumbnails.

FIGURE | 6–22 |

The Brush options—choose the Soft Round Pressure Size brush and set its size to 27 pixels.

FIGURE | 6–23 |

Position the Clone Stamp tool over an area, hold down Option/Alt, and click to take a picture (sample) of the pixels.

6. Position the pointer over one of the stained areas of the image, and click once to apply the saved picture over the stained area. Click and drag (brush) lightly over the stained area to blend it into the background pixels. See Figure 6–24. Note that when you click and drag over an area, a crosshair comes up. The crosshair indicates the area that is being copied by the brush in another area. Huh? Frankly, at first this relationship between the crosshair and the brush can be somewhat confusing, but once you understand how the tool works, it does make sense. The first picture taken with the Clone Stamp tool (when you hold down Option/Alt) is applied to a new area when you click elsewhere on the image. The crosshair indicates the relative starting point of what it will continue to pick up as you click and drag (brush) over the area. See Figure 6–25.

7. On the menu bar, go to Window > Clone Source to open the Clone Source panel. See Figure 6–26. This panel lets you save samples in the upper five squares by the one of them and setting a clone source (when you hold down Alt/Option) in the image.

FIGURE | 6–24 |

Blending the area into the background pixels.

FIGURE | 6–25 |

First picture applied to a new area.
Note the crosshair on the boy's nose.
The pixels in this area are being
applied by the brush above and to
the left.

FIGURE | 6–26 |

Options in the Clone Source
panel.

The first square already has a saved sample from our first attempt at cloning. Also, the
Show Overlay at the bottom of the panel will reveal a ghost image of the clone source
(the crosshair) over the original image.

8.   Continue to take samples of clean areas of the image and apply them to the stained or
     scratched areas. You might want to change your brush size, depending on the area size
     you are sampling. To do this quickly, click on the right and/or left bracket keys on the
     keyboard. Once you have made your adjustments to the brush, press Enter to exit the
     menu. See Figure 6–27 (on the next page). The bracket [ ] keys offer another quick way of
     changing brush sizes. The [key decreases the size of the brush while the] key increases it.

FIGURE | 6–27 |

Adjust brush size with Ctrl-click (Mac) or right-click (Windows) or using the bracket keys.

FIGURE | 6–28 |

The Smudge tool is located under the Blur tool in the toolbox.

FIGURE | 6–29 |

Hiding blemishes with the Smudge tool.

9. Select the Zoom tool and zoom in on the scratch on the boy's knee on the left side of the photo.

10. For another retouch tool that might do the trick, select the Smudge tool in the toolbox. See Figure 6–28.

11. Gently blend the darker pixels of the boy's knee into the light scratched area. See Figure 6–29.

12. Zoom out to 100% magnification—to do this quickly, double-click on the Zoom tool in the toolbox. Note that Mike's face is dark under his hat. Zoom in on his face.

13. Select the Dodge tool in the toolbox (see Figure 6–30) and in the Options bar set Exposure to 5%. In the Options bar, also adjust your brush size, if necessary (we chose 5 for the brush size—quite small).

14. Gently brush the Dodge tool over Mike's cheeks to lighten them slightly.

15. Zoom out to 100% magnification to see the subtle result. If you dodged too much, either undo actions in the History panel or use the Burn tool (under the Dodge tool in the toolbox) to redo the darker effect.

FIGURE | 6–30 |

The Dodge tool in the toolbox.

16. Using your newly found tools, retouch other areas of the photo. See also Exploring on Your Own, item #4, at the end of this chapter for an explanation of more retouching tools that you can play with.

> Note: *When working with the retouch tools, individual clicks or very short drags with the tools can be more successful than brushing over large areas all at once.*

17. Save your document.

Effect

1. With the Effect step you can add any sort of inspiration to a photo. For the Mike photo, let's make a frame. See the after version of Figure 6–11, for example.

2. In the menu bar, go to Layer > Flatten Image. This will unite the **Levels 1** and **Photo Filters 1** layers and the **mike_photo** layer into one layer.

3. Select the Elliptical Marquee tool in the toolbox. Position the cursor on Mike's belt buckle, hold down Shift and Option/Alt, and then click and draw from the center a circle around the three figures. If you wish to reposition the selection, click inside the selection area with the Marquee tool still active and move it.

4. Choose Select > Inverse to inverse the selection area; marching ants appear around the edges of the photo.

5. Choose Edit > Stroke, select a color to your liking, and choose 4 pixels. See Figure 6–31. Click OK.

FIGURE | 6–31 |

Add a stroke to the photo frame.

6. While the selection is still active, choose Filter > Texture > Texturizer. The Photoshop Filter Gallery window appears with Texturizer options open. In the Texturizer menu, choose the Canvas option (see Figure 6–32) and set the Scaling and Relief to your liking. Click OK when completed.

FIGURE | 6–32 |

Add a texture to the selected frame area.

Note: *You can preview the changes being made directly on your document without closing the Texturizer Filter Gallery.*

7. Choose the Hue/Saturation option in the Adjustments panel. See Figure 6–33. Adjust the Hue slider to any color you wish.

Save

1. Save a Photoshop version of your corrected image (maybe even two or three versions along the way). Choose File > Save As and save a final .psd version in your **lessons** folder.

2. Let's save two more versions for different output. For print, choose File > Save As and under Format, select TIFF. Click Save. In the TIFF Options box, select NONE for Image Compression and select Discard Layers and Save a Copy for Layer Compression. (The Discard Layers and Save a Copy option will save a flattened copy of your image, but the image you are currently working on is still the "original.") See Figure 6–34.

3. Let's save another version for the Web. Choose File > Save As, Format: JPEG. Click Save. Set the Image Options Quality to 8, so there is some compression placed on the image, but not enough to ruin its quality. Click OK.

> **Note:** *You can also choose File > Save for Web & Devices to save in JPEG format. However, this opens up another big dialog box of choices you don't have to deal with right now. We will get into that in Chapter 11.*

You're done with the image-correction process.

FIGURE | 6–33 |

Add a color to the frame using a Hue/Saturation adjustment.

FIGURE | 6–34 |

Save the file in the TIFF format.

SUMMARY

A whole new world—blemish-free—has opened up to you in this chapter. With the powerful image-correction tools and processes available in Photoshop, every photograph has the potential for perfection.

▶ IN REVIEW

1. What are the six basic steps for image correction?

2. Why is it important to check the resolution setting of an imported photograph or image?

3. Why might someone choose the RGB Color mode over other modes?

4. What are you adjusting when you move the sliders in the Levels histogram?

5. What keyboard command must you press to take a pixel sample with the Clone Stamp tool?

6. When working with the retouching tools, why would viewing your cursor as Brush Size be helpful? Where do you go to make this setting?

7. What is the advantage of using an adjustment layer to make color or tonal corrections on an image?

8. Why would you save backup copies of the original photograph before retouching it?

▶ EXPLORING ON YOUR OWN

1. Play further with the Adjustments panel and image-correction presets. Open a photograph that you have that needs some tonal correction (some examples can also be found in the **chap06_lessons/samples/ color_tonal** folder). Select the Essentials workspace. Docked in the panels on the right is the Adjustment panel (if you don't see it, choose Window > Adjustments). See Figure 6–35. A list of icons is located at the top of the panel. Roll over each icon to reveal its adjustment type Levels, Color Balance, Exposure, etc.). We explored the Hue/Saturation adjustment in previous lessons. Click on an

FIGURE | 6–35 |

Roll over the icons in the Adjustments panel to reveal its text equivalent.

adjustment and play with its options. To get back to the adjustments list, click the back arrow in the lower left corner of the panel. See Figure 6–36. Also experiment with the Presets located in the lower portion of the Adjustments panel (see Figure 6–35). Finally, go to the Layers panel and note how each adjustment made has its own adjustment layer. To remove an adjustment, delete its layer. To edit an adjustment, click on the adjustment layer and the information related to that adjustment appears in the Adjustments panel. See Figure 6–37.

2. In the Photoshop Help files (Help > Photoshop Help), expand your knowledge of levels and discover the wonders of curves. See the sections on "Making color and tonal adjustment."

FIGURE | 6–36 |

Click the arrow to go back to the adjustments list.

FIGURE | 6–37 |

Click on an adjustment layer to reveal its options in the Adjustments panel.

FIGURE | 6–38 |

Other photo retouching tools to explore.

FIGURE | 6–39 |

1. Photo before retouching with the Spot Healing Brush.
2. Photo after correcting pixels with the Spot Healing Brush.

3. Explore color correction using a color version of the Mike photo. Using the Channel Mixer, remove the red overcast in the **chap6L1** file. For information on using the Channel Mixer, consult the Help files.

4. As you learned in the lesson, the Clone Stamp tool can correct imperfections or duplicate areas of an image by sampling pixels elsewhere on the image or from other images. There are three other photo retouching tools that work similarly to the Clone Stamp tool, but with slight variations in effect: Healing Brush, Spot Healing Brush, and Patch tool. The Patch tool is best for areas without a lot of detail. See Figure 6–38.

Executed like the Clone Stamp tool, the Healing Brush tool matches the texture, lighting, transparency, and shading of the sampled pixels—determined by the size of the brush you choose—to the pixels being healed. As a result, the repaired pixels blend seamlessly into the rest of the image. The Spot Healing Brush tool offers the same effect as the Healing Brush tool. However, there is no requirement to specify (take a snapshot of) a sample spot to apply elsewhere. The Spot Healing Brush tool automatically samples the pixels by Proximity Match (by assessing the pixels that surround the edge of the retouched area), or by Create Texture, using the pixels in the selection to create a texture in which to fix the area. It's amazing, really! See Figure 6–39.

The Patch tool works just like the Healing tools, but instead of defining a retouch area with a chosen brush size, you draw a selection around the source or destination area you want to sample and then repair that selection from another area or pattern. The Patch tool is best for areas without a lot of detail. See Figure 6–40.

To practice these tools, retouch the photo of a dilapidated shack in **chap06_lessons/samples/patch.jpg**.

5. Found in the same area of the toolbox as the Healing and Patch tools, the

FIGURE | 6–40 |

1. Photo before using the Patch tool.
2. Photo after using the Patch tool.

Red Eye tool is worth a try. To quickly remove red eye from flash-photographed people, or the white and green reflections in flash photos of animals, select the Red Eye tool and click on the unwanted area. For practice with this tool, use the **red_eye.jpg** in the **chap06_lessons/samples** folder.

6. Another tool to play with in the Photoshop toolbox is the Color Replacement tool. Using brush strokes, this tool simplifies replacing specific colors in your image. Select the tool (see Figure 6–41), choose a brush size in the Options bar, select a foreground color or take a sample of color (Alt/Option) in the image, then brush the color onto the area of the image you would like to modify.

FIGURE | 6–41 |

The Color Replacement tool.

adventures IN DESIGN

PHOTOMERGE

P hotoshop's Photomerge command smartly combines several photographs into one continuous image. For example, you can take several overlapping photographs of a landscape, and then assemble them into a panorama. It can assemble photos that are tiled horizontally as well as vertically.

PROFESSIONAL PROJECT EXAMPLE

I was asked to assemble three overlapping photos taken at Monhegan Island in Maine to be printed on a large canvas. See figure A–1. For Photomerge to properly detect and blend the contiguous area of a series of images, the original photos taken must overlap sufficiently— represented by the color overlays in figure A–1.

FIGURE | A–1 |

To view all the photos at once, the 3 Up option was chosen from the Arrange Documents command in the Application bar. Note the areas in the three photos that overlap (highlighted in transparent yellow and red).

First step in the process was to choose File > Automate > Photomerge in Photoshop, select the Auto Layout option and browse to find the photos needed. The photos can have any file name and can be selected in any order and Photomerge will automatically detect the order in which they should be assembled. See Figure A–2.

If there is a discrepancy in how Photomerge detects the blend and it doesn't look quite the way you want it, you can select the blended pieces individually in the Layers panel and transform them as you would any other object. For the Monhegan Island photos, a seamless composition

Photomerge

Layout
- Auto
- Perspective
- Cylindrical
- Spherical
- Collage
- Reposition

Source Files

Use: Files

middle.jpg
left.jpg
right.jpg

Browse...
Remove
Add Open Files

OK
Cancel

☑ Blend Images Together
☐ Vignette Removal
☐ Geometric Distortion Correction

FIGURE | A–2 |

The Photomerge dialog box. There are many layout types to choose from (Auto, Perspective, Cylindrical, etc.). I chose the Auto option and it worked wonders for my project.

LAYERS

Normal   Opacity: 100%
Lock: Fill: 100%

middle.jpg
left.jpg
right.jpg

FIGURE | A–3 |

In the Layers panel each assembled piece can be selected and modified, if necessary.

was created and no transformations needed to be done. See Figure A–3.

Then, although Photomerge correctly blended the three photos, I had to do some retouching and color correction on the final panorama. I cropped the image, then saved it. Then, I flattened the image and from the Adjustments panel applied an auto levels correction. See figure A–4. I then blended the color of the sky with the Clone tool. See **final_merge.psd** in **aid_examples/photomerge_examples** on the CD.

YOUR TURN

Using the sample files **left.jpg, middle.jpg,** and **right.jpg** in the **aid_examples/photomerge_examples** folder found in the **lessons** folder on the back of the book CD, you will assemble your own panorama.

Photomerge Project Guidelines

1. Choose File > Automate > Photomerge.

2. In the Photomerge dialog box, under Layout, choose Auto. For Source Files select the Files option. Browse for the **left.jpg, middle.jpg,** and **right.jpg** in the **aid_examples/photomerge_examples** folder. Be sure the Blend Images Together option is selected at the bottom and choose OK.

3. Photoshop will think for a bit and then the assembled images will appear as an "untitled" file. Save the file.

4. At this point, feel free to crop and enhance the panorama as you see fit.

Things to Consider

For future explorations with the Photomerge command, consider the following:

Your source photographs play a large role in panoramic compositions. To avoid problems, follow these guidelines when taking pictures for use with Photomerge (extracted from the Photoshop Help files):

▶ **Overlap images sufficiently** Images should overlap by approximately 25–40%. If the overlap is less,

FIGURE | A–4 |

Color correction (Auto Levels) and retouching were done on the panorama to improve its final appearance.

Photomerge may not be able to automatically assemble the panorama. However, keep in mind that the images shouldn't overlap too much. If images overlap by 70% or more, Photomerge may not be able to blend the images. Try to keep the individual photos at least somewhat distinct from each other.

▶ **Use one focal length** If you use a zoom lens, don't change the focal length (zoom in or out) while taking your pictures.

▶ **Keep the camera level** Although Photomerge can process slight rotations between pictures, a tilt of more than a few degrees can result in errors when the panorama is assembled. Using a tripod with a rotating head helps maintain camera alignment and viewpoint.

▶ **Stay in the same position** Try not to change your position as you take a series of photographs, so that the pictures are from the same viewpoint. Using the optical viewfinder with the camera held close to the eye helps keep the viewpoint consistent. Or try using a tripod to keep the camera in the same place.

▶ **Avoid using distortion lenses** Fish-eye and other distortion lenses can interfere with Photomerge.

▶ **Maintain the same exposure** Avoid using the flash in some pictures and not in others. The advanced blending feature in Photomerge helps smooth out different exposures, but extreme differences make alignment difficult. Some digital cameras change exposure settings automatically as you take pictures, so you may need to check your camera settings to be sure that all the images have the same exposure.

Explorer PAGES

Michael Dwyer

"With design it's not a pure art . . . it's not self-expression totally. You are fulfilling a purpose for a client, which is business. You must blend the art and business together. And you have to have a thick skin to take criticism . . . even if you know in your heart it's wrong. You have to educate your clients, but at some point you have to bend to their vision . . . adapt, compromise with the client and the design."

 Learn more about this artist via an audio interview found on the book's CD.

About Michael Dwyer

Michael Dwyer studied fine art at SUNY Purchase and the School of the Museum of Fine Arts (Tufts) in Boston, MA. On the road of sculpture and public art he took a detour to graphic design. During the last 14 years he has worked for large corporations and small studios, most notably YOE! Studio in Peekskill, N.Y. At YOE! he designed logos, packaging, ads, magazines, Web sites, and animations for clients such as the Discovery Channel, Pepperidge Farms, Golden Books, Mudd Jeans, Cartoon Network, and AOL.

Currently he is the creative director at EZ Marketing Group (EZMG) in Harrison, N.Y. EZMG's clients include the *New York Times*, Universal News, and Nuttin' But Stringz.

Michael teaches graphic design courses online for the Art Institute of Pittsburgh and Westwood College. In his spare time he produces short documentaries, including his most recent, *Mom and Pop Shop*.

To see more of his work, visit *http://www.crackanegg.com*.

About the Work of Michael Dwyer

In his own words, Michael shares his experience working with the Discovery Channel:

"One of the most successful and fun clients I have had the opportunity to work with has been the Discovery Channel's *Crocodile Hunter* program. When Discovery first approached

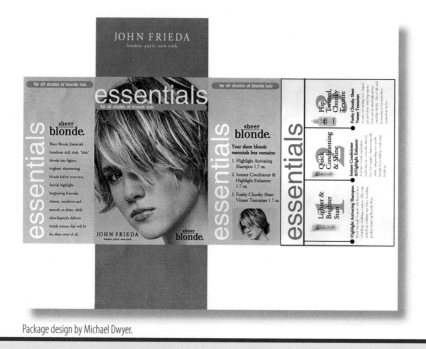

Package design by Michael Dwyer.

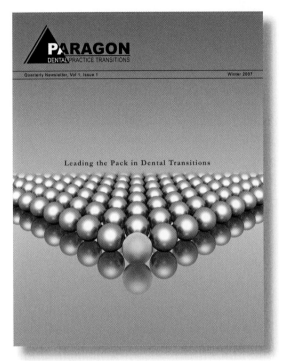

Newsletter cover for a dental practice transition company.
Compliments of Michael Dwyer.

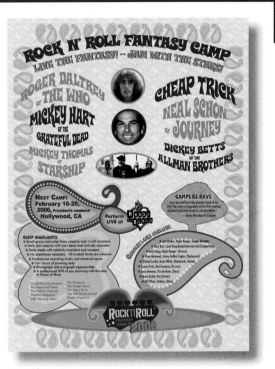

Print ad for a guitar magazine.
Compliments of Michael Dwyer.

Poster design for Discovery Channel.
Compliments of Michael Dwyer.

the studio they had a very popular show and a logo, but that was about it as far as a brand or defined image of the show. I developed three possible 'looks' or directions that they could pursue. One approach emphasized the dangerous elements of the show, the second had a comic book/superhero feel, and the third focused on the environmental aspects of Steve Irwin's work, which is ultimately the direction they chose to develop."

"Once the basic direction had been chosen I worked with a team of designers and an illustrator to develop an entire style guide for the client. I prefer working in a collaborative environment where all the designers can feed off each other's ideas. An atmosphere of sharing makes the project seem more like play than actual work."

"A style guide typically includes logos, a color panel, fonts, type treatments, patterns, textures, and final art. The style guide allows other artists or third parties to create any variety of merchandise and still maintain a cohesive and coherent brand."

| Drawing and Painting |

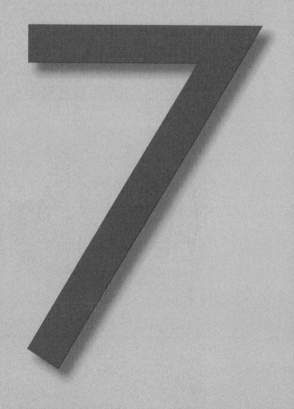

charting your course

So far, we have spent a lot of time working with photographs in Photoshop—cropping, selecting, and transforming them, and altering tonal values and color. In this chapter, you get an introduction to the drawing and painting tools. These tools advance the possibilities of what you can do in Photoshop to another creative level. With little doubt, as you play with the Brush, Pencil, Pen, and Shape tools—not to mention path and type options—you may get lost in what can be a complex amalgamation of colors and shapes. It's like looking into a kaleidoscope, where complex patterns and designs allure you into amazement.

If you were to take the kaleidoscope apart, however, you would find that this amazing eye candy is but an artifact of a simple design—a few reflective mirrors, some light, and a myriad of objects: confetti, beads, jewels, glass, and pressed flowers. The same goes for drawing and painting in Photoshop, except instead of spinning objects making these dazzling images, it is another type of back-lit object. Yes, you guessed it: pixels.

goals

In this chapter you will:

▶ *Master pixel painting with the Pencil and Brush tools*
▶ *Recognize how vectors serve as a temporary mold for more flexible and free-form drawing and offer cross-compatibility support between pixel-based and vector-based programs*
▶ *Make geometric and free-form shapes using paths, fills, and strokes*
▶ *Draw a nonrepresentational art piece*

PIXELS—A CONTEMPORARY ART MEDIUM

With pixels, you can simulate art styles through the use of the Pencil and Brush tools (and filter effects, discussed later in this chapter). Want to paint with watercolors or an airbrush? Draw with charcoal or chalk? With a mouse or pressure-sensitive digitizing tablet, you can. In addition, you can paint other elements, such as textured grass, scattered leaves and flowers, swirls, and patterns using the brush libraries. And with custom brushes you can paint just about anything else. You can change brush sizes, opacity, blending modes, and flow attributes. (If you are the doodling type, you may never get beyond this chapter!)

FIGURE | 7–1 |

Pencil and Brush tools in the toolbox.

USING THE PENCIL AND BRUSH TOOLS

The Pencil and Brush tools are found in the toolbox. See Figure 7–1. These tools let you paint with any foreground color you choose. In general, the Pencil tool creates hard-edged, freehand lines of color, and the Brush tool creates soft strokes of color. To compare and contrast the same styles used with both the Pencil and Brush tools, see Figure 7–2 and Figure 7–3.

I recommend that you set your cursor preferences to reflect the brush size you are using. To do this, go to Photoshop > Preferences > Cursors (Mac) or Edit > Preferences > Cursors (Windows) and,

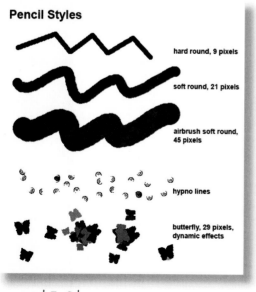

FIGURE | 7–2 |

A small sampling of pencil styles and sizes.

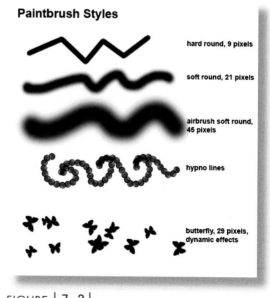

FIGURE | 7–3 |

A small sampling of brush styles and sizes.

under Painting Cursors, choose Normal Brush Tip. There are several places to make adjustments and add variations to your Pencil or Brush tool; for example, look in the Options bar (see Figure 7–4), in the Brush panel (Window > Brush, Figure 7–5), and in the context menu when you Ctrl-click (Mac) or right-click (Windows) over an area with the tool. See Figure 7–6 (on the next page).

FIGURE | 7–4 |

The Brush tool's Options bar (Pencil tool options are similar).

FIGURE | 7–5 |

The Brush panel (also used with the Pencil tool). On the left-hand side you can click on an effect name to bring up its properties (i.e., for Color Dynamics choose the Color Dynamics title). To apply the effect to your brush, check the box to the left of the effect's name.

FIGURE | 7–6 |

Context menu for the Brush tool. As you paint, you can quickly change the tool's diameter, hardness, or style.

In the chapter lesson, you will get to practice with the Pencil and Brush tools, but that is still a few pages away and the temptation to start messing around with these tools is usually urgent. So, let's do it—pronto!

1. In Photoshop, choose File > New and create a document of any size.

2. Check the preferences to make sure that under Cursors, the Normal Brush Tip painting cursor is selected.

3. Set a foreground color in the toolbox or the Color panel. This is the color you will draw with.

4. Select the Pencil tool in the toolbox. See Figure 7–1. In the Options bar, click on the second inverted arrow to open the Brush (also Pencil) Preset picker. Choose a pencil in the scrolling list and set a size of between 10 to 20 pixels. See Figure 7–7.

Note: *Alternatively, you can go to Window > Brush and open the Brush panel, which contains these options and more.*

For future reference, you can also adjust the Pencil tool's blending modes and opacity in the Options bar. Hold off on exploring these options until you feel comfortable with the basic settings.

5. Place the cursor over your blank document. Click and drag to start drawing.

Note: *To create straight lines, click with the Pencil tool, hold down Shift, and then click in another place on the document. (Do not click and drag, just click-click-click… while holding down Shift. If you do not hold it down, you'll just make dots. Try it and see!)*

6. Draw to your heart's content, changing colors and pencil attributes.

FIGURE | 7–7 |

Open the Brush (also Pencil) Preset picker. Note that in the Options submenu for the Preset picker, the view in this example is set to Stroke Thumbnail.

7. To erase, use the Eraser tool. See Figure 7–8. Like the Pencil tool's diameter (size), the Eraser tool's diameter can be set in the Options bar. Remember that the bracket keys will increase or decrease the diameter of the selected drawing tool on the fly. The background color you have chosen in the toolbox is the color the Eraser tool reveals. So, if your document started out with a white background, make sure white is set in the background color swatch of the toolbox (select D on the keyboard) to completely remove whatever you are erasing.

Note: *You can undo your strokes in the History panel.*

8. Select the Brush tool in the toolbox.

9. Select a Brush Preset in the Brush Presets panel (Window > Brush Presets). For more options (not that you need them right now), click the arrow with four horizontal lines in the upper-right corner of the panel and, from the drop-down Options menu, choose another brush library from the list at the bottom (i.e., from Dry Media Brushes or Special Effect Brushes). To add the brush library to the current list of brushes in the Brush panel, select Append when the dialog box comes up. See Figure 7–9.

FIGURE | 7–8 |

The Eraser tool. The color it reveals is determined by the background color.

Adobe Photoshop

Replace current brushes with the brushes from Wet Media Brushes?

Ps

(Append)   (Cancel)   (OK)

FIGURE | 7–9 |

Choose Append to add brushes to your existing brush style list.

> **Note:** *In the Brush panel's Options submenu are settings for how you might like to view the brush styles in the Panel window. Such settings include Text Only, Small or Large Thumbnail, Small or Large List, or Stroke Thumbnail.*

10. Paint with your chosen brush. Alter the brush options in the Options bar. Change the brush tip size and colors, and experiment with the Opacity and Flow settings. See Figure 7–10.

> **Note:** *From the Photoshop help files: Opacity sets the transparency of color you apply. Flow sets the rate at which color is applied as you move the pointer over an area. As you paint over an area, pressing the mouse button, the amount of color will build up based on the flow rate, up to the opacity setting.*

FIGURE | 7–10 |

Adjust the Flow setting of the brush and see what effect this has when you paint.

11. Play with the adjustments in the Brush panel; try Scatterings, for example. Click on the Scattering option on the left-hand side of the panel (it highlights in blue and a check mark appears in its checkbox). Then adjust its settings in the options area to the right. See Figure 7–11. To turn off Scattering, click on the checkbox to the left of the Scattering option.

FIGURE | 7–11 |

Adjust settings for the Scattering effect in the Brush panel.

MAKING A CUSTOM BRUSH

Photoshop has provided a plethora of brush styles, but inevitably, there will
be a need for something more and different. This is where making custom
brushes comes in handy. A sample selection from any image or photograph
can be used as a custom brush. First, marquee the area of the image you
would like to use as a brush (be sure the correct layer in the Layers panel is
selected), choose Edit > Define Brush Preset, and give your brush a name.

The custom brush shows up in the Brush Presets list (Window > Brush Presets).
See Figure 7–12 and Figure 7–13. You can also draw or paint a pattern or shape,
select it, and then choose Edit > Define Brush Preset. See Figure 7–14.

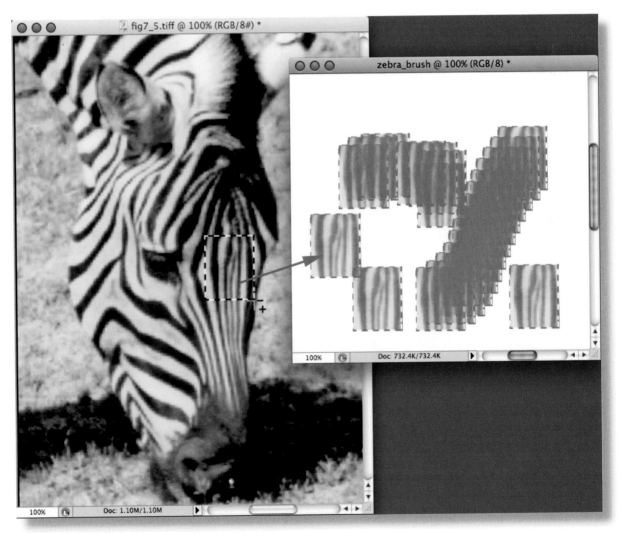

FIGURE | 7–12 |

Need a brush of zebra stripes? Make a selection of part of a zebra picture and save it as a custom brush.

FIGURE | 7–13 |

The zebra brush is saved in Brush Presets (Window > Brush Presets). Note that this screen shot shows the Brush Preset window set to Small Thumbnail view. To set the view, click the arrow with four horizontal lines in the upper-right corner of the panel and select a view option (Small Thumbnail, Large Thumbnail, Small List, etc.) from the drop-down menu.

FIGURE | 7–14 |

Draw your own shapes (i.e., crazy flowers) and make them into custom brushes.

VECTORS—A GUEST APPEARANCE

I wish I could make it simple and tell you it is all black and white when learning this program, but there are gray areas to be addressed. Even though Photoshop is the pixel master, it can work with vectors on a minimal level—enough to use as a temporary solution for creating more flexibility in your drawing and for compatibility purposes when importing and exporting between programs. It is temporary in the sense that you can draw and make shapes using vector attributes, where no pixels are associated with the paths drawn, but that is only until the objects become rasterized (turned into pixels) with a fill or stroke color.

> **Note:** *For a review of the differences between vectors and bitmaps, see Chapter 3. In several places and processes within the program, vectors make a guest appearance, such as when you use the Pen tool and create paths, with vector masks, with type, and when you save in vector-supported file formats.*

PATHS

Paths are vector lines you draw in Photoshop. They are used to define areas of an image and make new shapes or selections. You make paths using the Pen tool (see next section) or Shape tools, or by converting a selection into a path. To see created paths, go to Window > Paths. See Figure 7–15.

Let's make some paths so you can experience how they work.

1. Create a new document, and make it about 500 by 500 pixels in size.

2. Press Shift-Tab to hide unneeded panels, if necessary.

3. In the toolbox, set your foreground and background colors to their defaults (black foreground, white background) by pressing the D key.

4. Choose Window > Paths to open the Paths panel, if not already open in the Essentials workspace. Note that no paths are indicated in the panel—yet.

5. Select the Freeform Pen tool in the toolbox. See Figure 7–16.

> **Note:** *The ways of the Pen tools are vast and somewhat complicated (see the next section). For now, using the Freeform Pen tool is a good way to start.*

6. In the Options bar for the Freeform Pen tool, choose the Paths shape option, which is the second icon (the square with the Pen symbol in the middle). See Figure 7–17 (on the next page).

FIGURE | 7–15 |

The Paths panel.

FIGURE | 7–16 |

Select the Freeform Pen tool.

FIGURE | 7–17 |

Choose the Paths shape option.

7. Click and drag the Freeform Pen tool on your blank canvas, making a random, closed shape. To close a shape, approach the beginning of the path; an O-shape will appear near the tool. The shape is indicated as a work path in the Paths panel. See Figure 7–18. A work path is temporary. Unless you save it, it will be replaced when you draw another path.

8. Before you save a path, first replace the work path with another path. Try this: select the Rectangular Marquee tool. Click and drag on your canvas to define the rectangle. Right now, it is considered a selection (indicated by marching ants). In the Paths panel, click on the arrow with four lines in the upper-right corner to open its options, and then choose Make Work Path. See Figure 7–19. Set the Tolerance (smoothness) of the path to 2.0. Note in the Paths panel that the work path you made before has been replaced by a new, rectangular work path. Congratulations, you just created a path made from a selection!

FIGURE | 7–18 |

A path is indicated as a temporary work path in the Paths panel.

9. With a work path you can modify the path freely (using vectors) before committing to the final, bitmapped version. Choose the Direct Selection tool in the toolbox. This tool lets you select individual points on the path to modify it. See Figure 7–20. Click on a line of the rectangular work path to select it. Note the points on each corner (called anchor points). Click and drag one of the corner points to modify the rectangular shape into a triangular shape. See Figure 7–21. The work path is updated in the Paths panel.

FIGURE | 7–19 |

In the Paths panel, change a selection into a work path.

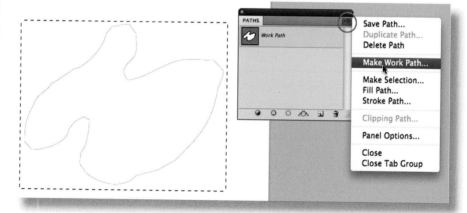

10. From the Paths panel's options (click on the arrow in the upper-right corner of the panel), choose Save Path. Name it **mytriangle**.

11. Let's rasterize this shape—cast it in stone, so to speak. Choose Window > Layers, if not already open. Double-click on the Background layer to release it to a layer that can be edited.

12. Go back to the Paths panel and select the **mytriangle** path. From the panel's options, choose Fill Path. See Figure 7–22. Click OK. A copy of the triangle path becomes a permanent bitmap object in the current layer. In other words, you cannot use the Direct Selection tool to select individual points on the filled shape. In the Paths panel, however, the **mytriangle** work path is still available for modification. See Figure 7–23.

FIGURE | 7–20 |

Choose the Direct Selection tool in the toolbox to select individual anchor points on a path.

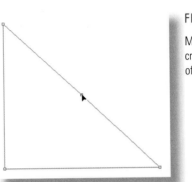

FIGURE | 7–21 |

Move an anchor point to create a triangular shape out of a rectangular shape.

FIGURE | 7–22 |

Make a work path a bitmapped object by filling the path.

FIGURE | 7–23 |

A path becomes a bitmap object in the Layers panel.

THE PEN TOOL

Ahh, the Pen tool, an instrument that either wreaks havoc or invokes joy, depending on your experience with it. I am not going to delve into the intricate workings of this tool in this book. While it is an available option for drawing in Photoshop, it is best utilized in a vector-robust program, such as Adobe Illustrator. In fact, it is such an important tool in that program that I spend almost a complete chapter on the Pen tool in my book *Exploring Adobe Illustrator CS5*.

In brief, the Pen tool lets you draw straight and curved vector segments and paths, defined by anchor points. With each click of the tool, anchor points are deposited and can be selected and modified with the Direct Selection tool (what you experienced in the last section on Paths). Through direction lines and direction points (together called direction handles), anchor points define the position and curve attributes of each line segment. See Figure 7–24. Because it is so precise, the Pen tool is excellent for tracing around complex shapes. In the following steps, practice drawing straight and curved lines with the tool, first randomly to get a feel for it and then more precisely to trace images.

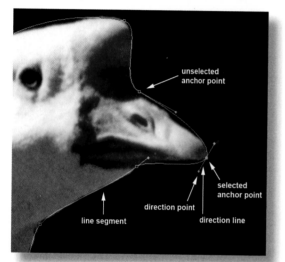

FIGURE | 7–24 |

Anatomy of a path.

1. In Photoshop, choose File > New and make a new, blank document (any size).

2. Select the Pen tool in the toolbox. See Figure 7–25.

3. As if you are doodling on a piece of paper, randomly click to place anchor points on the document. To create straight-line segments, click the Pen tool and then pick it up and click somewhere else; keep clicking to make straight lines.

FIGURE | 7–25 |

Select the Pen tool in the toolbox.

4. To end the path, Command-click (Mac) or Ctrl-click (Windows) away from all objects, or click on the first point of your path to close it.

5. To make curved lines, click and drag, keeping the mouse button pressed. Continue to click and drag to make curves. Fun, huh?

6. With no objective, continue to make straight and curved lines. Use the Direct Selection tool to select and modify individual anchor points. Use the Path Selection tool (see Figure 7–26) to select a complete path, so you can move it or delete it with the Delete key.

FIGURE | 7–26 |

Select the Path Selection tool.

7. Now for more precision drawing. Open **pen_practice.psd** from the **chap07_lessons** folder.

8. In the Layers panel make sure **drawing_layer** is highlighted. See Figure 7–27.

9. Select the Pen tool in the toolbox.

10. In the Options bar for the Pen tool, choose the Paths shape option. See Figure 7–28.

11. Click once on a corner of one of the diamonds in the first shape. This action makes an anchor point. Click the next corner, then the next, and then close the shape by clicking on the first anchor point again. See Figure 7–29. If you make a mistake (which is likely when you first attempt to use this tool), select the previous step in the History panel or choose Edit > Step Backward. If you are a perfectionist and want perfect, straight-line segments between anchor points, hold down Shift as you click on each point to constrain them to 45-degree angles.

12. Practice creating straight-line segments on the other three diamond shapes. Choose Window > Paths to view the work paths you have created.

13. On the next tile shape (resembling a sunburst), click once with the Pen tool on a tip of one of the teardrop shapes, and then click and drag horizontally on the rounded head of the tear-drop to create a curve. (With your finger still on the mouse you can continue to drag the direction lines out to create a rounder curve and also move the direction handle up-down or in-out to make the line tangent with the tracing image.) See Figure 7–30 (on the next page). Click again—do not drag—on the anchor point at the bottom of the teardrop to close the shape.
Continue tracing the other teardrop shapes, and the circle in the middle. For fun: can you draw the circle in the middle using only two anchor points?

14. Continue your Pen practice on the flower shape.

15. Change your vector shapes into bitmapped shapes. First, choose a foreground color for the fill. Next, select the **Work Path** layer in the Paths panel. Click on submenu in the upper-right corner of the Panel window, choose Fill Path, and click OK.

16. See **pen_practice_final.psd** in the **chap07_lessons** folder for a completed version of this exercise. View the work paths in the Paths panel. The paths were stroked with a brush style with color dynamics turned on. To apply the stroke to your own work, choose Stroke Path from the Paths panel's options menu or click on the shortcut at the bottom of the Panel window. See Figure 7–31 (on the next page).

FIGURE | 7–27 |

The **drawing_layer** selected.

FIGURE | 7–28 |

Choose the Paths shape option in the Options bar.

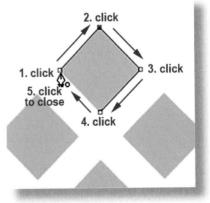

2. click
1. click
3. click
5. click to close
4. click

FIGURE | 7–29 |

Each time you click with the Pen tool, you create an anchor point.

FIGURE | 7–30 |

Create a curved-line segment by clicking and dragging with the Pen tool.

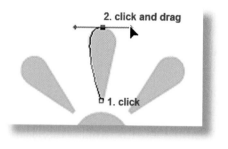

VECTOR MASKS

Since I am currently covering the different ways to work with vectors, I want to briefly mention vector masks. Masks in Photoshop are a way to hide and reveal areas of an image without permanently changing it. They are very useful in image editing and can create interesting effects (see Chapter 8).

FIGURE | 7–31 |

To quickly apply a stroke to a work path, select the shortcut at the bottom of the Paths panel.

Vectors produce graphics with clean, harp edges (not pixelated). To take advantage of this attribute, Photoshop offers you the ability to create vector masks. On a layer, vector masks produce a sharp-edged shape that is useful when you want to add a graphic element with clean, defined edges or when you wish to export your image into a vector-based program, such as Adobe Illustrator. The vector mask is defined in the Layers and Paths panels. See Figure 7–32. Use the Pen or a Shape tool (see later section in this chapter) to draw a work path, and then define its vector mask by choosing Layer > Vector Mask > Reveal All or Hide All.

FIGURE | 7–32 |

A vector mask is defined in the Layers and Paths panels.

TYPE

Have you ever noticed that when you print a text document from a word processing program, such as Microsoft Word, that the text is very clean and crisp looking, and no matter what size you make it—12 pt or 60 pt—it always looks great? On the other hand, when you print a piece of clipart that was scaled really big on the document, it looks kind of blurry and pixelated. Why? Well, the type contains vector data that keeps the letter shapes sharp and that can be scaled large or small because, as you discovered in Chapter 3, vectors are not dependent on resolution. Therefore, when type is printed on a printer that supports this vector data, it's perfect and easily readable. In contrast, the clipart is constrained by its resolution (because it is composed of pixels) and must remain a particular size to preserve its crispness when printed.

FIGURE | 7–33 |

The Horizontal Type tool in the toolbox.

Type in Photoshop works very much like type in a word processing program. When first created, it is placed on its own layer. It also contains vector data, so you can easily modify it without worrying about how good it is going to look when printed. To apply type to a Photoshop document, select the Horizontal Type tool (see Figure 7–33), click within the document, and begin typing.

You can adjust a type's font, size, orientation, and color in the Options bar, similar to editing type in a word processing program. Alternatively, choose Window > Character and Window > Paragraph for more formatting choices. See Figure 7–34.

FIGURE | 7–34 |

Format text in a Type tool's Options bar and Character panel.

▶ DON'T GO THERE

Although I have compared how type works in Photoshop to how it works in a word processing program, I do not recommend using Photoshop as a word processing program, especially if you need large bodies of text in an image or layout. For adding headlines and body copy, use a layout program, such as Adobe InDesign or QuarkXPress. These programs support type characteristics much better. Use type only as a design element in Photoshop.

FIGURE | 7–35 |

When saving in EPS, the vector data can be preserved (indicated by a check mark), but note the warning. It will not be preserved when reopened in Photoshop, only when opened in a fully vector-supported program, such as Adobe Illustrator.

VECTOR COMPATIBILITY

As presented in Chapter 3, some image formats support vector data and some do not. When you work in Photoshop's native format (PSD), any vector masks, work paths, and type you create is preserved in that state until it is rasterized, which you might need to do to add certain effects and filters to the object. When you save your work, however, you must decide whether you want to keep the vector data in the file. This depends on where it is headed. If you save a file in the EPS or PDF formats, the vector data is preserved when the file is opened in a vector-based program, such as Adobe InDesign or Illustrator (see Figure 7–35). You can select and edit individual objects and the anchor points that define them.

If saved in a TIFF or JPEG format and opened in a vector-based program, the vector data is rasterized (flattened into pixels). See Figure 7–36 and Figure 7–37. The **chap07_lessons/samples** folder contains several saved versions of an image in different formats. If you have Adobe Illustrator, for instance, you can import these versions into the program and then select the image or image parts to see what vector attributes of the image have remained. You can also open each version in Photoshop and see what happens. Does the vector data remain intact, or is everything rasterized?

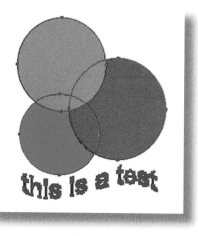

FIGURE | 7–36 |

This EPS-formatted version of a file was saved in Photoshop and opened in Illustrator. When you click on the grouped item, you can see the editable, individual anchor points that comprise vector objects.

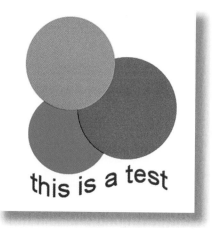

FIGURE | 7–37 |

This JPEG-formatted version of a file was saved in Photoshop and opened in Illustrator. Because JPEG does not support vector data, when opened in Illustrator or Photoshop it is composed of bitmapped pixels only.

MAKING SHAPES

In almost any art class you learn how to draw geometric shapes, and in previous chapters you have made shapes. However, now that you have learned about the characteristics of drawing with vectors and bitmaps, you can better understand the shape-making tools and options. One way to make shapes quickly is to make a selection (i.e., draw with the Marquee or Lasso tools) and then fill or stroke the shape by choosing Edit > Fill (or Stroke). There is also a set of Shape tools (see Figure 7–38) that provides you with selections to choose from in the Options bar. See Figure 7–39. Such selections include the type of shape (shape layers or vector masks, paths, or fill pixels), the characteristics of each of which were covered in the last sections on drawing with vectors versus pixels. And depending on what shape type you choose, you also have the ability to add, subtract, exclude, and intersect shapes as well as add styles (premade effects).

FIGURE | 7–38 |

The Shape tools available in the toolbox.

FIGURE | 7–39 |

The Shape tool's Options bar.

The following steps will familiarize you with the Shape tools.

1. Create a new file about 500 by 500 pixels in size. Make sure the background content is white.

2. Select the Rounded Rectangle tool in the toolbox. See Figure 7–38.

3. In the Options bar, select the Fill pixels style option. See Figure 7–40.

Note: *In the Options bar, you can modify the geometric options for the selected shape by clicking on the second inverted arrow. See Figure 7–41.*

FIGURE | 7–40 |

Select the Fill pixels option to make rasterized shapes.

FIGURE | 7–41 |

You can alter the geometric options for a selected shape in the Options bar.

4. Set a foreground color in the toolbox.

5. Click and draw a rounded rectangle on the blank canvas.

6. Open the Layers panel. Note that the rectangle is a rasterized image on the Background layer.

7. Select the Paths style option in the Options bar. See Figure 7–42.

FIGURE | 7–42 |

Select the Paths style option.

8. Select the Polygon tool.

9. Draw a polygon on the document. It is a temporary work path you can alter.

10. Open the Paths panel to see the work path.

11. Select the Shape layers style option in the Options bar. See Figure 7–43.

FIGURE | 7–43 |

Select the Shape layers style option.

12. Choose a new foreground color.

13. Select the Custom Shape tool and, in the Shape Options drop-down menu, choose a custom shape. See Figure 7–44.

> Note: *You can also make your own custom shapes to add to these choices. See the Photoshop Help files for details.*

FIGURE | 7–44 |

Select a custom shape.

14. Draw the shape on the document. Note in the Layers panel a new layer appears containing the shape and its vector mask.

15. Select Subtract from shape area in the Options bar, and then draw another custom shape overlapping the first custom shape you made. See Figure 7–45 and Figure 7–46.

Explore the other shape modification options, such as adding, intersecting, or excluding a shape from another.

FIGURE | 7–45 |

Select Subtract from shape area in the Options bar.

FIGURE | 7–46 |

The shape of one object subtracted from another.

16. Select a Style option from the Options bar. See Figure 7–47. The selected shape is updated with the style. Pretty slick, eh?

FIGURE | 7–47 |

Select a shape style.

LESSON: NONREPRESENTATIONAL ART CREATION

You will be surprised to find that this lesson contains very little step-by-step instruction.

Since painting and drawing can be such an exploratory medium, I thought I would leave most of this lesson to your imagination. Using the various tools and techniques you learned in this chapter, create a nonrepresentational digital art piece—an art creation that doesn't reference anything in nature or reality. See Figure 7–48.

As described in the book *Artforms* (Revised Seventh Edition), by Duane Preble and Sarah Preble (revised by Patrick Frank), "Nonrepresentational art (sometimes called nonobjective or nonfigurative art) presents visual forms with no specific references to anything outside themselves. Just as we can respond to the pure sound of music, we can respond to the pure visual forms of nonrepresentational art."

1. In Photoshop, use the toolbox to set the background color to any color of your choice.

2. Create a new file about 500 by 500 pixels in size. Set Color Mode to RGB Color, and the resolution to 150 ppi. For Background Contents, choose Background Color, which is the color you specified in the first step.

3. Open the Layers panel.

4. Make a new layer and name it **painting**.

FIGURE | 7–48 |

An example of nonrepresentational art using Photoshop. See also the chapter opening image.

5. Select the Brush or Pencil tool. Set the brush style to your liking and start to paint on your canvas. It does not matter what you paint—if you don't like it, there is always the History panel. Open the Brush panel (Window > Brush) to explore more options.

6. Create another layer and name it **shapes**.

7. Create any number of fill shapes using the Shape tool.

8. Make other shapes, using vector shape layers and paths.

9. Save your file, if you have not already (save often!).

10. Add some text as a graphic design element to the canvas.

11. Use Layer styles on any of the layers you have created, such as Drop Shadow, Bevel and Emboss, and Pattern Overlay. To do this, highlight the layer you want to affect in the Layers panel, and choose Layer > Layer Style from the menu bar or by clicking on the fx icon at the bottom of the Layers panel.

12. If you recall how from previous lessons, place blending effects and filters on any of the layers you have created. (For more specifics on the "what" and "how" of blending effects and filters, see Chapter 9.)

13. Create another layer and name it **frame**. Draw or construct (using the Shape tool options, such as Subtract or Intersect) a frame around your masterpiece.

14. Save your file in the JPEG format, set the quality amount to about 8, and e-mail your art to a friend.

SUMMARY

After this chapter, there should be no such thing as a blank Photoshop canvas. Usually it only takes a quick introduction to the drawing and painting tools and processes in this program to initiate a creative spark.

▶ IN REVIEW

1. What is the main difference between the Pencil and Brush tools?

2. Name at least three features in the Brush panel.

3. Does the Eraser tool erase with the foreground color or background color?

4. Why would having some vector support in Photoshop be useful for drawing and painting?

5. Name three areas (features/tools) in Photoshop that incorporate the use of vector technology.

6. What is the difference between a "click" action and a "click and drag" action when you are using the Pen tool?

7. What are paths in Photoshop? How do you make them? What tools do you use to select a complete path or parts of a path?

8. What file formats preserve vector data?

9. In what three styles (ways) can you create shapes in Photoshop?

10. Describe nonrepresentational (nonobjective) art.

▶ EXPLORING ON YOUR OWN

1. Create your own custom brush out of your signature. See Figure 7–49.

    ▶ Make a new document. For Background Contents, choose Transparent.
    ▶ Select the Pencil tool in the toolbox.
    ▶ Choose a brush style with a small diameter (1 to 5 pixels in size).
    ▶ Choose a foreground color.
    ▶ Write your signature on the document.

- ▶ Choose Edit > Define Brush Preset, and name your custom brush.
- ▶ Set your brush settings in the Brush panel (look for your custom brush in the Brush Tip Shape area).
- ▶ Paint with your signature.

2. In the Photoshop Help files (Help > Photoshop Help), do a search for "brush dynamics" and find out what this feature does.

3. In the Help files, find out what the Convert Point tool does.

4. Using the Pen tool, trace around the images (**goose.tif** or **peacock.jpg**) provided in the **chap07_lessons/samples** folder.

5. Practice creating some type on a path.

- ▶ Using the Pen tool, draw a simple path on your document.
- ▶ Select the Type tool, and set the typeface and font size in the Options bar.
- ▶ Click with the Type tool (the little I-beam) on the path and start typing some text.
- ▶ Adjust the type by selecting it and modifying its formatting options in the Options bar.
- ▶ Adjust the path the type is on and the starting point of the type by using the Direct Selection tool. See Figure 7–50.

6. Discover the wonder of kaleidoscopes. Visit these sites:

- ▶ Amazing Software Kaleidoscopes: *http://bindweed.com/kaleidoscopes.htm*
- ▶ Kaleidoscopes Heaven: *http:// kaleidoscopeheaven.org/*
- ▶ Kaleidoscope Collector (how they work): *http://www.kaleidoscopesusa.com/how.htm*
- ▶ Make your own Kaleidoscope: *http://familycrafts.about.com/cs/ toystomake/a/blconnkaleid.htm*

FIGURE | 7–49 |

Use the Scattering option in the Brush panel with your new custom signature brush.

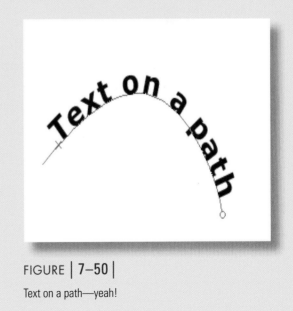

FIGURE | 7–50 |

Text on a path—yeah!

7. Try the Rotate View tool.

The Rotate View tool is located in the Tools panel, underneath the Hand tool. See Figure 7–51. Select the tool, then click and drag on an image (a compass should appear on top of the image). The OpenGL performance of Photoshop provides the performance necessary to display the image view in a rotated state, including rapid updates during drawing and painting. This tool is great for tablet sketch artists who prefer to rotate an image view to match the more natural arrangement of pencil and paper.

FIGURE | 7–51 |

Select the Rotate View tool.

8. Watch a video on the use of Content Aware technology - now available on a minimal level in CS5. Go to www.youtube.com and do a search for "Content Aware".

adventures
IN DESIGN

DODGE AND BURN

In traditional photography, "dodge and burn" is a technique whereby, using light, a photographer can selectively darken (burn) areas in a photograph and selectively lighten (dodge) shadowed areas to bring out details. In glorified form, this technique is provided for you in Photoshop with the Dodge and Burn tools. Using any selected brush tip, these tools offer the artist localized and precise tonal control of the pixels in an image. See Figure B–1.

FIGURE | B–1 |

The Dodge and Burn tools (along with the Sponge tool) offer localized tonal control on a photograph.

In the toolbox, the Dodge and Burn tools are grouped with another tonal control tool: the Sponge tool. These tools are great for localized manipulation of the highlights, mid-tones, and shadows in a photograph. For more global control, use the Levels or Curves command. It is a wonderful thing to be able to use the Dodge and Burn tools to create subtle adjustments to the brightness and contrast in a photograph, and it's a simple way to paint more spatially enhanced objects. With these tools you can paint dimensional illusions quickly, as you will see in the next section.

PROFESSIONAL PROJECT EXAMPLE

If you have ever taken a traditional drawing or painting class (which I wholeheartedly recommend!), you have probably been assigned the onerous task of rendering an egg—in all its proportionally rounded splendor—using hard and soft lead pencils, charcoal, or a paintbrush. It sounds easy enough; after all it is only an egg. However, after some initial sketches, you might realize—at least I did—that rendering an egg involves a very subtle play of dark and light pencil strokes and finger smudging to make the egg look somewhat realistic, rather than flat or oddly deformed. Using the Dodge and Burn tools in Photoshop, the digital art professional has a more, shall we say, quick and dirty solution to breathing life into a flat image or photograph.

Figure B–2 is a photograph of some eggs. There are obvious lights and darks in the photo, but what happens if we enhance these tones for an even more dimensional look? With the Dodge tool and a soft-tipped brush (or airbrush), areas of the eggs can be further lightened. See Figure B–3. Moreover, with the Burn tool and a soft-tipped brush (or airbrush), areas of the egg can be further darkened. See Figure B–4. The result is two

FIGURE | B–2 |

A digital photograph of some eggs without photo retouching.

FIGURE | B–3 |

With a soft-tipped brush, lighten areas of a photograph with the Dodge tool.

With a soft-tipped brush, darken areas of a photograph with the Burn tool.

A photograph of two eggs made more "golden-looking" using the Dodge and Burn tools.

Go from flat to spatial. Draw a dimensional-looking egg shape using the Dodge and Burn tools.

"golden-looking" eggs. See Figure B–5. This same technique can be applied without a photo reference. Start with a gray-toned elliptical shape and build the shadows and highlights with varied brush strokes and tip sizes. See Figure B–6.

YOUR TURN

Using the sample file **eggs.psd** in the **aid_examples/ dodge_burn_examples** folder, you will paint your own realistic eggs with a metallic sheen. If you like, you can further enhance the image with layer styles and/or artistic brush stroke or sketch filters.

Dodge and Burn Project Guidelines

1. Open the **eggs.psd** file from the **aid_examples/ dodge_burn_examples** folder.

2. View the Layers panel, and be sure the **overlay_ adjustment_layer** is selected. See Figure B–7. This is the layer you will paint on with the Dodge and Burn tools. It is a special layer filled with a 50% gray background and set with an Overlay blending mode, located above, thus protecting the original photo you are about to enhance.

FIGURE | B–7 |

Select the **overlay_adjustment_
layer**.

3. Select the Burn or Dodge tool in the toolbox, and set your brush tip size. For starters, I suggest a soft brush with a diameter of about 45 pixels. For Range in the Options bar of the tool, select Midtones. See Figure B–8. You can also play with the Exposure setting to adjust the amount (or intensity) of lightness or darkness applied with each brush stroke.

4. After enhancing the egg photo, save your file in your lessons folder. Then hide **overlay_adjustment_
layer** and **egg1** in the Layers panel. This reveals another egg example: flat, elliptical shapes.

5. Expand the **other_egg_samples** layer set by clicking on the triangle next to the folder icon, and select the **hand_drawn_egg1** layer.

6. Use the Burn and Dodge tools with soft-tipped brushes to bring the egg to dimensional life.

7. Add a drop shadow for further spatial impact via Layer > Layer Style > Drop Shadow.

8. Enhance the other egg example in the **hand_
drawn_egg2** layer.

9. Save your golden eggs.

Things to Consider

For future explorations with drawing and painting, as featured in this "Adventures in Design," consider the following:

▶ Whenever possible, use an adjustment layer to work on over your original image to protect it. When working with localized tonal control tools, create a new layer with a 50% gray fill and set to the Overlay blending mode (as in the egg.psd file). To make global tonal adjustments, such as Levels and Color Balance, choose Layer > New Adjustment Layer.

▶ There are hundreds of artist's tips and techniques for using Photoshop. Step-by-step instructions are plentiful on the World Wide Web. Do a global search for "Photoshop tips and techniques" or a more refined search for the name of a Photoshop tool or function, such as "dodge and burn." Also, a helpful book to consider is *Best Practice: The Pros on Adobe* Photoshop, by Toni Toland.

FIGURE | B–8 |

Set options for the Dodge or Burn tools, such as Brush Size, Range, and Exposure.

Explorer PAGES

Kevin Burke

"When I can get to the point where the tools seem to disappear from the process, creativity can flow more readily."

Jazz at Pink's Alley #1. Courtesy Pawblo LLC and Kevin Burke.

About Kevin Burke

Kevin Burke was born in Rapid City, SD and raised in Springfield, MA. As a grade school and high school student, he was always intrigued by graphic arts. How someone could get a whole story in one logo amazed him. A two-year stint in the Army made it possible to attend Keene State College in Keene, NH, focusing in printmaking, sculpture, and ceramics. While at Keene State, he attended the College of York St. John in York, England, where—through a miscommunication about academic courses—he studied only ceramics and printmaking. Shortly after returning from England, he began working as a production potter for a local pottery. After a couple of years, he began showing his work in galleries in New England and Europe.

Snowboarding came along and Kevin started to get involved with judging snowboard events and eventually coaching these athletes. He is presently a Snowboard Coach with

Okemo Mountain School, where he also teaches computers and is the resident techie.

Kevin, after a few years of changing jobs and starting a couple of non-art-related businesses, decided it was time to get back into focus with his art. Starting Pawblo LLC in 2000, this became the vehicle to begin working in technology and the arts. In 2004, he attended Marlboro College Graduate Center in Brattleboro, VT, and received a Masters of Science degree in Information Technology Management. During this time it became apparent that the bug for graphic design never left, and so he started concentrating on merging art and technology.

Kevin now resides in Wardsboro, VT, with his wife, Jenna. He is building a studio where he will teach technology to all levels of learners. The primary focus will be to teach art skills to techies and techie skills to artists.

See more of Kevin's work at *http://pawblo.com*

About the Work of Kevin Burke

Kevin shares his process working on the Women's Film Festival poster: "The Women's Film Festival is a non-profit group that raises money for the Women's Crisis Center in Brattleboro, VT. I volunteered my time to do this piece, as well as the brochure, catalogue, postcards, and website. Domestic violence is something we still need to bring awareness to. This piece was done entirely in Photoshop. The process is not complex. There are many layers with some gradients as well as the use of the resize/warp tool.

"The main image came from a still in the movie *Companeras*. The face and the sombrero were irresistible but because of the horizontal nature of the image, I was wondering how to get the poster into a vertical layout without losing the image. While looking at Apple's 'flow' display in iTunes, the reflection made perfect sense. The rest was organizing the information around this so as to enhance the picture and still get the information across. I came up with about 5 variations and this one won."

Kevin speaks of his love for drawing: "I have been drawing ever since I can remember, but deliberately from when I was about 9 years old. My tools have always been the traditional tools of pencil, paper and eraser.

"As soon as computers became fast enough, I began experimenting with drawing, using a Wacom pen tablet and Photoshop. Drawing usually depends on the light, not only for the subject, but to be able to see the paper, so drawing in dark places on paper is sort of a pain, but with a backlit screen on my computer, life is much easier and I can now draw in the dark. One of my favorite pastimes is to go and listen to live jazz at Pink's Alley in Manchester [Vermont], and draw while the band plays. This is a great exercise for getting proficient at Photoshop because I like to get the drawings done fairly quickly. I am getting to the point where the keyboard commands make life so much easier, and I no longer have to think about where the tools are."

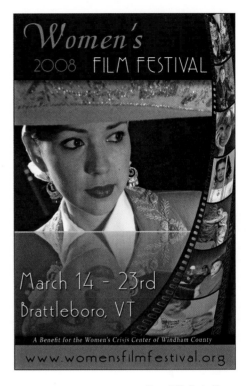

Women's Film Festival Poster.
Courtesy Pawblo LLC and Kevin Burke.

Jazz at Pink's Alley #2. Courtesy Pawblo LLC and Kevin Burke.

| Masking |

8

charting your course

When the power of masking in digital illustration and design was first developed, people wondered how they managed so long without it. Masking is a technique for hiding or revealing areas of an image. Similar to how masking tape protects window trim as you paint around it, a digital mask reveals or hides areas of an image as you apply effects to unmasked areas.

Masks are used often in animation and digital video editing. A scene transition where one frame wipes away another is a moving mask. A computer-generated character interacting with a human actor is superimposed into a scene using masks. There are several types of masks in Photoshop for use in digital imagery. Each contains specific attributes for different purposes.

In this chapter, I cover how a mask works and the various types of masks that can be created in Photoshop, including layer and vector masks, type masks, clipping masks, and quick masks.

goals

In this chapter you will:

▶ *Learn what a mask is and discover how it works and is used in Photoshop*

▶ *Explore the types of masks available in Photoshop*

▶ *Paint full and partial selections using quick masks*

▶ *Hide and reveal content with layer and clipping masks*

UNMASKING MASKS

How does a mask work? First, I will give you an overview, and then I will describe it in depth. Examine the four steps in Figure 8–1. Step 1 shows an original photograph taken at the rustic Palmela castle in Portugal. Step 2 shows part of the photo with a layer mask applied. My face in the cardboard character was selected with the Elliptical Marquee tool, and then Layer > Layer Mask > Hide Selection was chosen. Step 3 indicates the layer (a picture of Max from Chapter 4) that will be affected by the mask created in Step 2. In Step 4 the "Max" layer is placed below the mask layer, whereby Max's face replaces mine. All of this magic was done without damaging the original photo.

To clarify a few things for you—or maybe to confuse you further—let me give you a closer look at the characteristics of a mask. Masks get easier to grasp when you actually

FIGURE | 8–1 |

This four-part example shows how a mask can replace an area of a photograph with another photograph behind it. The mask "protects" the original image—so it appears as if you have cut out (deleted) selected parts of an image without actually destroying it. It is just an illusion.

play with them (like anything else, of course!). So when you reach the end of this chapter and have had some experience with masks, you might want to review this section.

When Step 2 was executed on the photo example (see Step 2, Figure 8–1), the mask became attached to the photo's layer in the Layers panel. Now note the mask thumbnail in the layer **cardboard_character** in Figure 8–2.

FIGURE | 8–2 |

The layer mask thumbnail located on the same layer in which the mask is applied.

FIGURE | 8–3 |

Unlink the mask layer from the original object it was masking.

Check it out for yourself! Open **example_mask.psd** in the **chap08_ lessons/samples** folder. Then open the Layers panel and take a look. The black dot in the layer mask thumbnail shows the part of the mask that's to be transparent; in other words, the selected area is hidden. An important distinction to make here is that the mask is not *deleting* the selection but *hiding* it. You can disable or delete a mask and still keep the original photo or artwork intact. To do so in this example, click on the mask thumbnail in the Layers panel (it will have a black outline around it when selected), and then choose Layer > Layer Mask > Disable (a big X appears over the thumbnail). To turn it back on, choose Layer > Layer Mask > Enable. Here are a few other things to do with masks:

FIGURE | 8–4 |

Move an unlocked mask elsewhere on the image.

► Unlink and move a mask to hide other areas of an image or photograph: In the example layer mask, unlink the mask thumbnail in the Layers panel from the photo it was masking by clicking the link icon, selecting the layer mask thumbnail, and moving it to a different location using the Move tool. See Figure 8–3 and Figure 8–4.

► Disable or delete a mask without damaging the original work. See Figure 8–5.

FIGURE | 8–5 |

Disable or delete a mask without damaging the original image.

► Make masks out of any selected shape. See Figure 8–6.

► Load and save a selection from a mask: You can store and reload selections as alpha channels. Alpha channels are located in the Channels panel, and they have many uses. See "Note" on page 181. When you examine an alpha channel in Photoshop (see Figure 8–7), the black indicates the area you can see through the mask (like a window, it is transparent), and the white is the opaque area. Figure 8–8 shows how the black and white areas of an alpha channel can hide or reveal (mask) areas of an image. There can also be semitransparent masks at all different levels of transparency, which is indicated by varying shades of gray. See Figure 8–9. You will learn how to create these soft transparency effects using a quick mask in the section "Quick Masks."

FIGURE | 8–6 |

Make masks out of any selected shape, like that of Max's body.

FIGURE | 8–7 |

An alpha channel, saved in the Channels panel, can be used to mask out areas of an image.

FIGURE | 8–8 |

On the left, the background is revealed (black) and Max remains isolated from the mask. On the right, the background is revealed through Max (black) and the rest of the background remains protected.

FIGURE | 8–9 |

A gradient of grays can become a mask—each level of gray creating more or less transparency. Here, the ostrich is softly being revealed through the gradient mask.

Some file formats, such as TIFF, will support an alpha channel in an image. This is useful when you want to use an alpha channel (i.e., a mask) in another program (other than Photoshop) that supports the use of alpha channels, such as Adobe InDesign, Illustrator, Flash, or After Effects. See Figure 8–10.

FIGURE | 8–10 |

The option to preserve an alpha channel appears when you save a file to the TIFF format.

TYPES OF MASKS

Although the concept of masking in Photoshop is consistent, there are different types of mask you can use, including layer and vector masks, clipping masks, type masks, and quick masks.

> Note: *A little more about alpha channels: You can get into some sophisticated image editing and manipulation with alpha channels—something to look into in your more advanced studies of Photoshop. For now, keep in mind that channels, and alpha channels in particular, have these properties (taken directly from the Photoshop Help files):*
>
> ▶ Each image can contain up to 56 channels, including all color and alpha channels.
> ▶ You can specify a name, color, mask option, and opacity for each channel. (The opacity affects the preview of the channel, not the actual image.)
> ▶ All new channels have the same dimensions and number of pixels as the original image.
> ▶ You can edit an alpha channel using painting tools, editing tools, and filters (see Figure 8–11).
> ▶ You can convert alpha channels to spot color channels.

FIGURE | 8–11 |

From left to right: alpha channel without filter effect, alpha channel with filter effect, and result of alpha channel as a mask on the Max photograph (the edges of his body are transparent and appear "alien-like").

LAYER AND VECTOR MASKS

Layer masks let you create a mask that is linked to an object on the same layer, which, therefore, directly affects the object. A layer mask was used in our first example, shown in Figure 8–1. Vector masks are a variation on layer masks. They are created in much the same way. However, because vector masks consist of vectors, the edges of a selection being used for the mask are much more crisp and clean-looking. To quickly make and edit a layer or vector mask, you can try these steps (or just review them for later reference):

1. Select an area on an image or photograph using any shape Marquee tool or Lasso tool. Note that if you select the Background layer, you must double-click on the layer to turn it into a standard layer (Layer 0) for the next step to work.

2. Choose Layer > Layer Mask or Layer > Vector Mask, and determine whether you want the mask to reveal or hide the selection.

3. To edit a mask, Command-click (Mac) or Ctrl-click (Windows) on the layer mask thumbnail in the Layers panel to load the mask shape as a selection.

4. Turn on Edit in Quick Mask Mode in the toolbox. Add or subtract from the selection with the painting tools (details to follow in the section on quick masks).

CLIPPING MASKS

Clipping masks are a quick way to attach a sequence of layers to be masked by another layer. Here is how it is done:

1. Decide what item you want to use as a mask—text, shape, any filled object—and place it on its own layer.

> **Note:** *When using shapes, be sure the Fill pixels option is selected in the Options bar.*

2. Place items you want to be revealed through the mask in their own layers above the mask layer.

3. Hold down Alt/Option and place the cursor between these two layers. A funky icon of two circles, one atop the other, appears. Click on this edge line and the top layer will indent above the lower layer. The clipping mask has been executed. See Figure 8–12. Alternatively, you can select the items you want to be revealed through the mask and choose Layer > Create Clipping Mask.

FIGURE | 8–12 |

Create a clipping mask.

Note: *A clipping mask can be applied to several layers.*

HORIZONTAL AND VERTICAL TYPE MASK TOOLS

You can make masks out of type with the Horizontal Type Mask or Vertical Type Mask tools. It is quite easy:

1. In the toolbox, choose either the Horizontal Type Mask or the Vertical Type Mask tool. See Figure 8–13.

2. Set the type's formatting options (font, size) in the Options bar.

3. Click on the document and type a word or phrase. While you type, you will be sent into Edit in Quick Mask Mode, indicated by the transparent red overlay.

4. Press Enter on the numeric pad (not the main keyboard) or click on a selection tool to create the type selection.

5. Create a new layer in the Layers panel. Note that the type becomes a selection—but only temporarily—on the document for you to fill, add effects to, and use as an object for layer or clipping masks. See Figure 8–14.

FIGURE | 8–13 |

The Horizontal Type Mask and Vertical Type Mask tools in the toolbox.

FIGURE | 8–14 |

The selected text is filled, has a layer effect added to it, and is assigned a clipping mask that reveals a photographic texture through the letter forms.

QUICK MASKS

As mentioned in Chapter 4, there is a direct relationship between selections and color in Photoshop. The dynamics of this relationship allow very versatile and sophisticated mask-making with the use of Photoshop's quick mask feature. A quick mask is not really a mask but a temporary mode in which to define and edit selections with the Painting tools, or even a Photoshop filter effect. Paint with white to select more areas of an image; paint with black to deselect areas; paint with an opacity setting or shade of gray to create a semitransparent mask that is useful for soft-edged, feathered effects. (You can also uniformly soften selection edges with the Feathering option, accessed via the selection tool's Options bar or Select > Modify > Feather.)

Note: *When you paint with black and white, the selection is either indicated or not by marching ants once you exit Quick Mask mode. But, when you paint with an opacity setting or a tonal color, a selection may or may not be visible. A dialog box might appear. See Figure 8–15. However, although you cannot always see the marching ants of a semitransparent selection, the selection will be indicated by a level of gray when viewed as an alpha channel (saved mask).*

FIGURE | 8–15 |

The "selection edge not visible" warning.

When I designed the Max lesson in Chapter 4, I used a quick mask to extract the background from the photograph, so I could replace it. The original background was composed of many shadows and highlights, so, regrettably, I couldn't just click on it with the Magic Wand tool and be done with it. Moreover, I was determined to protect Max's body from the extraction. See Figure 8–16.

To get into Quick Mask Mode, I cursorily selected as much of the background as I could with the Lasso (or Magic Wand) tool. Then I chose Edit in Quick Mask Mode in the toolbox. See Figure 8–17.

Photoshop covers the nonselected areas of the image in a translucent color, which by default is red, like rubylith. (I could change this color by double-clicking on the Edit in Quick Mask Mode icon in the toolbox. See Figure 8–18.) I then selected the Brush tool in the toolbox. The swatches in the toolbox automatically become black and white, ready to edit by color my selected or nonselected areas when I paint. I painted with white to add to my selection (remove the translucent color) and black to delete areas of my selection (add the translucent color). Flipping between Edit in Standard Mode and Edit in Quick Mask Mode (toggle between the two modes by clicking on the Edit in Quick Mask Mode button or typing the letter Q) allows me to see how I was doing—showing what areas were selected. See Figure 8–19.

FIGURE | 8–17 |

The Edit in Quick Mask Mode option in the toolbox.

FIGURE | 8–18 |

Double-click on the Edit in Quick Mask Mode icon in the toolbox to get to its options.

FIGURE | 8–16 |

The original photo of Max taken near a window with my digital camera. Admittedly, not the most professional setup.

In Standard Mode, I saved a permanent version of my final selection to an alpha channel (in case I wanted to use it again or edit it later) by choosing Select > Save Selection. Last, I created the layer mask out of the selection, made a new background on a separate layer, and placed it below the mask layer. The result is shown in Figure 8–20 (on the next page).

FIGURE | 8–19 |

Move between Standard and Quick Mask Modes to see how the selection process is going.

LESSON: LISBON VIEW

In this lesson, you will create a new background in a photograph using Quick Mask Mode and a layer mask. See Figure 8–21.

Setting Up the File

1. Open the file **chap8L1.psd** in the folder **chap08_lessons**.

2. Choose View > Actual Pixels.

3. Press Shift-Tab to hide unneeded panels.

Making and Refining a Selection

1. With the Rectangular Marquee tool, draw a rectangle covering the top-left open area of the window; the selection does not need to be perfect. Hold down Shift and keep adding to the selection by selecting the other window panes. For the window with the figure in it, select only the top area with the rectangular shape. See Figure 8–22.

2. Click Edit in Quick Mask Mode in the toolbox. See Figure 8–23.

3. Zoom in close to the window area with the silhouette figure.

4. Select the Brush tool and choose a hard brush about 9 pixels in diameter. See Figure 8–24. Make sure the brush's opacity setting is set to 100% in the Options bar.

FIGURE | 8–20 |

The final Max image used in the Chapter 4 lesson. Compare with Figure 8–16.

FIGURE | 8–21 |

The lesson before and after a mask effect.

5. Make sure white is the foreground color swatch in the toolbox.

6. Add to the selection by painting away the translucent areas of the open window. You might need to change brush tip sizes to more accurately select the corner crevices of the window. Leave a halo of the translucent color around the head and flying hair strands of the figure. See Figure 8–25 (on the next page).

> Note: *If you get overly zealous with your painting, you can undo brush strokes in the History panel, or paint with black to deselect areas. Pressing the X key will toggle between the foreground and background colors. This is a great way to switch between black and white instantly!*

7. Click the Quick Mask icon to switch to Standard Mode so you can see what you have selected.

8. To refine this selection, switch back to Edit in Quick Mask Mode. Set your brush to a soft, round brush about 9 pixels in size. See Figure 8–26 (on the next page). Adjust its opacity setting in the Options bar to 92%. Paint carefully around the edge of the figure's head and over the flying strands of hair. You will not see it in the selection, but by using a softer brush and adjusting the opacity setting (or, alternatively, painting with a shade of gray), you can create a softer, more realistic mask effect around the hair (you will see this in a later step).

9. Keep refining the selection with the brush tools to your liking. All open parts of the window should be selected.

10. Go to Standard Mode and choose Select > Save Selection from the menu bar. Enter a name for the new alpha channel. See Figure 8–27 (on the next page).

11. Choose Window > Channels to view the alpha channel mask you just saved.

12. Save the lesson in your lessons folder.

FIGURE | 8–22 |

Select the open window areas with the Rectangular Marquee tool.

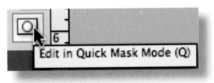

FIGURE | 8–23 |

Select Edit in Quick Mask Mode in the toolbox.

FIGURE | 8–24 |

Select an appropriately sized paintbrush.

FIGURE | 8–25 |

Keep part of the translucent color around the figure's head.

FIGURE | 8–26 |

Set the brush with a softer tip to produce subtle, semitransparent mask areas.

Create a Layer Mask

1. In the Layers panel, highlight the **lisbon_view** layer. Your windows should still be selected. If not, choose Select > Load Selection and select the alpha channel you created from the Channel pop-up menu, then click OK.

2. Choose Layer > Layer Mask > Hide Selection.

3. Choose File > Open and from the **chap08_lessons/ samples** folder open **background1.jpg**.

4. Click the Arrange Documents button on the Application bar and choose the 2 Up option.

5. Move a copy of the background image to the lesson file: with the Move tool, drag the image over the **lesson** file and let go of the mouse to drop the copy.

6. Place **Layer 1** (with the new background image) below the **lisbon_view** layer by clicking and dragging it. Position the background image to your liking behind the **lisbon_view** layer mask.

7. With the background revealed through the mask, you might notice your mask needs a little touch-up. Select the layer mask thumbnail in the Layers panel. Select a brush (set the opacity to 100%) and paint with black to reveal more of the background (the black, transparent area of the mask) or with white to hide more of the background (the white, opaque area of the mask).

8. Save the file in your **lessons** folder. Feel free to try other background images (more are provided in the samples folder).

FIGURE | 8–27 |

The saved alpha channel mask is located in the Channels panel.

SUMMARY

This chapter uncovered the mystery of masks. Methods for how to use layer, vector, type, clipping, and quick masks were examined, and practical applications for their use were revealed.

▶ IN REVIEW

1. What is the advantage of using masks to hide and reveal content?

2. Name at least four types of masks in Photoshop.

3. When you save a selection, where does it go?

4. Describe a trick (or two) for making soft-edged effects or semitransparent masks in Photoshop.

5. What is the difference between a layer mask and a clipping mask?

6. What is the shortcut key to define a clipping mask in the Layers panel?

7. What first two steps must you take before you can see a quick mask?

8. In Quick Mask Mode, how do black, white, and gray tonal colors affect the selection process?

▶ EXPLORING ON YOUR OWN

1. Explore your own mask effects on the sample cardboard character photographs located in the **chap08_lessons/samples** folder (**cardinal.jpg**, **pope.tif**, and **explorer.jpg**).

2. Access the Help > How to Work with Layers and Selections > Soften the edges of selections how-to in the menu options. Read the related topics in the how-to.

3. Create textured mask effects with the words earth, wind, and fire, using the Horizontal Type Mask or Vertical Type Mask tool.

4. Do an Internet search for "image masking" and find at least two examples that demonstrate the technique of masking.

Explorer PAGES

Joe Summerhays

"If I was starting again right now . . . well, everybody and their dog is learning Photoshop. In fact, Photoshop is being taught in the fourth grade. When I started out I knew Photoshop was huge. Someone would find out I knew it and would say, 'You know Photoshop? Come on in!' So that's the challenge now: to be able to distinguish yourself as a quality artist, as an expert user of Photoshop."

 Learn more about this artist via an audio interview on the book's CD.

About Joe Summerhays

Joe Summerhays is an award-winning media designer for clients such as HBO, MTV, VH1, AOL, Tribeca Film Festival, Jazz at Lincoln Center, and other innovative media organizations. He has developed more than 30 software titles for children, written over 35 books, and produced broadband properties for Granada, MTV, and Comedy Central. Additionally, he has guided the production of more than 200 animated short films by young people. His program Animation: Minds in Motion! has been used to teach more than 2,000 elementary school pupils the art of animated filmmaking. Joe has lectured on animation, visual intelligence, and broadband content development. He is currently designing animation workshops for children for the Tribeca Film Festival.

About the Work of Joe Summerhays

Joe shares his process in creating the "After" animation, a personal project that represents the basic steps he takes in preparing many of his animations:

"The point of the 'After' bit was to have Santa relaxing in front of his TV after a long night of flying, only to be bombarded by infomercials, each addressing his myriad conditions (i.e., balding, wrinkles, abdominal exercise, Viagra). Zamphir and his pan flute is the first commercial he hears, which does not address one of Santa's insecurities, and the bit ends with him dialing the 800 number for a Zamphir album.

"As always, I start with a rough sketch and scan it in. See Figure 1.

Figure 1: The initial idea is sketched on paper.
Joe Summerhays Productions

Figure 2: Photoshop's Multiply blending mode is used to clean up the sketch. Joe Summerhays Productions

"I want the TV glow on Santa to change colors, so I keep the glow on its own layer above the Santa painting in preparation for color cycling in After Effects. [Color cycling is the process of rapidly changing an object's colors to achieve the illusion of smooth movement.] This glow is painted in with bold brush strokes, then . . . good old Gaussian Blur helps create the haze of late night TV in a dark room. Now it is set; it's ready to be imported into After Effects for color cycling and animation. See Figures 4 and 5."

"Then, in Photoshop, I make a new layer underneath the sketch layer. I turn on what is called the Multiply ink effect on the sketch layer, so the blacks maintain and the whites drop out. I also reduce the opacity of the sketch layer, allowing me to see the painting I'm doing on the layer below. See Figure 2.

"After much painting I turn off the sketch layer and use the smudge tool to blend all my bold color strokes into soft gradients and painterly strokes. I also make new layers for arm positions to be animated later in Adobe After Effects (*http://www.adobe.com/products/aftereffects/*). See Figure 3.

Figure 3: Color effects are painted in. Joe Summerhays Productions

Figure 4: Image is now prepared to be imported into Adobe After Effects. Joe Summerhays Productions

Figure 5: A single frame of the final animation viewed with the Quicktime player. Joe Summerhays Productions

CRANIA

AUSTRALOPITHECUS AFRICANUS
ARCHAIC HOMO SAPIENS BROKEN HILL
CHIMP
MODERN HOMO SAPIENS CRO-MAGNON
GORILLA-F
GORILLA-M
HOMO ERECTUS-3733
HOMO ERECTUS-JAVA
HOMO HABILIS-1470
NEANDERTHAL-LA CHAPELLE
MODERN HOMO SAPIENS
NEANDERTHAL-MT-CARMEL
PARANTHROPUS BOISEI
ARCHAIC HOMO SAPIENS-STEINHEIM

FEMORA

CHIMPANZEE-FMR-LFT
CHIMPANZEE-FMR-RT
HOMO ERECTUS
HOMO HABILIS
HOMO SAPIENS-LFT
HOMO SAPIENS-RT
NEANDERTHAL-FMR

PELVES

AUSTRALOPITHECINE
CHIMPANZEE
HOMO SAPIENS

CRANIA
FEMORA
PELVES

A COMPARATIVE COLLECTION

| Layers, Compositing, and Process |

9

charting your course

The previous chapters have focused almost exclusively on specific concepts, tools, and ways of doing things in Photoshop. You learned how to get around Photoshop's interface, how to manage color, select and transform pixels, retouch photos, draw and paint shapes, use type, and mask areas of an image. Chapter 9 covers the process and methods by which to layer, composite, link, blend, merge, and organize graphic elements into more complex images or graphic layouts. It includes a significant overview of image compositing and the design process, using layers and alignment tools, merging images with blending modes and filter effects, acquiring content, and producing a CD cover. In this chapter, you can freely utilize all that you have studied thus far in the program.

goals

In this chapter you will:

► *Learn workflow and organizational techniques for developing image compositions and layouts*
► *Gain a better understanding of the role the Layers panel plays in organizing a Photoshop project*
► *Review the options for content acquisition and copyright compliance*
► *Composite images together with blending modes, the Liquify effect, and filter effects*
► *Define the sequential steps of a basic design process*
► *Construct a mock CD cover for a client*

ABOUT COMPOSITING AND COMPOSITION

It is important to make a distinction between image compositing and composition in regard to using Photoshop. In his book, *Digital Retouching and Compositing: Photographers' Guide*, David D. Busch describes image compositing as ". . . combining two or more images or portions thereof, to create a new image that didn't exist in that form previously." Otherworldly images by artist Tim Warnock—found on the Explorer Pages in this book—are good examples of images constructed by compositing. Also, see in this book the Adventures in Design: From the Imagination.

Composition, on the other hand, ". . . refers to the aesthetic arrangement of elements within a work of art," according to Lois Fichner-Rathus in his book *Understanding Art* (Seventh Edition). It is the artful use of design elements—line, shape, value, texture, and color—in a visual image or page layout, such as a Web page, brochure, or poster. See Adventures in Design: Wine Box Composition in this book. *Exploring Adobe Photoshop CS5* does not cover design elements specifically, but *Exploring Adobe Illustrator CS5* does in relation to using Adobe Illustrator. *Exploring Adobe Photoshop CS5* places more emphasis on image compositing. However, the next section does provide a brief overview of the work process by which a layout or composition might be constructed.

A DESIGN PROCESS

As much as we might like to snap our fingers in an instantaneous epiphany and have an idea materialize from our heads to reality (that would truly be magic), it does not work that way. From thought to conception to actuality is a process; there is no way around it. So you might as well make the process your modus operandi. Of course, the process can take shape in many ways. You just need to find the one that is right for you as a graphic designer and fits the needs of your clients. (I am assuming your goal is to do work for hire, to actually make money playing with Photoshop.)

In this section, I introduce a general process by which to organize and produce an image composition or layout, and I share some of the tools available for organization and workflow. There are five parts to this process: start with an idea, make a comp (thumbnail sketches), gather content, assemble content, fine-tune, and output.

START WITH AN IDEA
A design starts with a vision or idea. Sometimes the idea is perfectly realized in your mind and it is simply a matter of making it tangible. Other times, the idea is fleshed out as you progress through the design process. Either way, you have to start with an idea, something that drives you to make it "real."

MAKE A COMPREHENSIVE LAYOUT (COMP)

Have you ever made a collage out of magazine clippings? Usually, before you permanently glue everything down, you take your pile of clippings and artfully arrange them. You move and rotate things around, group clippings based on topic or color, and inevitably place the most interesting clipping in the center for visual impact. What is happening at this stage of development is your comprehensive layout, or comp; you put thought into the actual design of the collage and the initial placement of elements. At this point, nothing is set in stone, but you consider multiple options for how something will look best.

The idea slowly forms into something tangible. Often, it starts as a cursory sketch, or several of them (often referred to as thumbnail sketches); it is then reproduced as a more detailed drawing. Many artists will sketch the idea on paper, scan it, and then use the sketch as a template for constructing the digital version. Others, who feel really comfortable drawing on the computer, construct their vision digitally, utilizing the flexibility of undo and redo and saving multiple copies. See Figure 9–1 and Figure 9–2. When the comp is arranged to your liking, or to your client's, you move to the next steps: gathering the content to be used in the chosen design and assembling it into the final product.

FIGURE | 9–1 |

Design comp of a Web site home page.

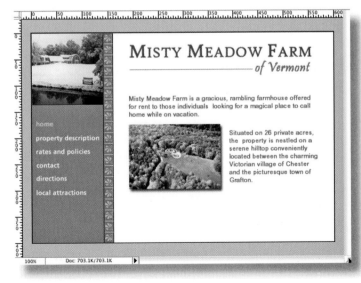

FIGURE | 9–2 |

Design comp of a Web site home page.

GATHER CONTENT

The comp gives you a better idea of what kind of content you need for the final design. Gathering content for your layout can be the most time-consuming and challenging part of the process, so leave plenty of time for it in your project timeline. You may be in a situation where you must create all of the content—images and copy— yourself, or procure the content from other sources, such as your client or an outside resource (i.e., another artist or writer, image, or font repository). At this point, you must consider the issues of copyright and content format.

Copyright Issues

If you create your own content or use copyright-free material, don't worry about the permission process. However, to reuse others' material, such as a company's logo or a photo of a famous person, you need the correct permissions. As an example, every digital image in *Exploring Adobe Photoshop CS5* is protected by copyright law whether explicitly indicated or not. As soon as it is created, copyright is automatically implied; no copyright notices or procedures are required to protect the image from unauthorized reproduction.

It certainly does not hurt, however, to register your work through the U.S. Copyright Office (that is, if you made your creation in the United States) at *http://www.copyright.gov*. You should at least put a copyright notice (©, date, your name) on your work to deter individuals from using it without your permission. I requested permission and/or paid for the artwork and photographs used in this book that I did not create myself. I also had to acknowledge that permission was granted (i.e., "Printed by permission of..." or "Courtesy of...").

With the proliferation of digital content in our society, copyright protections have come under renewed scrutiny. It has become easier than ever to procure and edit content without giving thought to the original artist. In regard to the protection of digitized content and its use for educational purposes, laws have been enacted, such as the Digital Millennium Copyright Act (for information, see Exploring on Your Own).

You should know about a provision in U.S. copyright law called "fair use." Fair use delineates the use of creative works for educational or nonprofit purposes, such as the photographs provided for the lesson project in this chapter.

When determining whether to use someone else's work as part of your own, ask yourself, "Will copying this image—or text, typeface, music, video, or data—make me money or take money out of someone else's pocket?" If the answer is "Yes," proceed with caution: get permission and credit the artist.

Format

Another aspect of content gathering is getting the content into the right format for your use. For example, if Photoshop is to be used as the medium for assembling your image (see next section), be sure the content can be successfully imported into the program. Are the images and photos you want to use in the correct file format for Photoshop or any other program you might be using? Is the written copy translatable in the digital environment? I am not going to go into great detail about each of the importable file formats supported by Photoshop. However, the available formats appear in Adobe Bridge, the File > Open dialog box, or the File > Place dialog box. The following is an abbreviated list: Photoshop, BMP, Photoshop EPS, CompuServe GIF, JPEG, PCX, Photoshop PDF, PICT file, PNG, Targa, TIFF, and Wireless Bitmap (WBMP).

ASSEMBLE CONTENT

Once you have gathered the content, you assemble it in your layout program, which could be Photoshop or a more layout-friendly program (i.e., Adobe Illustrator, InDesign, or QuarkXPress).

There are two parts to integrating content into your final layout: properly importing content from outside the program, and accurately positioning it within the intended composition using placement and organization tools.

Import

When you have the content in an importable format, you bring it into Photoshop in one of two ways: Use the Open or Open Recent commands, or Adobe Bridge (File > Browse, or click on the Bridge option on the Applications bar), or copy and paste between other applications. You have been taught how to open files in the lessons in this book, but is the quick review:

1. Choose File > Open.

2. Select the name of the file you want to open. If the file does not appear, select the option for showing all formats or documents from the Files of type (Windows) or Enable (Mac) pop-up menu.

3. Click Open. A dialog box might appear, letting you set format-specific options. If a color profile warning message appears, specify whether to convert the pixels based on the file's color profile or not.

> Note: *For image preview and file compatibility options, choose Photoshop > Preferences > File Handling (Mac) or Edit > Preferences > File Handling (Windows).*

Generally when you import native file formats—such as Illustrator (AI) or Flash (FLA)—from one program to another, it is a hit-or-miss proposition. Sometimes the version of the program you are importing the file into will support it, sometimes not. Keeping files in more generic file formats—EPS for vector-based files, or TIFF for bitmap-based files—might prove a better solution, even if—on occasion—you lose some information in translation.

Another importing issue will occur if you attempt to open a newer version of a Photoshop file in an older version (i.e., CS5 to version 7). You usually get a dialog box looking like that shown in Figure 9–3. The conversion usually works, but you might lose some information. When you go to import artwork and cannot

FIGURE | 9–3 |

Attempt to import a Photoshop CS5 file into Photoshop 7. It will work, but some information might be lost.

access the file you want, even after you have chosen All Formats from the Files of type (Windows) or All Documents from the Enable (Mac) pop-up menu, you know the file has been saved in a format Photoshop cannot read.

Organizing

After importing your content into Photoshop, or creating it in the program, you should organize it. I emphasize the word "should" here, because it is optional whether you want to organize your content or not. However, I highly recommend it. You cannot leave all of your content in a series of unnamed layers and expect to find what you need quickly and without frustration. Features to keep your work organized while integrating content in a document include Layers, the alignment commands, rulers, the grid, guides, and the Snap feature.

Layers: The Layers panel is your organizational Mecca, as you have probably surmised from working through past lessons. You might be wondering why I have waited until this chapter to impart this important information. Well, the best way to learn how to use this panel is to practice using it, which you have had several chances to do in previous chapters. You have already explored using specific compositing techniques and effects when items are on individual layers, including layer styles (i.e., Drop Shadow, Bevel and Emboss blending modes, and filters). These techniques and effects are officially covered in this chapter. The anatomy of the Layers panel (Window > Layers) is labeled for quick reference in Figure 9–4.

FIGURE | 9–4 |

The Layers panel is where you keep track of all the images and text elements in a document.

Note: *By default, every document in Photoshop starts on the Background layer. To change a Background layer into a regular layer (much more versatile), double-click on the Background layer in the Layers panel and give the layer a name. See Figure 9–5.*

New Layer

Name: Name your layer!

☐ Use Previous Layer to Create Clipping Mask

Color: ☐ None

Mode: Normal   Opacity: 100 ▼ %

☐ (No neutral color exists for Normal mode.)

OK   Cancel

FIGURE | 9–5 |

Give your layers intuitive names, so you can find what you need in the Layers panel.

Layers are transparent except for any filled content that is placed on them, making it easy to move layers above and below one another for dimensional reasons and for overlapping combinations of images and effects. See Figure 9–6.

Items on any layer can be selected as a group by highlighting the layer and then Command-clicking (Mac) or Ctrl-clicking (Windows) on the layer's thumbnail. See Figure 9–7.

Layers can be selected and linked together temporarily to transform or align objects as a group. To select more than one layer, hold down Command (Mac) or Control (Windows). You can also merge selected or visible items into one layer, or group layers in subfolders, called Layer Sets. See Figure 9–8.

For more information on layers, go to Help > Photoshop Help > Layers.

FIGURE | 9–6 |

Layers can be selected and dragged up and down the layer stack, sending objects in front or in back of each other.

FIGURE | 9–8 |

You can merge selected or visible layers into one layer, if necessary.

FIGURE | 9–7 |

To select all the areas on a layer, Command-click (Mac) or Ctrl-click (Windows) on the layer's thumbnail.

The Alignment Commands: The alignment commands are located in the Move tool's Options bar (select the Move tool to view). They align objects on linked layers horizontally (right, left, or center) or vertically (top, bottom, or center). They also horizontally or vertically distribute content evenly on linked layers, using the objects' edges for spatial reference. You can also get the alignment and distribution options by choosing Layer > Align or Layer > Distribute from the menu bar. If you are precision oriented, you will use these commands frequently. See Figure 9–9 and Figure 9–10.

FIGURE | 9–9 |

The alignment commands are located on the Move tool's Options bar.

FIGURE | 9–10 |

Before-and-after example of using the alignment commands. The buttons and text on the right are horizontally centered, with a vertically centered distribution of space between each object.

FIGURE | 9–11 |

The Ruler Tool and Count Tool in the toolbox.

In addition to alignment commands, there are two tools for measuring precisely: the Ruler Tool and the Count Tool. See Figure 9–11. These tools are found under the Eyedropper tool in the toolbox. The Ruler tool (Analysis > Ruler Tool) analyzes angles and distances across the image, with the results shown in the Info panel (Window > Info). The Count tool (Analysis > Count Tool) counts off with each click of the mouse.

The Auto-Align Layers button (Edit > Auto-Align Layers) is also located in the Move tool's Options bar. This alignment tool analyzes overlapping elements in selected layers to align similar content. This is a great way to create panoramic images (using Auto, Perspective, or Cylindrical options) or piece together scanned segments of a larger image (using the Reposition Only option). See Figure 9–12. Once the images are combined, use Auto-Blend Layers (Edit > Auto-Blend Layers) to smooth out any visible seams.

Rulers: Rulers are designed to accurately measure and place objects in the Photoshop workspace. They are toggled on and off by choosing View > Rulers. Both a horizontal ruler and a vertical ruler are made visible along the top and left edges of the document. You can change a ruler's measurement by Ctrl-clicking (Mac) or right-clicking (Windows) over a ruler and selecting a new measurement from the drop-down menu. See Figure 9–13.

Alternatively, you can go to Photoshop > Preferences > Units & Rulers (Mac) or Edit > Preferences > Units & Rulers (Windows). In the upper-left corner of the document, where the vertical and horizontal rulers meet, you can also set what is called the ruler origin. Setting the ruler origin is useful when, for example, you are working on an object that is 2 by 3 on an 8.5-by-11-inch document. You can set the ruler origin at 0, 0 in the upper-left corner of the 2-by-3 area, rather than the 8.5-by-11 area, for more precise positioning. To set the ruler origin, move the cursor into the upper-left corner of the document where the rulers intersect, then click and drag the crosshair to the new origin edge. To restore default settings, double-click on the upper-left corner where the rulers intersect.

Grid: The Grid function is located under View > Show > Grid. A grid of lines or dots appears behind your artwork. The grid can be used to position objects symmetrically. Grids do not print. To adjust grid settings (i.e., color, style, and subdivisions), choose Photoshop > Preferences > Guides, Grid & Slices (Mac) or Edit > Preferences > Guides, Grid & Slices (Windows).

Guides: Guides are incredibly useful for aligning your work. To quickly create guides, choose View > Rulers and drag guidelines from the horizontal and vertical rulers on the sides of the document. See Figure 9–14. Alternatively, choose View > New Guide. You can lock/unlock and clear guides in the View menu, and show guides under View > Show > Guides. Guides do not print. To adjust guide colors and style, choose Photoshop > Preferences > Guides, Grid & Slices (Mac) or Edit > Preferences > Guides, Grid & Slices (Windows).

FIGURE | 9–12 |

Options for the Auto-Align Layers feature.

FIGURE | 9–13 |

Ctrl-click (Mac) or right-click (Windows) over a ruler to change the measurement.

FIGURE | 9–14 |

Drag guides from the horizontal and vertical rulers.

Snap: Snap allows for exact positioning of selection edges, shapes, and paths. Often, however, the Snap feature—on by default—is more a hindrance than a help, preventing you from properly placing items. Luckily, snapping can be enabled or disabled under View > Snap. With Snap enabled you can snap to particular elements, such as the grid (when visible), guides (when visible), and document bounds. Choose View > Snap To

Guides, Grid, Layers, Slices, or Document Bounds. To position items more accurately while Snap is enabled, use the arrow keys on your keyboard.

FINE-TUNE AND OUTPUT

The fine-tuning stage is where you fix the fine details of your image or layout, including adjusting colors, incrementally aligning items, and playing with subtle formatting of text (such as line and character spacing). In short, you make the document look as perfect as possible. At this time, you will also prepare your work for its intended output, including choosing the proper color mode and settings for either screen or print.

BLENDING MODES, STYLES, AND EFFECTS

If you have spent significant time playing in Photoshop, you have probably already found and delved into the blending modes, layer styles, filter effects, and Liquify function. These are easy-to-use features with high visual impact (addictive, really) that work miraculously with image compositing.

BLENDING MODES

Blending modes work with layers and layer sets. A blending mode is specified for a selected layer that affects (blends with) the layer below it or within a layer set.

Blending modes offer true compositing of images on different layers, determining how pixels blend with underlying pixels in an image. See Figure 9–15.

> Note: *Blending modes are also available for the Brush options, found in the Brush tool's Options bar.*

To experience pixel blends, open **chap09_lessons/samples/blend.psd**.

1. Open the Layers panel.

2. Two layers are already created for you. Highlight the layer **painted-image**. From the blending mode drop-down menu in the Layers panel, choose the Multiply blending mode—a blend that simulates a look of transparent markers. See Figure 9–16 (on page 204). Explore the other modes. (Alternatively, you can get to the blending modes under Layer > Layer Style > Blending Options.) If you are using Photoshop on Windows, you can also click on the blending mode drop-down menu in the Layers panel and use the up and down arrow keys to cycle through the list of blending modes.

3. For an overview of what each blending mode looks like and its description, examine Figure 9–15 and see Painting > Blending Modes > Blending Mode Examples in the Photoshop Help files.

FIGURE | 9–15 |

The blend image is on a layer above the base image, and it contains the specified blending mode. There are many blending modes to choose from.

FIGURE | 9–16 |

Multiply blending mode.

LAYER STYLES

A layer style—such as a Drop Shadow, Inner and Outer Glow, Bevel and Emboss effects, and Strokes—can be applied to items on any selected layer. Go to Layer > Layer Style to choose a style. A dialog box comes up, where you can modify and add or remove a style. To get to the options of any style, click on the style name on the left—not just the check mark, but the actual name—and the options for that style will appear on the right. See Figure 9–17.

FIGURE | 9–17 |

The Layer Style dialog box—a lot to tinker with in here!

FILTER EFFECTS

Photoshop is famous for its extensive gallery of filters. Filters directly distort and manipulate the pixels in an image. See Figure 9–18. Keep your image in the RGB Color mode to have the full range of filters available. (Once the filter is applied, you can change to another color mode.) To view all the filter choices and preview what they will look like on your image, choose Filter > Filter Gallery from the menu bar. See Figure 9–19. A sample file is provided for you to try out filters: **chap09_lessons/samples/filter.psd**.

FIGURE | **9–18** |

Filter examples—there are many to choose from!

FIGURE | **9–19** |

The Filter Gallery. Take your pick and preview.

The Lighting Effects filter is used often by artists and photographers and is not to be missed. It allows you to create different light styles and properties for your image. To check it out, choose Filter > Render > Lighting Effects. See Figure 9–20 (on next page).

If there comes a time when you want to change how your filters are applied to a layer, the answer is Smart Filters. See Figure 9–21 (on next page). Smart Filters let you apply filters nondestructively to a layer. This allows you to change the stacking order of filters by clicking and dragging, and changing any filter setting simply by double-clicking on the appropriate filter. To add Smart Filters, select the layer and choose Filter > Convert for Smart Filters. If a warning message appears, click OK to accept. A small icon appears in the corner of the layer's thumbnail to show it is now a Smart Object. Now, feel the freedom of adding and experimenting with different combinations of filters without fear of damaging the original image!

FIGURE | 9–20 |

The ever-popular Lighting Effects filter.

FIGURE | 9–21 |

Use of Smart Filters in the Layers panel.

LIQUIFY FUNCTION

Last in our tour of special effects is the Liquify feature—it is sweet. With Liquify you can distort pixels with various Liquify commands, such as Bloat, Pucker, and Warp. To open the Liquify menu, choose Filter > Liquify. Select tools from the toolbox to the left of the window and specify adjustment options at the right. See Figure 9–22 and the sample file under **chap09_lessons/samples/liquify.tif**.

LESSON: CD JACKET PROJECT

Now that you have gotten a handle on using Photoshop, here is your chance to break from the step-by-step study, explore some of the blending and filter effects, and begin to flex your artistic muscle.

You have been approached by PaleoExcavators Inc., to design a CD jacket (a cover, both front and back) for its new comparative collection CD of skeletal remains. See Figure 9–23. The client has provided a few guidelines and some content (text and photographs) for the project but, in general, is open to the possibilities of what can be done. The client has also provided some examples of its previous CD jacket designs. See Figure 9–24 (on page 208) and Figure 9–25 (on page 208).

FIGURE | 9-22 |

The Liquify tools in action.

FIGURE | 9-23 |

Skeletal remains to be incorporated into a CD jacket design. All photographs are courtesy of Joel Hagen, graphics design instructor at Modesto Junior College, California.

Project Guidelines

1. Required text and a selection of photographs are provided in the **folder chap09_ lessons/assets/CDproject**. Photographs are categorized in folders for what each contains: crania, femora, and pelvic skeletal remains. The text for the front and back covers is provided. You need to include and format the text. For text-formatting options in Photoshop, choose a Type tool to bring up its Options bar, and make use of the Window > Character and Window > Paragraph panels.

> Note: *For your viewing fun, some Flash SWF movies have been provided in the assets folder as an example of what will be on the mock CD. You will need the Flash Player (free from http://www.adobe.com) to view the movies on your computer.*

2. You are welcome to use a combination of your own acquired raster- and vector-based images.

FIGURE | 9–24 |

CD cover project example 1, designed by a Photoshop student at Modesto Junior College, California.

FIGURE | 9–25 |

CD cover project example 2, designed by a Photoshop student at Modesto Junior College, California.

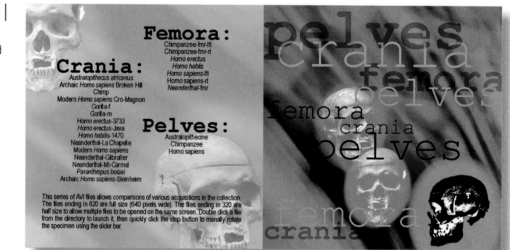

3. Dimension specifications for the jacket are the following:

- ▸ *Width:* 9.5 inches
- ▸ *Height:* 4.6875 inches
- ▸ *Resolution:* 200 pixels/inch
- ▸ *Color mode:* RGB Color (eventually to be converted to CMYK for printing)

4. Before assembling the final designed piece, hone your design ideas by sketching them by hand or mocking them up digitally. Provide an overall potential "look and feel" for the jacket, including font and color possibilities and a general layout of text and images.

5. Save your final work in both PSD and TIFF format.

SUMMARY

Chapter 9 offered the big picture of the image compositing and design composition processes. In addition, it went over often-used organizational and workflow features of Photoshop, and got you hooked (I hope!) on its unique blending, Liquify, and filter effects. Work out that imagination muscle!

▶ IN REVIEW

1. Describe image compositing. Describe composition in design.

2. List five steps in the design process.

3. What question should you ask yourself when deciding whether to use someone else's work?

4. Name at least five features of the Layers panel.

5. How do you change a background layer to a regular layer?

6. To align items on separate layers, what must you do?

7. Most filter effects are only available in what color mode?

▶ EXPLORING ON YOUR OWN

1. Study about copyright online:

   ▶ U.S. Copyright Office (copyright basics): *http://www.copyright.gov/circs/*
   ▶ Specifics of the Digital Millennium Copyright Act: *http://www.copyright.gov/legislation/dmca.pdf*
   ▶ Copyright Web site: *http://www.benedict.com*
   ▶ Stanford University Libraries, Stanford Copyright & Fair Use Center: *http://fairuse.stanford.edu/*
   ▶ Copyright Clearance Center to access copyright permission for millions of publications worldwide: *http://www.copyright.com/*

2. Design a CD cover or promotional poster for a band or theater company in your area.

3. Create a home page design for a Web site.

4. Explore the Adobe design center at *http://www.adobe.com/designcenter/* and vailable videos, *http://www.adobe.com/designcenter/video_workshop/*.

adventures IN DESIGN

FROM THE IMAGINATION

Photoshop can bring out the mad scientist in us all. It is a digital laboratory where instruments are used to piece together pixels, rather than strands of DNA, into new life forms that come alive on screen or paper, tabloid covers, DVD or video game splash screens, or in this book's Explorer Pages. Enter an adventure in design for the wild imagination.

PROFESSIONAL PROJECT EXAMPLE

Our experiment begins with an example brought to you from the digital artist, "Mad Scientist," Jeffrey Moring. Jeffrey reveals the secrets used to bring about his optical vision titled *Yesterday, Today, Forever*. See Figure C–1.

FIGURE | C–1 |

Artist Jeffrey Moring's altered self in his image *Yesterday, Today, Forever*. Printed with permission of Jeffrey Moring.

"The first step in creating this piece was getting the right digital images to work with," said Jeffrey. "I took some photographs of myself, then photographed many different skulls. (The biology department of your school should have such skulls.) After picking the right digital photos, I brought them into Photoshop. See Figure C–2 and Figure C–3. The most important techniques for this kind of digital manipulation are selecting areas and your ability to blend two different images together. The tools that I used were the Smudge tool, the Eraser tool, and the Clone Stamp "tool." See Figure C–4.

"Getting a good selection of the image you are using is critical," said Jeffrey. "Each picture should be on a different layer when building such images. This is also critical. See

FIGURE | C–2 |

A self- portrait was taken and imported into Photoshop. A black background was added.

FIGURE | C–3 |

Photographs of skeletal remains were taken, brought into Photoshop, and their background pixels selected and removed.

Figure C–5. Being able to change one part at a time is a timesaver and gives great effects. I then scaled down each skull and began placing them over the face layer, changing the opacity and using the blending tools. I left many of my own facial features but also used the main skull features and blended the two. Feathering the selections can help soften an image, but be careful not to feather a selection too much. The tool I probably used the most is the Eraser tool. After you place one layer on top of the other, you can erase (with a soft-tipped brush) what you do not want. See Figure C–6. The more comfortable you get with the mouse, the better you can blend the images."

FIGURE | C–4 |

Tools used to blend the images: the Smudge, Eraser, and Clone Stamp tools.

YOUR TURN

Using some of the tools and techniques recommended by Jeffrey, create your own freak of nature or otherworldly vision of yourself.

FIGURE | C–5 |

Each item—including each bone selection—
is placed on its own layer.

FIGURE | C–6 |

Choose the Eraser tool with a soft brush tip to
create a seamless blend between layered images.

Self-Project Guidelines

1. Import a photograph of yourself into Photoshop.

2. With the Selection tools or Quick Mask feature, extract the background from the photograph and replace it with a solid color or fantasy-like backdrop.

3. With their backgrounds already removed, bring in other images (with either hard or feathered edges) to composite with the self-portrait. Put each image on its own layer. Duplicate and flip images you might like to use on both sides of the portrait (like the bat wings on Jeffrey's image).

4. Hide and reveal areas of images using Layer Masks or the Eraser tool.

5. Blend images with the layer blending modes, if needed.

6. Add Liquify or filter effects to individual layers for more distorted and/or textured looks.

Things to Consider

For this Adventure in Design and future experimentations such as this, consider the following:

▶ For photographs of objects where the background will eventually be removed, shoot the picture against a matte-finished, even-colored backdrop. This, of course, will make it easier to remove the pixels in Photoshop.

▶ Take high-resolution digital photos, or scan in photos at a high resolution, so you have plenty of pixels from the beginning.

▶ Sketch some of your creature designs on paper.

▶ Practice mastering the tools (and their many options) you think you will use—such as the Smudge, Eraser, Dodge, Burn, and Clone Stamp tools—on a separate, blank document.

▶ Save your work often and back it up.

Explorer PAGES

Jim Carroll

"While the computer has offered creative people a powerful and seductive tool, we must remind ourselves that the creation does not happen in that box but rather in our minds and spirits. Work hard but always remember to go outside and play."

About Jim Carroll

One night back in 1992, Jim had lucid dream about a machine that allowed him to manipulate the world all around as if it were made of clay. The next morning a friend called and asked him to come over and check out a cool new computer program. It was Adobe Photoshop. Jim's background as an illustrator, photographer, and print maker allowed him to take full advantage of the new possibilities that this software offered.

Over the years, Jim and his artwork have been featured in many books and magazines including: *Zoom, How, Print,* and *Communication Arts*. Working primarily in the publishing field, Jim has been honored by the Society of Illustrators and was awarded first place for a book cover at the New York Book Awards. In 2008, the Society of Children's Book Writer's and illustrator's awarded him the Grand Prize for his illustration portfolio. His work has been displayed around the world, including at the Leonardo da Vinci Museum of Science and Technology in Milan and at the United Nations in NYC.

Jim has been an instructor at The School of Visual Arts and The Massachusetts Museum of Contemporary Art. He has a BFA from SUNY Purchase and currently lives in upstate NY with his wife and three children.

Learn more about Jim at:
http://www.jameschristophercarroll.com/

Paris 08. Courtesy of Jim Carroll

Marley's Little Sister. Courtesy of Jim Carroll

Explorer PAGES, *continued*

About the Work of Jim Carroll

Jim shares his work process: "Not since the invention of photography has any other event been so instrumental in shaping the way visual artists create than the introduction of Adobe Photoshop. This technological 'gift' has not only changed the process of the way we work and forever altered the look of the pictorial landscape, it has also encouraged us to think in a much more comprehensive manner when creating. In a traditional sense this methodology is much like collage. The pleasure of paint on a canvas, the dusty charcoal that makes our fingers dirty, the sharp marks and lines of ink on crumpled paper, our photographs rich in reality or distorted with lens and atmosphere, the textures of leaves, bones and bike-parts, all come together digitally and play a role in the final picture. Certainly as much happens off the computer as does within it.

"This collage method is the basic approach used to create the image of the baby in the nest (*Nuthatch*). Beginning with a sketch to help map out my picture, I then began to collect the parts. Background clouds were drawn with charcoal on rough paper, an edge border was painted in gouache on glass with rubbings of Victorian lace as accents. Hills were built from scanned pieces of moss, a fallen robin's nest was photographed, and the flower was composited from three different photos. The moon stars, and kite were sketched in pencil, while the baby grew from drawings and two separate photos. All of these components were brought together in Photoshop and then the messy magic began. The possibilities with filters, layer interactions, and manipulation tools are endless. Any detailed explanation of my process would be impractical."

Nuthatch. Courtesy of Jim Carroll

Bucky on the Roof. Courtesy of Jim Carroll

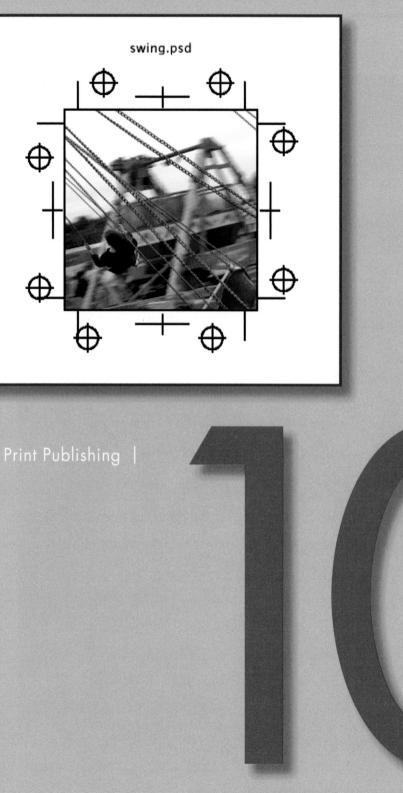

swing.psd

| Print Publishing |

10

charting your course

Eventually, you will want to format your artwork so you can share it. Chapters 10 and 11 help you do that. There are many possibilities for where your digital images can appear, including on screen, such as in a Web page, an interactive learning environment, a kiosk, or mobile device (see Chapter 11); and on paper, such as in a glossy magazine ad, a flyer, brochure, or poster. Print media publication is what we explore in this chapter.

goals

In this chapter you will:

- ▶ *Learn about the different methods of printing*
- ▶ *Discover why color management makes a difference*
- ▶ *Understand the halftone and color separation process*
- ▶ *Learn what questions to ask when consulting a print service bureau*
- ▶ *Get familiar with the Print command*

PRINTING METHODS

There are several ways to get your artwork onto paper: directly from a desktop printer or digital printing press, from a film negative that is used to create a metal plate for a commercial press, or in the form of a Portable Document File (PDF) or PostScript file.

Let us briefly describe each of these output methods, and then in the section, Output Compatibility, we will show you how to set up your print job in Photoshop's Print window.

DESKTOP PRINTING

Without a doubt, you will want to print your work from a desktop printer—if not the final version, at least some proofs for mock-up and revision purposes. Desktop printers differ by manufacturer and have different levels of printing capabilities. A low-end ink jet printer, for example, deposits ink onto a page much differently than does a high-end laser printer. You should read the specifications for your particular desktop printer, so you can accurately gauge whether a printer problem is something you can fix on the Photoshop side of things or is unavoidable with your type of printer.

You also need to know what resolution your printer will support and what will give you the best quality, which can vary depending on the type of printer and the paper used. Much of the process of determining this is trial and error—print it and see how it looks. In general, laser printers have a resolution of about 600 dots per inch (dpi). For printers, dpi is the resolution measurement, whereas for computers the measurement is pixels per inch (ppi). Ink jet printers have a resolution of between 300 and 2880 dpi.

> **Note:** *If you need to review the subject of resolution, or want to know more about it related to Photoshop, go to Help > Photoshop Help and do a search for resolution. Also, refer back to Chapter 3.*

DIGITAL PRINTING

A digital printing press is a beefed-up version of a typical desktop printer. As digital printing technologies improve, digital printing services are becoming a more prevalent alternative to traditional offset printing. Digital printers can yield quality output with a quick turnaround, because they rasterize PostScript data (print directly from a computer file) rather than go through the intermediary film or metal plate stage (see next section, Commercial Printing). Digital printing is ideal for targeted printing jobs and short-run projects that need to be done quickly, but at a much higher quality than a desktop printer can offer. The resolution needed to properly print from a digital printing press is the resolution of the particular output device.

Consult the printing service for the resolution at which your document should be set.

COMMERCIAL PRINTING

The traditional method for getting your virtual work to hard copy is using a commercial or mechanical printing press, the most common being offset printing. A digital file is transferred to a film negative, which is then used to "burn" a metal printing plate. The metal plate carries the image the press transfers to paper. If you are printing a photograph or illustration with more than one or two colors in it, things get a little more complicated and expensive. To simulate a full range of colors (four-color process printing), mechanical printers deposit the four ink colors (CMYK) dot-by-dot, called halftones. See Figure 10–1.

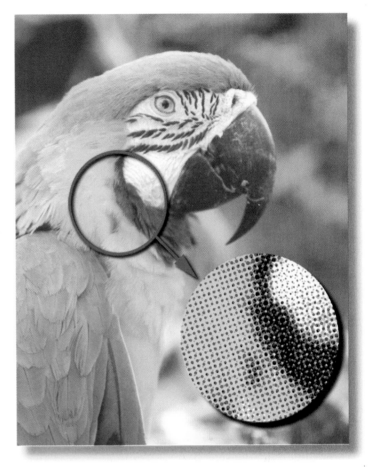

FIGURE | 10–1 |

Magnifying a section of the parrot, you see its color is produced by halftone dots composed of CMYK ink colors.

To create continuous-tone color using the halftone method, each color must be inked and pressed separately to the paper. In short, the colors are separated and then layered back together. To do this, each color must have its own metal plate (one plate inked with cyan, one with magenta, one with yellow, and one with black). The plates are produced from four separate files or film negatives. This is the process of color separation.

The individual colors produced by the mixing of CMYK colors are called process colors. You can also print with spot colors or custom inks. Spot colors are special colors composed of premixed inks that require their own printing plate(s) in addition to the ones used for four-color processing.

For pr]inters using the halftone procedure, Photoshop provides options in the Print dialog box for preparing your image for color separation and the subsequent printing process.

PORTABLE DOCUMENT FILE (PDF)

With Photoshop you can also print a file as a Portable Document File (PDF)—a popular, PostScript-based format developed by Adobe that supports vector and bitmapped data. Printing to PDF is a convenient way to maintain all attributes of

FIGURE | 10–2 |

The Save Adobe PDF dialog box.

your original Photoshop file in a cross-platform compatible format. Often, print service bureaus will request a PDF version of your file. To set the PDF options, choose File > Save As, specify a file name, and choose Photoshop PDF as the file format. Click Save. The Save Adobe PDF dialog box appears (see Figure 10–2), where you can indicate compression, output, and security options. For information on these settings, visit the Photoshop Help files, Saving and exporting images > Saving PDF files.

OUTPUT COMPATIBILITY

If you were to travel to the moon, you'd need to prepare for the change in atmosphere. This means wearing a special space suit with weighted boots so you stay on the moon's surface, as well as a pressurized helmet shaped like a fish bowl so you can breathe. Just as you must give consideration to the outer space environment, you must assess the printing environment when you decide to take your Photoshop work and land it on a piece of paper, so to speak. In general, three areas need to be considered when you are going to print: the image's color, resolution (size and quality), and format. This applies if you are outputting to a printing device (see section Printing Methods) or are importing into another program first (i.e., one that works with page design, such as Adobe InDesign and QuarkXPress).

> **Note:** *Programs specifically designed for page layout are quite savvy in setting up your document properly for print. Although Photoshop is able to do this, programs such as Adobe InDesign and Illustrator are more appropriate for this kind of translation.*

I have discussed color, resolution, and formats in previous chapters, but understanding them is so important I need to mention them again (and again in Chapter 11) as they relate to the printing process.

COLOR

If you recall from Chapter 5, different devices (whether screen- or print-based) have different color gamuts—the range (or limits) of color that can be reproduced. Therefore, it is important to prepare your image to match the specific color profile of whatever device or other application to which you are going to output. This workflow process is called color management. Admittedly, it is impossible to match colors between a monitor and a printer perfectly; one is using light to make colors, the other is using ink. However, you can get close by creating profiles for your monitor, printer, and printer papers. With these color spaces set, Photoshop's built-in color management system can correctly transform the color from one working color space to another. You can explore the fine points of color management to a great extent in the Photoshop help files (you can even purchase complete volumes on the subject), but for now, you will be well on your way if you learn how to set up color profiles and calibrate your monitor.

About Color Profiles

A printer's output quality is determined by its color profile—sometimes called destination profile or output profile. This profile determines how many colors and to what degree of color accuracy a given device can produce. There are many types of color profiles you can work with, usually identified by the name of the company that designed them or the country that has standardized them, such as Adobe RGB (1998), U.S. Web Coated (SWOP) v2, or Euroscale Uncoated v2. You determine what profile you need by consulting the specifications of your particular printer or, if you are printing commercially, ask your prepress specialist. If you are not sure what to do, stick with Photoshop's default working color space. When working in RGB, and eventually converting to CMYK and going to print, this would be the Adobe RGB (1998) setting. Use this space when you need to print work with a broad range of colors. See Figure 10–3 (on the next page).

FIGURE | 10–3 |

To set your specific
working space,
choose Edit > Color
Settings.

Color Settings

For more information on color settings, search for "setting up color management" in Help. This term is searchable from any Creative Suite application.

Settings: **Custom**

Working Spaces

RGB: Adobe RGB (1998)

CMYK: U.S. Web Coated (SWOP) v2

Gray: Dot Gain 20%

Spot: Dot Gain 20%

Color Management Policies

RGB: Preserve Embedded Profiles

CMYK: Preserve Embedded Profiles

Gray: Preserve Embedded Profiles

Profile Mismatches: ☐ Ask When Opening   ☐ Ask When Pasting

Missing Profiles: ☐ Ask When Opening

Description

OK

Cancel

Load...

Save...

More Options

☑ Preview

There are several places in Photoshop where you will encounter options for setting color profiles. Let's open an image and visit each place.

1. In Photoshop, be sure the Essentials workspace is set and then open the file **swing.psd** in the folder **chap10_lessons/assets**. Note that the status tab at the top of the image indicates that it is set in the RGB Color mode. See Figure 10–4.

2. Choose View > Print Size to see what dimensions the image will be when printed. For exact dimensions and resolution, choose Image > Image Size. See Figure 10–5.

3. Let's indicate global color settings for the current document and any new document you create. Go to Edit > Color Settings. Choose the More Options button. Then, under the Settings option, choose North America Prepress 2. Note in this pop-up window the other presets available. See Figure 10–6.

FIGURE | 10–4 |

At the top of any open file you can check what color mode it is in.

FIGURE | 10–5 |

To get the exact dimensions of a document, dependent on its resolution, go to Image > Image Size.

Image Size

Pixel Dimensions: 4.12M

Width: 1200   pixels

Height: 1200   pixels

OK
Cancel
Auto...

Document Size:

Width: 4   inches

Height: 4   inches

Resolution: 300 pixels/inch

☐ Scale Styles
☑ Constrain Proportions
☐ Resample Image:

Bicubic (best for smooth gradients)

FIGURE | 10–6 |

Indicate a color profile preset in the Color Settings dialog box.

Color Settings

For more information on color settings, search for "setting up color management" in the Suite...

OK
Cancel
Load...
Save...
More Options
☑ Preview

Settings

Custom
✓ North America General Purpose 2

Monitor Color
North America General Purpose 2
North America Newspaper
North America Prepress 2
North America Web/Internet

Spot: Dot Gain 20%

Color Management Policies

RGB: Preserve Embedded Profiles

CMYK: Preserve Embedded Profiles

Gray: Preserve Embedded Profiles

Profile Mismatches: ☐ Ask When Opening ☐ Ask When Pasting
Missing Profiles: ☐ Ask When Opening

Description

North America General Purpose 2: General-purpose color settings for screen and print in North America. Profile warnings are disabled.

4. Under Working Spaces, note that each color mode (RGB, CMYK, Gray, and Spot) has its own profile. As mentioned previously, when in doubt about where your document will eventually be printed, keep your file in RGB Color mode with the Adobe RGB (1998) setting. To read a description of this mode and any other setting in the Color Settings dialog box, move your cursor over the item you want described and view the description at the bottom of the dialog box. Click OK.

5. Choose Edit > Assign Profile to open the Assign Profile dialog box. See Figure 10–7. In this box you can choose color management options specific to the selected image. The options include using Don't Color Manage This Document, keeping it at the setting you chose in the Color Settings dialog box, or selecting a specific profile for the particular printer and paper quality you will be using. For now, keep the profile the same as what was chosen under Color Settings—Working RGB: Adobe RGB (1998). Click OK.

> Note: *If you choose to embed a different profile in Assign Profile than what is indicated in Color Settings, be aware that a dialog box will come up the next time you open this document reminding you of this setting and asking what you would like to do next. See Figure 10–8. If no Color Settings have been indicated (Missing Profile), you will get a dialog box asking what you would like to do with the document's settings. See Figure 10–9.*

6. To set your document to print a proof of a color profile other than the image's assigned profile, choose File > Print. Under Color Management on the right side, choose Photoshop Manages Colors under Color Handling. Then make a selection under Printer Profile. (See the section, Print Command.)

7. Close **swing.psd**. Hopefully, now you have a better idea of the color profile settings in Photoshop.

> Note: *Keep in mind that there are also color profiles for input devices (sometimes called a source profile), such as digital cameras and scanners. Creating an input profile to match your working space can get complicated, and there is the question of whether it is essential for producing consistent color. For information on this topic, see Help > Photoshop Help and search in the index for color management, working with color profiles, and about monitor calibration and characterization*

FIGURE | 10–7 |

Assign a profile for your selected document. Note here that one profile I can choose is Canon printer software Canon MP470/MX300/MX310 series SP4 because that's the type of printer I have. Depending on your brand of desktop printer, there will be different profiles available.

Embedded Profile Mismatch

The document "swing.psd" has an embedded color profile that does not match the current RGB working space.

Embedded: sRGB IEC61966–2.1

Working: Monitor RGB – iMac

What would you like to do?
- ● Use the embedded profile (instead of the working space)
- ○ Convert document's colors to the working space
- ○ Discard the embedded profile (don't color manage)

Cancel   OK

FIGURE | 10–8 |

Dialog box indicating a file has an embedded profile mismatch, and asking what you would like to do.

Missing Profile

The document "swing.psd" does not have an embedded RGB profile.

What would you like to do?
- ○ Leave as is (don't color manage)
- ● Assign working RGB: Adobe RGB (1998)
- ○ Assign profile: Canon MP470/MX300/MX310 series SP4
    - ☐ and then convert document to working RGB

Cancel   OK

FIGURE | 10–9 |

If no color settings have been indicated for a document, a dialog box will appear indicating the missing profile and asking what you would like to do.

Monitor Calibration

Monitors are the lighted windows through which you view your digital work. Like printers, they need to be identified with a particular color profile that, ideally, is consistent with the profiles you have set in Photoshop. Although identifying and changing the color profile of your monitor—through calibration—was not the first thing I talked about in the color management process (I wanted to explain what a color profile was first), it should be the first profile you create—even before choosing color settings in Photoshop. To do this you can use a visual calibrator provided as part of your computer's operating system, such as Monitor Calibrator for the Mac OS, or products from other manufacturers like Color Wizzard (for Windows), or Pantone Huey (for Mac or Windows). See Figure 10–10.

RESOLUTION

Argh! Here we are again on the topic of resolution—that elusive concept that pretty much determines everything about your image's final quality and size (both dimensionally and in file size). For output to printers using halftone dots to render images (see the section, Commercial Printing), consideration must be given to the number of dots to be printed within a given area or screen—in other words, the dpi or resolution. This process is like working with the resolution of bitmap images, which, similarly, are composed of a given amount of pixels on a bitmapped grid. In Photoshop, you specify halftone screen attributes before producing a film or a paper output of the image. This applies particularly when you are working with commercial

FIGURE | 10–10 |

Example of the calibrating program provided as part of my Mac's operating system (System Preferences > Display > Color). These programs will take you through the calibration process.

printers. Consult your print specialist for the recommended resolution and screen (frequency, angle, and dot) settings.

Halftone dots are deposited on paper based on a screen ruling—the amount of lines or rows within a given screen. Screen rulings for halftones and separations are measured in lines per inch (lpi). The frequency, angle, and size of dots are determined by the screen ruling. More lpi create smaller, tighter dots, like those seen in a glossy magazine or slick brochure. Fewer lpi create larger, rougher-looking dots that are easier to print, such as on newsprint. A general rule is that the resolution (ppi, or dpi, when referring to halftone printing) of a given piece of artwork is about 1.5 times and no more than 2.0 times the screen frequency. Did I just lose you here? Let me clarify. After consulting with your print specialist, you discover that the screen ruling for the glossy flyer you want to print is 150 lpi and needs to be in the TIFF format (an uncompressed bitmap format). This information gives you an idea of what resolution your TIFF file should be; somewhere between 225, and 300 dpi or ppi (hence, 150 lpi × 1.5 = 225 and 150 lpi × 2 = 300). Keep in mind that the resolution of an image and its screen frequency directly relate to what kind of paper it will be printed on and at what quality.

- ► Newspapers, or similar highly porous, coarse papers use screens of 85–100 lpi. Therefore, the artwork resolution should be at least 128–150 dpi or ppi.
- ► News magazines or company publications with medium coarseness use screens of 133–150 lpi. Therefore, the artwork resolution should be at least 200–225 dpi or ppi.
- ► Fine-quality brochures, books, and magazines with slick paper surfaces use screens of 150–300 lpi. Therefore, the artwork resolution should be at least 225–450 dpi or ppi.

> Note: *Photoshop has a nifty little feature that will automatically suggest a resolution for an image based on a screen frequency. Go to Image > Image Size and choose the Auto option. Enter a Screen frequency and Quality setting (Draft, Good, Best), and the resolution will be updated for the document. This option only specifies a resolution for a suggested screen frequency. To determine the final halftone screen ruling for printing, use the Halftone Screen dialog box, accessible through the Print command—select Output from the drop-down on the top right side (the default is set to Color Management), then select the Screen button at the bottom of the panel.*

FORMAT

Final output compatibility should be in the format in which the image is saved. Most likely you have been working on the image in Photoshop's native PSD file format, which maintains all of your layers and effects. Now you must save a copy of the file in a format specific to its output needs. For bitmapped images, TIFF is the best option because it uses minimal or no compression on the image (resulting in higher quality), flattens your layers in a more conveniently sized package (TIFF also gives the option to preserve layers), and will preserve alpha channel information. To preserve both vector and bitmapped data that might be in an image, the EPS format is a good choice. This format is especially useful when you plan to import an image into a vector-friendly program, such as Adobe Illustrator. More recently, print specialists prefer to save their images in the cross-platform compatible PDF format (see the section, Portable Document File).

You will quickly find there are many different formats in which to save your image. Each format has specific characteristics, depending on where it is going. As for Web-based formats, that is reserved for Chapter 11. An overview of common formats is also provided in Chapter 3. For practice, here are the steps for saving an image in the print-friendly TIFF format:

1. Open the file **swing.psd** from the folder **chap10_lessons/assets**.

2. Choose Image > Mode > CMYK Color to set the image into the CMYK color space. If you get a warning message that begins "You are about to convert to CMYK…," choose OK. You should always set your image to the CMYK color space if you plan to print the image using the traditional print process. However, if you simply want to make a quick print from a desktop printer, you can stay in RGB color mode.

3. Choose File > Save As and rename your file. Under Format choose TIFF (take note of the other available formats). Save the file to your **lessons** folder. Be sure the Embed Color Profile option is selected (if you assigned a profile to the image, this option should be checked automatically). Click Save.

4. A TIFF Options dialog box will appear. Here, you can choose a form of image compression. If the file size of the image is not an issue, stick with a compression setting of NONE to maintain the highest-quality image. LZW is another good choice for image compression, since it is a lossless form of compression (see the section, Compression, in Chapter 11). LZW works best on grayscale images or images with large areas of uniform color. However, LZW compression is not universally used by all programs, so if there is any doubt, keep it set to NONE.

> Note: *Depending on the image attributes, the choice of options in the TIFF Options box will vary. If, for example, your image contains more than one layer, you have a Layer Compression option. If your image has layers, you can choose the RLE or ZIP compression options and preserve the Photoshop layers in the TIFF, or reduce the file size of the image and discard the layers (flatten) and save a copy. Preserving the Photoshop layers in TIFF format will increase the file size.*

5. If you choose to flatten the layers of the image—which is going to happen in any case when you open the file in another program—be sure you save a version with the layers. You never know when you are going to need to reopen the image in Photoshop and make changes.

6. Click OK to close the TIFF Options dialog box. Out of interest, compare the file size of your PSD version to the TIFF version. To do this, find the saved files in your **lessons** folder (or wherever you saved them), right-click (Windows) or Ctrl-click (Mac) over each file icon, and choose Properties (Windows) or Get Info (Mac).

CONSULT THE PROFESSIONALS

If printing your artwork professionally, either via a digital or commercial press, is a "must," alleviate undue headaches and find yourself a reliable print specialist. A good specialist can identify your printing needs and offer appropriate solutions for getting the best-quality print job for your specific situation. However, do not underestimate the importance of understanding the printing process and its terminology—what was just covered in this chapter. Properly setting up your Photoshop file before handing it to the printer can save you time and money. Also, have a clear idea of what kind of paper the job requires. For instance, do you envision your creation on porous newsprint or slick, heavy card stock? Different types of paper produce varying color effects and require different specifications.

> Note: *Your print specialist can provide paper samples and color swatches to aid you in your decision.*

During the final output stages of your document, consult your printing service bureau to find out how best to prepare your file (i.e., color mode, resolution, and format). Also, be aware that the complexity of your artwork determines a lot about what you need to know to prepare it for print. Transparencies, alpha channels, spot colors, gradients, fonts, vector graphics, and duotones, for example, might require extra attention to print properly.

SETTING UP THE PRINT JOB

The easy way out of the printing process is to choose File > Print and be done with it. Yeah, right. If you want your print job to look professional, it can get more complicated than just choosing Print. (So, if you skipped the rest of this chapter and came directly here, I am assuming you already know about the quirks and conundrums of printing.) As previously covered, you first need to know where you are going to print your work (desktop printer, commercial printer, PDF). Second, you need to understand output compatibility, and third, you may need to contact a print specialist. With that in mind, you can go to the proper setup command in Photoshop. Do not simply go to File and choose Print; first consider the options presented when you select File > Print.

PRINT COMMAND

OK, you are ready to see your work on some papyrus material. In Photoshop, choose File > Print and see what is available. See Figure 10–11 (on the next page). (Note: If you want to do this right now, open **swing.psd** in the folder **chap10_lessons/assets** to use as an example.)

FIGURE | 10–11 |

Output options in the Print command window.

1. The first thing to notice is the option to scale your image (Scaled Print Size) to a print size other than what was originally specified under the image size area (Image > Image Size). You might want to do this if your original image is larger than the paper you are printing it on, or if you want a smaller, quicker proof for markup purposes. Remember, however, if the image is scaled larger the quality will deteriorate.

2. To the right of the image preview, designate Output as your option choice. Refer to Figure 10–11 again. For output, you can specify numerous goodies (i.e., a background color or border treatment). You can also make specifications necessary for a seamless printing endeavor, such as bleed amounts (if you have color extending right to the edge of your document), screen and transfer measurements, printer marks for proper registration of an image's color plates (see Figure 10–12), and film output options. For kicks, select the Border option and specify a border width. Also, choose Calibration Bars, Registration Marks, Corner Crop Marks, Center Crop Marks, and Labels. Note that each selection is shown on the image in the preview window.

3. Still in the Print window, switch the Output options selector to Color Management. Under the Print option you can choose a Document Profile or a Proof Profile. For each selection, set the options in the Options area. In the Options area, you can set Color Handling to Printer Manages Colors or Photoshop Manages Colors based on a specific Printer Profile.

swing.psd

FIGURE | 10–12 |

A PDF version of the file **swing.psd**. Registration, cropping, border, and bleed specifications were indicated in the Print command output area.

> Note: *Proof Profile, which we have not discussed, can be indicated for your document under View > Proof Setup. Consult the Help files for more on soft and hard proofs.*

4. If you are not ready to print but want to preserve your settings, choose Done. If you are ready to print, select where you would like to print your document from the Printer drop- down in the Print Window or under the Print Settings button. See figure 10-13. (on the next page) Save as PDF option under the PDF button or choose Adobe PDF under the Printer drop-down area, if available. Choose Print to execute the print action. See Figure 10–14 (on th next page).

5. Lastly, choose Print in the lower right corner of the window to execute the action.

> Note: *If your printer does not support PostScript data, a dialog box will come up indicating that some options chosen might not be available with the printer indicated. See Figure 10-15. (on page 233).*

FIGURE | 10–13 |

Options on my Macintosh for printing to a desktop printer or PDF document.

FIGURE | 10–14 |

Under Print Settings you can choose how to output your document via your printer or as a PDF document.

Note: *If you have printed a copy of your image to a desktop printer or saved it as a PDF document (which you can view using the Acrobat Reader), you will see the specifications set on the image, such as registration and cropping marks. See Figure 10–12 for an example.*

Adobe Photoshop

Some PostScript specific print settings (Interpolation, Calibration, Encoding) will be ignored since you are printing to a non-PostScript printer.

OK

☐ **Don't show again**

FIGURE | 10–15 |

Conflict dialog box that could come up if your printer does not support PostScript information.

▶ DON'T GO THERE!

As you roam through the various print dialog boxes, you might discover that you can set scaling options for your image in the print specifications dialog box of your particular desktop printer. See Figure 10–16. The recommendation is to not set the scaling options in this specific area, but rather in the Print window as reviewed previously.

Page Setup

Settings: Page Attributes

Format for: Any Printer

Paper Size: US Letter

8.50 by 11.00 inches

Orientation:

Scale: 100 %

Cancel   OK

FIGURE | 10–16 |

Page Setup for printers specifically installed on my Macintosh. To scale to print size, use the options under the Print command rather than the Page Setup box for your particular printer.

SUMMARY

With the wave of a wand, I wish I could make the printing process for your digital imagery totally seamless and stress free. But, as you learned, there are many variables to this. It is unlikely your print job will come out perfectly the first time, so be prepared to waste a few (or a dozen) sheets of paper trying to get everything just right. And, of course, it doesn't hurt to consult the professionals, get a proof or two created of your final work, and meticulously edit before printing the job in full.

▶ IN REVIEW

1. Briefly describe the four printing methods.

2. What are process colors?

3. Why might you output your image into a PDF?

4. What are the three areas that should be considered when preparing an image to go to print?

5. Describe color management and why it is important to understand.

6. What do you do in the Color Settings dialog box (Edit > Color Settings)?

7. Why calibrate your monitor?

8. What does halftone printing mean? What are halftone dots?

9. Describe what happens when an image is flattened.

10. Where is a good place to set alternate scaling options for a printed image?

▶ EXPLORING ON YOUR OWN

1. Access the Help > Photoshop Help menu and read the following topics related to printing: "Printing" and "Color Management > Keeping colors consistent." A word of caution: This is a ton of information to wade through—not necessarily bedtime reading, but rather something to be learned on a "need to know" basis.

2. Find out if your desktop printer supports PostScript and if you have the ability to specify options for color separations in the Print dialog box. If so, print separations for a document that has been saved in the CMYK Color mode (Image > Mode > CMYK Color).

3. Open the sample file **swing.pdf** in the folder **chap10_lessons/assets**. Take a look at the printer marks that have been specified around the artwork. In the Help files, do a search for "setting output options" or "to set output options." Investigate what each printer mark represents.

4. Call a printing service (or search online) and inquire about the printing services it offers and what file specifications it requires. Be specific with your questions and try out some of the terminology you learned in this chapter.

5. Explore options for making contact sheets (a feature that conveniently creates thumbnail versions of multiple images for proofing purposes) in the Adobe Output Module (AOM). AOM is a feature in the Adobe Bridge program. Here are the steps to give it a try:

   a. In Photoshop, click on the Launch Bridge icon in the Application Bar to open the program.

   b. Open Adobe Bridge CS5 > Preferences from the main menu. In Preferences, under Startup Scripts, check the Adobe Output Module option. See Figure 10–17. Close Preferences.

FIGURE | 10–17 |

Choose the Adobe Output Module in Adobe Bridge's Preferences.

c.   At the top part of the Bridge interface click the Output to Web and PDF option. See Figure 10–18. An Output panel opens to the right.

d.   At the top of the Output panel choose the PDF option, and under Template choose the 4*5 Contact Sheet. See Figure 10–19.

e.   On the left side of the Bridge program be sure the Folders panel is open. Scroll for a folder on your computer that contains images or photographs. Once the folder is selected, the images should appear in the Content panel at the bottom of the Bridge program. See Figure 10–20, #1 and #2 (on the next page).

f.   Hold down the Shift key on your keyboard and select any number of images in the folder for which you would like a contact sheet made. Refer to Figure 10–20 again.

g.   Scroll to the bottom of the Output panel, choose the View PDF after Save option, and click Save (refer to Figure 10–20, #3). The PDF document with thumbnails of the images will be created and opened in your Adobe PDF viewer. See Figure 10–21 for an example of a finished contact sheet.

For instructions on making Web Galleries (also a feature in the AOM), see Exploring on Your Own in Chapter 11.

FIGURE | 10–18 |

Choose Output to Web or PDF in the Bridge program.

FIGURE | 10–19 |

Under PDF choose a contact sheet template.

FIGURE | 10–20 |

1. Browse for some images on your computer. 2. Select the images in the Content panel. 3. Set options for the contact sheet and choose Save.

FIGURE | 10–21 |

An example contact sheet in the PDF format.

adventures
IN DESIGN

WINE BOX COMPOSITION

As you learned in, Chapter 9, assembling artwork pieces—photos, illustrations, and text—into an aesthetically pleasing whole is the art of composition. An experienced art director or graphic designer can envision the larger scope of attractively arranging elements, while simultaneously considering each element's minute design details. Moreover, a good handle on current computer graphics software programs and their tool sets is crucial for bringing an inspired vision to life. The work of art director Dave Garcez and the graphic artists at E. & J. Gallo

Winery in Modesto, California, is a good example of how composition is not just the bringing together of elements in one program, but also the coordination of elements among two or more programs. See Figure D–1.

PROFESSIONAL PROJECT EXAMPLE

The 5-liter wine box label shown in Figure D–1 was created for Gallo Winery using a combination of Photoshop and Illustrator. First, in Photoshop, photographs of glasses of wine were incorporated to achieve the most appetizing look. The final wine glass was then layered with a basket

FIGURE | D–1 |

A 5-liter wine box label was produced using Adobe Photoshop and Illustrator. Used with permission of E. & J. Gallo Winery.

FIGURE | D–2 |

Photographs were taken and layered in Photoshop.
Used with permission of E. & J. Gallo Winery.

FIGURE | D–3 |

The photographs were then incorporated
into a complete image. Used with
permission of E. & J. Gallo Winery.

and some grapes. See Figure D–2 and Figure D–3. The
logo was created in Illustrator. A hand-drawn sketch
was scanned and placed as a template into Illustrator.
The final logo design and photographic images were
incorporated into Photoshop and then saved and imported
into Illustrator, where additional typographic elements
were added and the whole file was prepared for print. See
Figure D–1. This same project is used as an Adventures in
Design in Exploring Adobe Illustrator CS5, emphasizing the
parts of the project (i.e., the logo design) that were done
in Illustrator. Now, I want to share the techniques used to
achieve the perfect look for the wine glass image.

The pixels of two of the wine glass photos were selected,
transformed, and blended to produce the most active and
realistic looking "swirl" of wine. See Figure D–2 and

FIGURE | D–4 |

Alpha channels were used to highlight and darken selections, creating more brightness and roundness to the glass: 1. The original wine glass photo; 2. Highlight outlines are drawn; 3. Alpha channel masks are created; 4. Final retouched photo.

Figure D–3. The glass was then retouched to produce a more appetizing glow and give it more roundness. To enhance it, the highlights on an empty glass were outlined and then saved into an alpha channel. Using a combination of the Dodge, Burn, and Airbrush tools, the selections (alpha channels) were then used to lighten highlighted areas and darken shadowed areas. See Figure D–4.

The grapes were also enhanced. The lower-right corner was darkened for more light contrast, and many berries were retouched to remove imperfections. They were then placed within the basket. See Figure D–5.

Another subtle improvement was done to the image. To make the stem of the glass appear in front of the stripe element at the bottom of the final design, another photo of the stem was taken. Then a color print of the grapes and basket was distorted and placed behind it. The areas around the stem were deleted. See Figure D–6.

Your Turn

Putting into practice your image compositing skills, it's your turn to create an attractive image that could be used on a wine box, label, or advertisement. The original photos for the Peter Vella wine box label are provided for your educational use in the **aid examples** folder (**basket.tif, grapes.tif**, **chard_glass1.tif**, and **chard_glass2.tif**), or you can photograph or find your own images.

Self-project Guidelines

1. Find a selection of images you might like to use in your image composition. They can be

photographs you have taken or borrowed for educational purposes, scanned illustrations, or the photos provided in the **aid_examples** folder. Some image ideas could include pictures of wine bottles or barrels, vineyards, other styles of wine glasses, or someone enjoying a glass of wine. Try to get the highest quality images possible.

2. On paper, sketch some ideas of how you see the images assembled into a completely new design.

3. Determine what techniques you know in Photoshop that will enable you to recreate the sketch you like best.

4. On a new document with a resolution of at least 150 pixels, import the photos into Photoshop. Put each image on its own named layer.

5. Work your pixel magic on the images using what you have learned in Photoshop. Adjust tonal levels and color, select and transform pixels, blend layers, and add effects and filters.

6. Save the file in PSD format and in a print-ready TIFF format.

Things to Consider

Here are some things to consider when working on your image compositions for this lesson and in your professional work:

► A design is never finished. Leave time to do revisions.

► Save often, and back up your work. I suggest saving different versions of your work, as in **wine_imagev1**, **wine_imagev2a**, **wine_imagev2b**, **wine_imagev3**, etc. You never know when you might want to refer to an earlier version.

► Get your document organized. In other words, use layers and name them intuitively.

► Print your image from a desktop printer (preferably color) to get a good idea of the image size and overall look.

► If you "borrowed" from another's work, or used another's image as a template in the creation of your own composition, resolve any copyright issues.

FIGURE | D–5 |

The grapes were retouched and incorporated with the basket.

FIGURE | D–6 |

An effect is created on the stripe element at the bottom of the design. The stripe is reflected through the wine glass stem.

Explorer PAGES

David Julian

Alphabet. © David Julian.

About David Julian

David Julian holds a BFA from Pratt Institute, and is a widely published and awarded photographer, illustrator, and mixed-media artist. His work has been commissioned for clients in all genres, and has appeared in over one hundred magazines including *Macworld, Sierra, Edutopia, Los Angeles Times, New York Times, Boston Globe, Baltimore Sun, Psychology Today,* *GEO, Nikon World, PRINT, Communication Arts, PhotoMedia, Zoom,* and *Archive.* He also authors articles for *Digital Photo Pro, PC Photo, Digital Photographer,* and *Double Exposure.*

When not working in his studio filled with eclectic collections, he travels and teaches creativity workshops across the continent. Dave's patient, intuitive teaching manner helps others develop the ability to reach their creative goals. Active

Transformation. © David Julian.

as a portfolio consultant, Dave is also on Adobe's Lightroom3 beta team and partners with Wacom and OnOne Software. He also co-leads a 840-member Photoshop User Group in Seattle. His images are represented by Corbis, and his work can be viewed at *www.davidjulian.com*.

About the Work of David Julian

"My main tools are a Macintosh MacPro, twin 23" Apple displays, and a Wacom Intuos 4 tablet. The Wacom is the most essential tool for my style of work as it allows fluid and variable retouching strokes and is perfectly integrated into the brush behaviors in Photoshop".

Transformation

"For *Transformation*, I began with a rough concept sketch to outline my idea. I made notes and a list of elements I needed to find in my archives or shoot for my Photoshop composite. I then assembled the elements, such as the girl, landscape, butterfly, and wings into an 'elements' folder on my hard drive. I prepared these for importing into the main layered

Explorer PAGES, *continued*

image in Photoshop by silhouetting objects from backgrounds and doing some basic retouching. Once I created a new file at poster size and at my printer's 360ppi resolution, I began my composite image with the key element of the woman. I added a different coat and retouched her face and hair using painted details and adjustment layers. Then I added the landscape, the full-moon sky, and a texture shot of an oil painting.

"I often reduce the element's opacity and play with layer modes to better visualize my options for composition and overall 'feel' of the evolving art. Once the main elements are in place and resized, I add shadow layers or use Layer Effects or dimension. Lastly, I fine-tune each element layer with masks and adjustment layers to balance color, opacity, effects, and mood. After so much effort, I generally move onto something else, returning several hours or a day later to fine-tune the composite using a refreshed perspective."

Heaven and Hell

"I created *Heaven and Hell* as a self-assignment after visiting several impressive cathedrals and cemeteries in Portugal. I sketched the basic idea and composed onto a canvas in Photoshop the four main photographic elements: the skulls, the sky with starlings, the cross, and the arched doorway. I left them in color, letting each layer overlap transparently until

Heaven and Hell. © David Julian.

the composition gelled in my mind. I then added a Black and White adjustment layer to the topmost layer so that all layers would appear colorless."

"Much masking and retouching was done with my Wacom pen to blend edges and fix distractions, and some brushed-in tone and blurring was used as well. Once the composition and tones were balanced, I added a Color Balance layer to the top of the stack to tone the image toward sepia. Lastly, I added the organic photographic edge as a layer (with mode set to multiply) from my collection of prints made long ago in the darkroom. The result is my darkly interpretative vision of a place between Heaven and Hell."

The Temple of Prambanan

"This is a huge Hindu temple complex in Java, Indonesia. I shot this image on color slide film for a series called Sacred Spaces. Years later, I scanned the slide at high resolution and recontextualized the image to fit into a series called Dreams and Visual Poems. In this series, all images are split-toned towards sepia and cool grey to lend a historical yet mystical feel. I added a Black and White adjustment layer, adjusting the sliders to best pump contrast into the features and to separate the sky from the temple. Three Curves adjustment layers were added, each carefully masked to balance the overall landscape and enhance or soften details."

"My original shot contained blurring at the edges due to hand-wiping mist from my lens, which caused a pleasing effect that I then added to in Photoshop. I achieved this by converting a duplicate image layer using Convert for Smart Filters from the Filters menu, and added more blur only to the edges by masking the blur filter. The edge was added as the topmost layer in multiply layer mode."

The Temple of Prambanan. © David Julian.

Karen Kamenetzky

Art Quilts Fiber Art Mixed Media

| Home | Gallery | Artist | Contact |

Recent Juried Exhibitions:

The Art and Soul of Quilting
January 18 - March 28, 2004
Anderson Art Center
Kenosha, WI

Art Quilts at the Sedgwick
April 3 - May 2, 2004
Sedgwick Cultural Center
Philadelphia, PA

Art Quilts: Elements
April 30-May 31, 2004
Page-Walker Arts Center
Cary, NC

Underground:Layers
Juried into "Art Quilts at the Sedgwick 2004"

| Web Publishing |

charting your course

Preparing images for the Web or screen-based publication is an important task in today's online world. Luckily for us, Web development tools come packaged with Adobe Photoshop and alleviate many of the headaches that occur when we try to find the right balance between an image that looks good but can also be quickly downloaded from the Internet for efficient viewing. For the avid Web designer, there is much to explore in Photoshop's Web tools, and it is not uncommon to find instructional books specific to this part of Photoshop. This chapter offers an overview of the three main features Web designers use in Photoshop: the Save for Web & Devices command (see the section by the same name); the ability to slice images for fast rendering and to create button and rollover effects (see the section "Image Slicing"); and the Animation panel (see the section "GIF Animation").

goals

In this chapter you will:

- ▶ *Optimize images like a pro*
- ▶ *Get a handle on Web file formats*
- ▶ *Examine the interrelationship among image color, format, size, and compression in the Web publication process*
- ▶ *Get hands-on experience with the Save for Web & Devices options*
- ▶ *Slice a Web page*
- ▶ *Create an animated GIF using the Animation panel*

ABOUT OPTIMIZATION

In part, Chapter 9 discussed the process of designing a print or Web page layout—the integration of many elements (such as text and graphics) into a pleasing visual display. I want to reiterate that the layout process usually involves working in more than one graphics program. For Web page design and development, this most likely includes the use of an image manipulation program to optimize images (i.e., Photoshop) and a layout program that assembles Web elements and codes them into a Web page fit for a browser to read (i.e., Adobe Dreamweaver or Flash).

When it comes to publishing graphics for the Web, it is all about optimization. Optimization, when referring to online artwork, is the process of preparing a functionally optimal graphic, which is an artful balancing act between the visual quality of an image and its quantitative file size. There are three interrelated areas to consider in the Web optimization process: image format, image color, and image size. These areas directly relate to image compression, which refers to reducing an image's file size so it looks good on screen and downloads quickly over an Internet connection.

COMPRESSION

An image's file size can be reduced by compression. If you compress a bitmap image too much—to make it smaller in file size—you can lose visual quality. For instance, it might lose its antialiased effect, which is the smoothing of pixelated edges through a gradation of color. It could dither, which occurs when colors that are lost during compression are replaced by colors within the reduced color palette. See Figure 11–1 and Figure 11–2.

FIGURE | 11–1 |

Close-up antialiasing creates a stair-step effect of color gradation. When viewed at a distance, the edge of the object looks smoother.

FIGURE | 11–2 |

Dithering attempts to simulate colors that are lost in the compression process. On the left is a close-up of an image without dither. On the right, with dither. The differences are subtle, but noticeable with certain images viewed at full magnification.

There are two basic types of compression: lossy and lossless (or "nonlossy"). Lossy compression discards data to make a file smaller. Let's say you are optimizing a line of pixels in the JPEG format, which uses lossy compression. Ten of the pixels are white, followed by a gray pixel, and then five more white pixels. With lossy compression the computer reads the line as 16 white pixels; the gray pixel, being the odd one in the sampling area, is converted to white.

Lossless compression does not eliminate detail or information. Instead it looks for more efficient ways to define the image, such as through the use of customized color tables (see the section "Image Color"). Ultimately, how compression is applied to an image varies greatly depending on the image's format, color, and size.

IMAGE FORMAT

Traditionally, most Web images are saved in the bitmap formats GIF, JPEG, or PNG. Bitmap images rely on resolution to determine their file size and quality. Therefore, bitmap images are generally larger in file size than vector graphics, and have a slower load time when viewed from the Web. Vector-based file formats—including Adobe's SWF and Scalable Vector Graphics (SVG) formats—have emerged that allow us to save and view graphics as streamlined paths, shapes, text, and effects in the online environment. Such graphics are scalable in size and easier to download. However, Photoshop does not handle these file types because it is the master of pixels, not vectors. Adobe Illustrator does a much better job at creating vector images. It also can support export of both the SWF and SVG formats.

> Note: *Adobe Flash and After Effects also have the ability to export bitmap images and animations to the SWF format. In the SWF format, the graphic can be posted directly to the Web or opened in Adobe's Flash. For information on SWF, do a search for SWF in the Photoshop Help files.*

The file format you choose for an optimized image depends on the color, tonal, and graphic characteristics of the original image. In general, continuous-tone bitmap images (images with many shades of color, such as photographs) are best compressed in the JPEG or PNG-24 formats. Illustrations or type with flat color or sharp edges and crisp detail are best as GIF or PNG-8 files. The following list outlines the characteristics of each Web-friendly format you can save in Photoshop including GIF, JPEG, PNG-8, PNG-24, and WBMP. Further clarification of these characteristics is presented in the next two sections.

GIF (Graphics Interchange Format) Format

- ▸ Supports an 8-bit color depth. Bit depth determines the amount and range of color an image can contain. A 1-bit image supports two colors, black and white; an 8-bit image supports up to 256 colors. A customized 256-color palette is referred to as indexed color.

- ► Works best compressing solid areas of color, such as in line art, logos, or graphics with type.
- ► Is supported by the most common Web browsers, such as Internet Explorer, Safari, and Firefox.
- ► Can be animated.
- ► Traditionally uses a lossless compression method. Lossless compression occurs when no data is discarded during the optimization process (see the section "Compression"). You can save a GIF file multiple times without discarding data. However, because GIF files are 8-bit color, optimizing an original 24-bit image as an 8-bit GIF will generally degrade image quality.

> Note: *Illustrator and Photoshop also allow you to create a lossy version of a GIF file. The lossy GIF format includes small compression artifacts—similar to those in JPEG files—but yields significantly smaller files.*

- ► Can be interlaced, so images download in multiple passes, or progressively. The downloading process of interlaced images is visible to the user, ensuring the user the download is in progress. Keep in mind, however, that interlacing increases file size.
- ► Includes dithering options: the process of mixing colors to approximate those not present in the image.
- ► Supports background transparency and background matting: the ability to blend the edges of an image with a Web page background color.

JPEG (Joint Photographic Experts Group) Format

- ► Supports 24-bit color (millions of colors) and preserves the broad range and subtle variations in brightness and hue found in photographs and other continuous-tone images (such as gradients).
- ► Is supported by the most common Web browsers.
- ► Selectively discards data. Because it discards data, JPEG compression is referred to as lossy (see the section "Compression"). The compression is set based on a range between 0% and 100% or 1 and 12. A higher percentage setting results in less data being discarded. The JPEG compression method tends to degrade sharp detail in an image, particularly in images containing type or vector art. Because of the nature of JPEG compression, you should always save JPEG files from the original image, not from a previously saved JPEG. A suggestion: before doing any compression on an image, save a copy in the PSD format. The PSD version becomes your original, uncompressed version that you can come back to if necessary.
- ► Can be interlaced, so images download in multiple passes.
- ► Does not support transparency.
- ► Does not support animation.

PNG-8 (Portable Network Graphics) Format

- ► Uses 8-bit color. Like the GIF format, PNG-8 efficiently compresses solid areas of color while preserving sharp detail, such as that in line art, logos, or graphics with type.

- ► Has not traditionally been supported by all browsers, but this is changing. It is advisable to test images saved in the PNG format on browser platforms that you and your audience might be using to view Web pages.

- ► Uses a lossless compression method, in which no data is discarded during compression. However, because PNG-8 files are 8-bit color, optimizing an original 24-bit image as a PNG-8 can degrade image quality. PNG-8 files use more advanced compression schemes than GIF, and can be 10% to 30% smaller than GIF files of the same image, depending on the image's color patterns.

- ► Can be indexed, like the GIF format, to a specific 256-color palette (such as Adaptive or Restrictive).

- ► Includes dithering options: the process of mixing colors to approximate those not present in the image.

- ► Like the GIF format, it supports background transparency and background matting: the ability to blend the edges of the image with a Web page background color.

PNG-24 (Portable Network Graphics) Format

- ► Supports 24-bit color. Like the JPEG format, PNG-24 preserves the broad range and subtle variations in brightness and hue found in photographs. Like the GIF and PNG-8 formats, PNG-24 preserves sharp detail, such as that in line art, logos, or illustrations with type.

- ► Uses the same lossless compression method as the PNG-8 format, in which no data is discarded. For that reason, PNG-24 files are usually larger than JPEG files of the same image.

- ► Like PNG-8, is not necessarily supported by all browsers.

- ► Supports multilevel transparency, in which you can preserve up to 256 levels of transparency to blend the edges of an image smoothly with any background color.

WBMP format

- ► Supports only 1-bit color, which means images are reduced to contain only black and white pixels.

- ► Standard format for optimizing images for mobile devices in the past (such as older cell phones and PDAs), which did not support viewing complex images in color.

IMAGE COLOR

Photographs and artwork to be viewed on-screen, such as on a Web page, must be saved in the RGB Color mode. (To review, read the characteristics of the RGB Color mode in Chapter 5.) To convert artwork to the RGB Color mode, choose Image > Mode > RGB Color. When it comes to the topic of image color, you need an understanding of color-reduction algorithms, covered in the following section.

Color-Reduction Algorithms

Photoshop uses color-reduction algorithms to generate a specific color table for an optimized image. You will get a better idea of how color tables work in a lesson later in this chapter. Color-reduction algorithms only apply to the GIF and PNG-8 formats. Because these two formats support the 8-bit format (i.e., an image with 256 colors or less), the color tables determine how the computer calculates which 256 colors to keep.

> Note: *If the original image has fewer than 256 colors, you can adjust the maximum number of colors that are calculated, further reducing the size of the image.*

Each color reduction palette produces slightly different results, so it is a good idea to understand how each type works its magic. The descriptions of the color tables that follow are taken from the Photoshop Help files. (Photoshop categorizes the color tables as dynamic, fixed, or custom.) Reading descriptions, however, will not give you the full effect of what these color tables do. This will only be possible when you see, later in the chapter, how the tables affect an actual image.

Dynamic options use a color-reduction algorithm to build a palette based on the colors in the image and the number of colors specified in the optimization setting. The colors in the palette are regenerated every time you change or re-optimize the image.

- *Perceptual:* Creates a custom color table by giving priority to colors for which the human eye has greater sensitivity.
- *Selective:* Creates a color table similar to the Perceptual color table, but favors broad areas of color and the preservation of Web colors. This color table usually produces images with the greatest color integrity. Selective is the default option.
- *Adaptive:* Creates a custom color table by sampling colors from the spectrum appearing most commonly in the image. For example, an image with only the colors green and blue produces a color table made primarily of greens and blues. Most images have a concentration of colors in particular areas of the spectrum.

Fixed options use a set palette of colors. In other words, the available colors are constant, but the specific colors in the palette will vary depending on the colors in the image.

- *Restrictive (Web):* Uses the standard 216-color color table common to both Windows and Mac OS 8-bit (256-color) palettes. This option ensures that no browser dither is applied to colors when the image is displayed using 8-bit color. (This palette is also called the Web-safe palette.) If your image has fewer colors than the total number specified in the color palette, unused colors are removed. Using the Restrictive palette can create larger than necessary files and is recommended only when avoiding browser dither is a high priority.
- *Black & White:* Builds a color table of only two colors—black and white.
- *Grayscale:* Creates a custom table of only grayscale pixels.
- *Mac OS and Windows:* Builds an 8-bit palette, capable of displaying 256 colors, using the color table of the system you select. If your image has fewer colors than the total number specified in the color palette, unused colors are removed.

The *Custom* option uses a color palette that is created or modified by the user. If you open an existing GIF or PNG-8 file, it will already have a custom color palette. When you choose the Custom color palette, it preserves the current perceptual, selective, or adaptive color table as a fixed palette that does not update with changes to the image.

> Note: *For future reference, you can lock, add, sort, delete, and shift colors in the generated color tables. You can also save and load color tables to apply to images.*

IMAGE SIZE

To discuss image size is to reintroduce the concept of resolution. For online display, an image's resolution need only match a standard monitor's resolution, which is 72 pixels per inch (ppi) for Mac and 96 ppi for Windows. This is a welcome relief considering what you learned in Chapter 10: the resolution of artwork going to print varies depending on where it is being printing and on what kind of paper stock.

Resolution is a moot point when working with vector-based graphics. These types of images are unique in their application to the Web. They are inherently scalable and compact in size. So, keep in mind that much of what we are talking about in regard to file size and compression applies to bitmap (or rasterized) images. Until more Web designers advance to using the latest online vector graphic formats, such as SWF and SVG, much of the graphics you see on the Web will be in bitmap format.

A bitmap image's size is directly related to its resolution. Image size can be referred to in two ways, and both impact optimization: the actual dimensions of an image (e.g., 5-by-5 inches or 400-by-600 pixels); and the image's file size (its actual amount in digital bits). This is measured in bytes, kilobytes, megabytes, or gigabytes. A byte is 8 bits, a kilobyte (KB) is 1,024 bytes, a megabyte (MB) is 1,024 kilobytes, and a gigabyte (GB) is 1,024 megabytes. How big is too big for a Web image? Well, it depends on how many images you have on a single Web page, whether they are bitmap or vector based, and whether they are dimensionally large or small.

I prefer to restrict my Web images, especially bulky bitmap ones, to no more than 10 to 20 KB each in file size. In fact, when I build Web pages it is not uncommon for a client to request that we keep the total file size of everything on a Web page under 30 KB for viewers with slow Internet connections. The ultimate, of course, is to actually post your optimized images to the Web and test how long it takes for them to download on different Internet connections—a process you can perform in the Save for Web & Devices area of the program.

SAVE FOR WEB & DEVICES

Think of the Save for Web & Devices option (File > Save for Web & Devices) as a fitness program for your graphics. Depending on your image's body type (format), you can try out various fitness regimens (compression schemes) to produce the best-looking and leanest image possible in the Optimized window view. A 2-Up or 4-Up window view lets you compare and contrast an image's optimization settings next to the original file. See Figure 11–3.

FIGURE | 11–3 |

The Optimized window view with the 4-Up window tab selected.

FIGURE | 11–4 |

Select a browser to view your image. If you do not have a browser selected, choose Other and find the browser of your choice installed in your applications folder, such as Safari, Firefox, or Internet Explorer.

In Save for Web & Devices you also can view your image using the selected specifications in a browser window of your choice (e.g., Safari, Firefox, Internet Explorer, whatever is installed on your computer). In the Save for Web & Devices window, this option is located in the lower-left corner of the box, next to the Device Central button. See Figure 11–4.

As discussed in the Image Format section, there are general guidelines for what artwork is best saved in what format—photos as JPEGs, line art as GIFs. However, to determine the right file size and quality, you need to subtly adjust the options in the Save for Web & Devices dialog box. A simple adjustment to the bit depth of a GIF image, for example, can reduce the file size of an image immensely, resulting in a much more efficient Internet download. There are multiple options to choose from in the Save for Web & Devices dialog box, but don't let that overwhelm you. When you are ready to learn about these options, review that information in the Photoshop Help files. For now, just learn some of the basics and trust your visual instincts when you start comparing and contrasting settings in the Save for Web & Devices dialog box—something you get the opportunity to do in Lesson 1: Preparing an Image for the Web.

OPTIMIZATION
WORKFLOW TECHNIQUES

If you understand how optimization works and how to save an image with proper optimization settings, you know 90% of the Web image publication process. However, for purposes of workflow—finding more efficient ways of doing a task—there are a couple of features related to optimization that might prove beneficial for you sooner rather than later. First is the ability to save and edit optimization settings (see Figure 11–5) and resize the image (pixel size) at export (see Figure 11–6).

Second, when you have many images that need to be saved with the same optimization setting, you can create a clever timesaver called a "droplet." A droplet is a small application that automatically applies specific settings

FIGURE | 11–5 |

Save and edit your optimization settings.

FIGURE | 11–6 |

Create a new size for the optimized image at export.

to a batch of images you drag over a droplet icon. Let's say you just received 50 high-resolution photos that need to be resized and converted to JPEG format, with a 60% compression. Moreover, the project needs to be done soon because the Web developer has to get the photos online (today) as part of the company's new spring catalog. With a droplet action, you record the optimization specifications on one of the photos and then have Photoshop diligently execute the steps on the rest of the images (while you take a long lunch break, of course). To make a droplet with specific optimization settings, record your optimization settings as an action. Then, to execute the action, choose File > Automate > Create Droplet. See Figure 11–7 (on the next page). When you're ready to execute the droplet action on images, drag a folder of images over the saved droplet.

I don't cover the topic much in this book, but Photoshop has an Actions panel (Window > Actions) where you can record a series of individual actions (commands)—like the steps for saving an image to a particular size and format— and then automatically run the action on batches of images. To practice creating a droplet in Photoshop, see the section Exploring on Your Own at the end of this chapter.

FIGURE | 11–7 |

The Create Droplet options
dialog box.

LESSON 1: PREPARING AN IMAGE FOR THE WEB

In this lesson, you'll optimally save a colorful photograph, originally in the TIFF
format, of a quilt created by Karen Kamenetzky. You'll use the settings in Photoshop's
Save for Web & Devices dialog box to prepare the image for Web publication.

Setting Up the File

1. In Photoshop, choose File > Open and open **chap11L1.tif** in the **chap11_lessons**
    folder.

2. Press Shift-Tab to hide unneeded windows.

3. Select View > Actual Pixels to be sure you are viewing the image at 100%.

4. Familiarize yourself with the file's specifications. Choose Image > Mode and be sure it is
    in RGB Color mode.

5. Choose Image > Image Size and note the document size and resolution. Right now the
    image is saved at 150 ppi. When optimized it will be reduced to 72 ppi—the standard
    resolution for screen-based graphics. Do not make any changes, just click OK.

6. Make a color adjustment to the image. Choose Image > Adjustments > Levels…, click
    on the Auto button and click OK, and then choose Image > Auto Color. Note the subtle
    but significant changes in the brightness and contrast (the vibrancy) of the image.

Setting the Save for Web Options

1. Choose File > Save for Web & Devices, and select the 4-Up option on the tab in the
    upper-left corner of the window. A four-window view of the image becomes available.
    See Figure 11–8 and Figure 11–9.

FIGURE | 11–8 |

Choose the 4-Up option to compare and contrast the image in four different windows.

FIGURE | 11–9 |

The full 4-Up window view.

2. Click on the top-left window to highlight it. A colored box appears around the image. Note that this window shows the original image at a file size of 456 KB. Also, note that Preset is set to Original in the information area to the right of the dialog box.

3. Click on the window to the right of the first window. A colored frame will appear around the image, and the setting options for the image become available at the top right of the dialogue box.

4. The viewing annotations at the bottom of the selected window provide valuable information about the optimization settings for that particular window. Those settings include format type, size, estimated download time, and Color table specifications.

5. Note that the download time is determined by a specified Internet connection speed. By default, this is set to the standard modem speed, 56.6 kilobytes per second (Kbps). To change this setting, click on the icon with the triangle and four horizontal lines to the right of the listed download speed and duration. See Figure 11–10 (on the next page).

FIGURE | 11–10 |

Change the Internet connection speed to see how it affects the image's download time.

FIGURE | 11–11 |

Set the optimization options.

6. Under Preset, leave it [Unnamed]. Then select the following options (see Figure 11–11):

▶ *Optimized file format:* GIF
▶ *Color-reduction algorithm:* Adaptive
▶ *Colors:* 256
▶ *Dither algorithm:* No Dither
▶ *Transparency:* Uncheck
▶ *Interlaced:* Uncheck
▶ *Matte:* None
▶ *Web Snap:* 0%
▶ *Lossy:* 0

7. The Color Table for the selected window indicates the colors being used in the image, which is determined by the color-reduction algorithm (Adaptive) and the maximum number of colors in the algorithm setting (256). Hover—do not click—your cursor over a swatch to reveal the color's attributes, which appear in a long rectangular box near the bottom of the window. See Figure 11–12.

8. Select the third (bottom-left) window and adjust the settings differently, as follows:

▶ *Optimized file format:* GIF
▶ *Color-reduction algorithm:* Restrictive
▶ *Colors:* Auto (the maximum number available)
▶ *Dither algorithm:* Diffusion
▶ *Dither:* 100%
▶ *Transparency:* Uncheck
▶ *Interlaced:* Uncheck
▶ *Matte:* None
▶ *Web Snap:* 0%
▶ *Lossy:* 0

9. In the Color Table for the selected window, the swatches with a diamond in the middle indicate Web-safe colors. (For more information on Restrictive [Web] algorithm, see the section Color-Reduction Algorithm.) The others are in the general RGB color space. Hover—do not click—your cursor over one of the diamond swatches, and the Web-safe hexadecimal color number is revealed in the box described in step 7.

10. Select the fourth window and alter its settings as follows:

▶ *Optimized file format:* JPEG
▶ *Compression Quality:* Maximum
▶ *Quality:* 100
▶ *Progressive:* Check

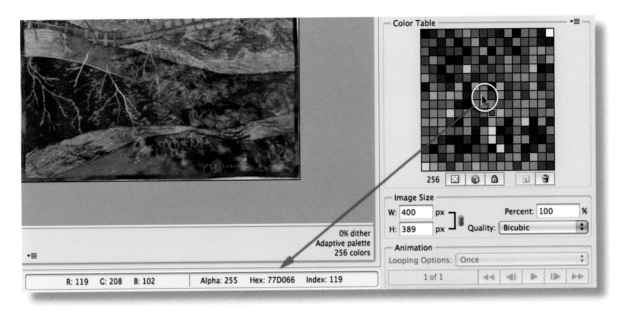

FIGURE | 11–12 |

Hover over a swatch to reveal the color's numeric attributes.

- ► *Blur:* 0
- ► *Matte:* None
- ► *Embed Color Profile:* Uncheck

Comparing and Contrasting Settings

1. Take a close look at what each optimization setting does to the image. Magnify the windows with the Zoom tool (located to the left of the Save for Web & Devices window) or with the Zoom level (at the bottom, left of the window above the Device Central button) and really examine the artifacts of each compression scheme. Use the Hand tool to move the magnified image around in a window.

2. Double-click on the Zoom tool icon to set the view of each window to the original image size. Which version looks best to you?

3. Compare and contrast the viewing annotations at the bottom of each window. What are the size differences? Is the one that looks best to you a reasonable size for a quick download from the Internet (i.e., under 20 K)?

Getting Picky

1. OK, let's fine-tune and reduce the file size of the image even more. It definitely needs it. It is a beautifully complex image that could be worth the download wait time, but let's make a version a user would be able to view relatively fast, even on a slower connection (i.e., 56 Kbps). Select the second window (top-right side).

2. Change the color-reduction algorithm to Selective, and reduce the colors to 128. The file size is reduced, but it does not look any better, and the file size is still too large. The gradients of color on the rock formations are getting splotchy. This is because gradients are composed of several shades of color, so when the color palette is reduced, so are the number of colors needed to make the gradient look smooth.

FIGURE | 11–13 |

Scale down your optimized image to decrease its file size.

FIGURE | 11–14 |

From the Select Browser Menu, select the browser in which you want to view the image.

3. Look at window 4—the JPEG. The gradient here looks good, but the file size is too big. How can we fix it?

4. Select window 4 and change the JPEG compression quality to Medium. Great! The file size is smaller and the image still looks relatively acceptable (compare it to the first window—the original file). It's still pretty big, however. Let's get it under 20 KB.

5. In the Image Size area (below the Color Table), reduce the resize percentage to 75%. See Figure 11–13.

6. Click the planet icon or the Preview button (both located at the bottom of the window) to view the optimized image in a browser. This is the ultimate test of how good it looks. See Figure 11–14 and Figure 11–15. Close the browser window.

> **Note:** *You might need to choose Other in the browser options menu (click on the double arrow next to the planet icon) to find a browser you have installed on your computer. I like to check my image in several browser types—Internet Explorer, Safari, and Firefox—because you never know which browser will be used to view the image.*

7. Make sure the bottom-right window is highlighted, and select Save to save this version of the file. Name it **webimage.jpg** and for format (Save as type), choose Images Only. Save the file in your folder **chap11_lessons**.

FIGURE | 11–15 |

Example of details revealed when an image is viewed in a browser window.

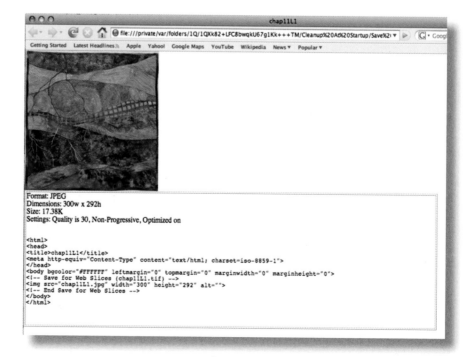

> **Note:** *If you do not want to save the file right away, choose Done rather than Save. This will close the Save for Web window but maintain your optimization settings.*

8. Save and close the lesson.

IMAGE SLICING

Image slicing is dividing up areas of an image or a complete Web page layout into smaller, independent files. If you are familiar with constructing Web pages, and working in HTML, you probably have an understanding of the benefits of slicing. If you are new to Web page design and development, this might seem like a somewhat crazy thing to do to your artwork, but slicing is useful for the following reasons:

▸ Creating accurate HTML table placement

▸ Creating independent files, each containing its own optimization settings

▸ Creating smaller, independent files for faster download

▸ Creating interactive effects, such as button rollovers

LESSON 2: SLICING A WEB PAGE NAVIGATION BAR

In this lesson, you prepare a navigation bar for placement in a Web page. Using Photoshop's Slice tool, you will slice and optimize areas of the layout for optimal Web performance.

Setting Up the File

1. Open **chap11L2.psd** located in the folder **chap11_lessons**. If a Missing Color Profile warning appears, click OK.

2. Choose View > Actual Pixels.

3. Press Shift-Tab to hide unneeded panels, if not already hidden.

4. Choose Window > Layers. Note that there is one layer available, called **nav-bar**.

5. To turn the guides on, choose View > Show > Guides, if not already checked. Guides have been created for you to indicate where the slices will be made. See Figure 11–16.

FIGURE | 11–16 |

The guides help to accurately create image slices.

FIGURE | 11–17 |

Select the Slice tool.

Making Slices

1. To turn the slices on, choose View > Show > Slices, if not already checked.

2. Select the Slice tool in the toolbox (located under the Crop tool). See Figure 11–17.

3. Position the pointed end of the Slice tool in the upper-left corner of the image and click and drag to the right, defining a box around the swirl logo and top header section (do not include the yellow bar of "nav" buttons at the bottom). See Figure 11–18. Note that a number for the slice is indicated in the upper-left corner of the defined box. To hide/show slices, choose View > Show > Slices.

> Note: *When you make slices, you do not actually "cut up" your artwork. Instead you create an overlay of divided areas that determines how the individual files will be created when saving the document. Slicing always occurs in a grid-like pattern. Even if you do not define a slice in a particular area, Photoshop automatically creates one to maintain the structure necessary for exporting into an HTML page.*

FIGURE | 11–18 |

Define a slice with the Slice tool.

4. With the Slice tool, slice around each button area in the lower part of the navigation bar. There will be six slices across the bottom: a slice defining each of the four buttons and one on each edge. Use the guides to get accurate placement. See Figure 11–19.

> Note: *Don't worry if you make a mistake. Just use Edit > Undo, or choose Edit > Step Backward a few times, if necessary and try your slice again.*

FIGURE | 11–19 |

Create six more slices, using the guides for accurate placement.

5. Each individual slice can be modified. From the toolbar, choose the Slice Select tool (under the Slice tool, as shown in Figure 11–20), and then click on the slice you want to alter. You can resize it with the handles in each corner of the selection, move it, or delete it.

6. With the Slice Select tool, select the Contact slice area.

7. There are also options for selecting individual slices. Double-click on the Contact slice area. In the Slice Options window, change the name for the sliced area to **contact_button**, make up a link (URL), such as **contactpage.html**, and an Alt Tag **contact_button**. Leave the rest of the options set to the defaults. Then, click OK. See Figure 11–21.

8. Choose File > Save for Web & Devices. Select Preview the optimized image in a browser option (at the bottom of window) and choose a browser to view the sliced image. Place your cursor over the word Contact to see that the area is now being interpreted as a link (the little hand cursor shows up). This occurs when you add a link (URL) to the slice in the Slice Options panel. Close the browser window and the Save for Web & Devices window.

9. Choose File > Save As, and save your file in your lessons folder.

Optimizing and Saving the Slices

1. To optimize and save the images, choose File > Save for Web & Devices.

2. Choose the 2-Up window option.

3. Select the Slice Select tool located on the left side of the window. See Figure 11–22.

4. Select slice number 1 in the lower window. It will highlight in yellow or appear with a lightened screen. Adjust the optimization settings of this sliced area. We chose JPEG, Medium, Quality: 50 because of the many gradations of color in the header and logo graphics.

5. Select the first button area (Home) and adjust the optimization settings. We chose GIF, Selective, No Dither, and reduced the Colors to 16, producing a very efficient graphic.

6. Select each of the other slices and optimize them to your liking. Balance the image file size with visual appeal.

7. To view the final, optimized work, turn off the Toggle Slices Visibility in the tools area to the left of the window. See Figure 11–23 (on the next page).

8. OK, we are almost there. Choose Save in the Save for Web & Devices window.

FIGURE | 11–20 |

Choose the Slice Select tool to select and modify slices.

FIGURE | 11–21 |

The Slice panel options to modify individual slices.

FIGURE | 11–22 |

Select the Slice Select tool.

FIGURE | 11–23 |

Option to toggle the Slices Visibility.

FIGURE | 11–24 |

The Saving Files options in Output Settings.

FIGURE | 11–25 |

Find your saved images on your computer.

Name
- contact_button.gif
- mynavbar_01.jpg
- mynavbar_02.png
- mynavbar_03.gif
- mynavbar_04.gif
- mynavbar_05.gif
- mynavbar_07.png

9. In the Save Optimized As box, enter the following:

   ► *Save As:* **mynavbar.jpg**
   ► *Format (Save as type):* Images Only
   ► *Where:* Your lessons folder
   ► *Settings:* Default Settings
   ► *Slices:* All Slices

10. Wait—before you hit Save, I want to show you something. Under Settings, choose Other. In Output Settings, choose the Saving Files option. In the Optimized Files options, make sure Put Images in Folder is checked and that **images** is indicated for the folder name. Then click OK. See Figure 11–24.

11. Hit Save to save the individual files to the images folder you specified. The images folder will be located in your **lessons** folder. Minimize the Photoshop program and find this folder. Open it up and, *voila*, all of your sliced images are there and ready to be placed into an HTML Web page. See Figure 11–25.

GIF ANIMATION

Photoshop offers features to create simple animations for Web publication.

LESSON 3: CREATING A WEB ANIMATION

In this lesson, you'll prepare an animated GIF for a vintage aircraft Web page. Using the Animation panel, you will move a number of elements to give the illusion of motion and flight.

Setting Up the File

1. Open **chap11L3.psd** located in the folder **chap11_lessons**.

2. In the toolbox, double-click on the Hand tool to expand the working window.

3. Double-click on the Zoom tool in the toolbox. Now, you have plenty of space to work in. See Figure 11–26.

4. Be sure View > Snap is checked. This option will allow you to snap the layers easily to the sides of the canvas.

5. Choose Window > Animation to open the Animation panel. By default, the Animation panel opens up at the bottom of the screen. Here you will see two frames: the first frame shows all of the layers, and the second frame shows only the Sky layer. See Figure 11–27.

Animating the Layers

1. Select the Move tool in the toolbox.

2. With the Sky layer highlighted in the Layers panel and your Move tool selected, click and drag the sky image in the working window slowly to the left. As you position the image, you will notice the image moves to the left and eventually snaps to the right edge. When it snaps, you are done with the move. Holding down Shift will keep it aligned top-to-bottom. See Figure 11–28.

> Note: *You may be thinking, "It looks exactly the same... what's going on?" Remember, looks can be deceiving. The reason for making them look exactly the same has to do with making the animation loop. Looping an animation is a great way to catch the attention of a viewer and minimize the file's size. You will soon find out what I mean.*

3. In the Layers panel, turn on the layer visibility (the eyeball) of the Background layer and highlight the layer. See Figure 11–29.

FIGURE | 11–26 |

Zoomed out version of the file—now, lots of room to work!

FIGURE | 11–27 |

Animation panel shows two frames.

FIGURE | 11–28 |

Move the sky image to the left until it snaps.

FIGURE | 11–29 |

Make the Background layer visible and select it.

FIGURE | 11–30 |

Snap the Background layer object into position.

FIGURE | 11–31 |

Snap the Foreground layer object into position.

FIGURE | 11–32 |

Snap the Foreground layer object into position.

4. Using the Move tool, click and drag the purple mountains to the left like the Sky layer previously. It may take multiple click-and-drags to move the mountains until they snap to the right edge. If the mountains (Background layer) suddenly disappear, and all you see is blue sky, choose Edit > Undo and move the mountains again but not as far to the left. You want to snap the bottom-right corner of the mountains to the bottom-right corner of the canvas. See Figure 11–30.

5. In the Layers panel, turn on the layer visibility for the Plane layer and Foreground layer.

6. Click on the Foreground layer to highlight it.

7. Again using the Move tool, click and drag the brown foreground cliffs to the left and snap the bottom-right corner of the layer to the bottom-right corner of the canvas. This is a long drag and may take multiple click-and-drags to move the cliffs all the way to the left. See Figure 11–31.

8. In the Animation panel, you will notice the two frames are identical. Now, we are ready to create the animation. See Figure 11–32. To do this, you will have Photoshop create additional frames between the two frames we just created. This is called "tweening" in the animation industry. Traditional animations, created by such studios as Disney and Warner Brothers, had many frames drawn in between key frames (the two frames in the Animation panel would be considered "key frames") to create the illusion of motion. These "tween" frames were drawn by artists called "in-betweeners."

9. In the Animation panel, click on the Tweens animation frames icon. See Figure 11–33.

10. In the Tween window, Tween With should be set to Previous Frame, Frames to Add is 58, Layers is All Layers, and all Parameters (Position, Opacity, and Effects) should be checked. See Figure 11–34. Click OK.

11. You will notice a lot more frames appear in the Animation panel. Those frames are created by our in-betweener—Photoshop. See Figure 11–35.

FIGURE | 11–33 |

Click the Tweens animation frames icon.

FIGURE | 11–34 |

Select options in the Tween window.

FIGURE | 11–35 |

Photoshop creates all the in-between frames—alright!

12. Want to see how it looks? In the Animation panel, click the Plays animation button. See Figure 11–36. There goes your plane flying through a canyon. Pretty nifty! Click the Stops animation button (same location as the Plays animation button). To learn more about the animation feature of Photoshop, choose Help > Photoshop Help > Video and animation.

Saving the Animated GIF

1. Choose File > Save for Web & Devices.

2. Under Preset, leave it [Unnamed]. Then select the following options (see Figure 11–37 on the next page):

▶ *Optimized file format:* GIF

▶ *Color-reduction algorithm:* Selective

▶ *Dither algorithm:* No Dither

▶ *Transparency:* Uncheck

▶ *Interlaced:* Uncheck

FIGURE | 11–36 |

Click play to view your animation.

FIGURE | 11–37 |

Save options for the animated GIF.

Preset: [Unnamed]

GIF

Selective   Colors: 16

No Dither   Dither:

☐ Transparency   Matte: None

    Amount:

☐ Interlaced   Web Snap: 0%

    Lossy: 0

- ► *Colors:* 16
- ► *Matte:* None
- ► *Web Snap:* 0%
- ► *Lossy:* 0

3. Preview the optimized image in a browser (select this option at the bottom of window), and choose a browser to view the animated GIF. See Figure 11–38. Close the browser window.

4. Click Save. Name it **plane.gif**. For Format (Mac) or Save as type (Windows), choose Images Only. Save the file in your **chap11_lessons** folder.

Format: GIF
Dimensions: 75w x 75h
Size: 0 bytes
Settings: Selective, 16 Colors, No Dither, 60 frames, Transparency off, No Transparency Dither, Non-Interlaced, 0% Web Snap

```
<html>
<head>
<title>chap11L3</title>
<meta http-equiv="Content-Type" content="text/html; charset=iso-8859-1">
</head>
<body bgcolor="#FFFFFF" leftmargin="0" topmargin="0" marginwidth="0" marginheight="0">
<!-- Save for Web Slices (chap11L3.psd) -->
<img src="BrowserPreview_tmp.gif" width="75" height="75" alt="">
<!-- End Save for Web Slices -->
</body>
</html>
```

FIGURE | 11–38 |

View the animated GIF in a browser.

SUMMARY

Yeah, I know, you are probably all excited now—at least, I hope so—about using Photoshop. Creating, adjusting, and preparing images for print and Web publication is no longer such a deep, dark secret.

▶ IN REVIEW

1. Describe image optimization. What three interrelated areas must be considered in the Web optimization process?

2. What is dithering?

3. Photographs are best saved in what format? What about graphics with solid colors and line art?

4. What image formats use color-reduction algorithms and why?

5. When would you use the WBMP format?

6. How many bytes are in a kilobyte? Why is that important to know?

7. Name at least two things you can do in the animation panel.

8. Name three useful things about slicing images.

9. Where do sliced images go once you save them?

10. What is so useful about a droplet?

▶ EXPLORING ON YOUR OWN

1. For information about Web graphics with Photoshop, spend some time in the Help files (Help > Photoshop Help > Web graphics).

2. Using what you have learned about the Save for Web & Devices window, decide which optimization settings are best for the example artwork, **fig1.tif**, located in the folder **chap11_lessons/samples.**

3. Automate the optimization process by learning how to make a droplet in Photoshop (File > Automate > Create Droplet). For more information about making a droplet, refer to Help > Photoshop Help and search

for "Create a droplet from an action." Use the batch of images located in the folder **chap11_lessons/samples**. See Figure 11–39.

4. Create a Web photo gallery. I admit, this is a really cool thing! A Web gallery is a quick way to create a Web page or presentation that showcases a series of digital images or photos. The features for making web galleries are now located in the Adobe Bridge program as part of the Adobe Output Module (AOM). For more details on getting to AOM in Bridge see Chapter 10's Exploring on Your Own section, #5. Once in the AOM in Bridge follow these steps:

a. Choose the Web Gallery option in the Output panel. Choose a Template and Style. See Figure 11–40.

b. On the left side of the Bridge program be sure the Folders panel is open. Scroll for a folder on your computer that contains images or photographs (For practice you may use the images located in the **chap11_lessons/samples** folder.) Once the folder is selected, the images should appear in the Content panel at the bottom of the Bridge program. See Figure 11–41, #1 and #2.

c. Hold down the Shift key on your keyboard and select any number of images in the folder for your web gallery. Refer to Figure 11–41, #2 again.

d. Scroll to the bottom of the Output panel to the Create Gallery section. Choose Save to Disk and browse to a location where you would like to save your web gallery (refer to Figure 11–41, #3). Click Save. An Adobe Web Gallery folder will be created in the location you specified. Go to the folder and double click on the HTML document inside to view the web gallery in a browser See Figure 11–42 for an example of a finished web gallery and also **chap11_lessons/samples/Adobe Web Gallery Example**.

FIGURE | 11–39 |

Drag a folder of images to a droplet to automatically optimize the images.

FIGURE | 11–40 |

The Output panel in Bridge with the Web Gallery option selected.

Note: *There are many other options in the Web Gallery panel that you can set before outputting your Web gallery, such as site information, color, and appearance. Also, be sure to try out the numerous templates available.*

FIGURE | 11–41 |

1. Browse for some images on your computer. 2. Select the images in the Content panel. 3. Set options for the Web Gallery and Save to Disk.

FIGURE | 11–42 |

An example of a Web gallery.

Explorer PAGES

Glenn Mitsui

"Learn aggressively. Make the technology end of what you do go away with your skill in the programs. This will allow you to create freely because you know what is possible. This is when the real magic happens. Think of the obvious, then throw it away. Your ideas have to be better, be two steps ahead. That's when you surprise people; that's when you surprise yourself."

About Glenn Mitsui

Glenn Mitsui was born and raised in Seattle, WA. He attended Seattle Central Community College, studying graphic design/illustration. One class short of graduating, Glenn took the graveyard shift at Boeing where he learned technical illustration on the computer. After earning enough money to buy a Datsun 280Z, he left Boeing and opened Studio MD in Seattle with friends Jesse Doquilo, Randy Lim, and Cindy Chin. Glenn became the studio illustrator, doing work for various magazines, newspapers, and corporations. Studio MD flourished for 10 years until 1.5 million gallons of water flooded the entire business in 1998. Since then, Glenn began looking at things differently as a close friend comforted him with these words, "This is a baptism, baby, time to start over."

Glenn continued to work as a freelance illustrator. His work concentrated on editorial illustrations for clients such as the *New York Times*, the *Wall Street Journal*, the *Los Angeles Times, Atlantic Monthly, PCWorld, Time,* and *Discovery Magazine*. His work has been honored by the Society of Illustrators, *HOW, Graphis,* and *Print*. In 2002, he was inducted into the NAPP Photoshop Hall of Fame. In his spare time, Glenn is president and co-founder of a program called LINK. Its aim is to bring various artists in the community together, connecting them with inner city high school students to help expand their art awareness in monthly Saturday workshops. For the past 11 years, LINK has provided funding to help over 50 students attend college.

Glenn's work has evolved from editorial illustration to fine art. It is used in concert settings, church services, and installation pieces. His latest venture, the Organica project, is a collaboration with musicians to visually score their music. It includes a full-length DVD of moving pictures set to the ambient music of Dan Phelps. Visit Glenn's Web site to learn more about his exciting work: *http://www.glennmitsui.com/*.

Upstream. Compliments of Glenn Mitsui.

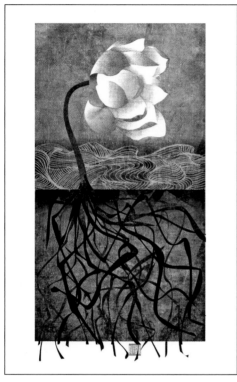

Family. Compliments of Glenn Mitsui.

About the Work of Glenn Mitsui

Glenn shares his process for creating the *Family* image: "The *Family* image is homage to a good friend's father who passed away. He was an amazing man who enjoyed life to the fullest and left behind a legacy of a wonderful family. His stem was not strong enough to support his petals, but his roots will grow forever.

"This piece was done entirely in Photoshop. The process is quite simple, no filters, no real amazing techniques. A lot of this piece is grounded in what feels right. The flower and roots were drawn with the Pen tool in Photoshop. The petals were also drawn using the Pen tool, then filled with a gradation. The wavy lines were drawn with a regular pencil on paper, then scanned. The textures are layered on top of each other until they look right. Cement, paper, linen, papyrus, rusted metal, paint, graphite streaks all combined till it feels right. I love the different variations you go through to get something you like. The trick is knowing when it is done, when can you walk away and feel satisfied. Then all you have to do is find someone who shares your sense of beauty."

Gesthemene. Compliments of Glenn Mitsui.

Explorer PAGES, continued

Charlene Chua

"I start sketching out my ideas, sometimes with a pencil and paper, and other times straight into Photoshop. I use a Wacom Cintiq, which is basically a monitor that you can draw on, and this allows me to directly convert the ideas in my head into a digital format."

About Charlene Chua

Charlene Chua spent her youth growing up in Singapore, where she divided her time between drawing, reading comics, and failing her Mandarin classes. She started her working life in 1998 as a Web designer, and went on to become a senior graphic designer, Web producer, and interactive project manager, with companies like Ogilvy Interactive and The Gate Worldwide. She decided to pursue illustration as a career in 2003, eventually moving to full-time illustration in 2006.

Since then she has worked with clients from North America, Europe, Singapore, and Australia on a wide variety of illustration projects. Her work has appeared in the Society of Illustrators of Los Angeles' Illustration West 43 and 45, American Illustration Tribute, and Ballistic Publishing's Exotique 4, as well as several other art books. She illustrated the children's picture book *Julie Black Belt* for Immedium Publishing, and the short stories "Eidolon" and "Worn" for Image comic's *Liquid City* anthology.

Courtesy of Charlene Chua.

Courtesy of Charlene Chua.

In 2007 she moved to Toronto, Canada, with her husband and two cats. She now spends her time illustrating, working on comics, watching video games, and telling people her last name is 'choo-wah', not choo, chui, choi, chew...

Learn more about Charlene at: *http://www.charlenechua.com*

About the Work of Charlene Chua

Every piece I do begins with an idea. My ideas are usually not very conceptual, but I do usually have to think about what I am going to do and start from there. Sometimes the idea is very simple and straightforward — a picture of a couple of kids eating ice cream, a landscape with trees, mountains, and forests.

Other times the idea is more complicated and abstract, requiring an interesting visual solution for conveying less tangible subjects, like emotions.

I start sketching out my ideas, sometimes with a pencil and paper, and other times straight into Photoshop. I use a Wacom Cintiq, which is basically a monitor that you can draw on, and this allows me to directly convert the ideas in my head into a digital format. Right now, I find I like coming up with ideas and compositions in rough thumbnails that I doodle on paper, and then creating a more polished sketch in Photoshop.

Once I have a working sketch, I import this into Illustrator and start creating the final colored artwork. Before discovering Illustrator (and prior to that, Freehand), I had been trying to teach myself how to work with the airbrush. I played around with that in my teens and loved it, but was also constantly frustrated by how difficult it was to control the tool. Freehand and Illustrator offered me a solution that let me achieve what I wanted to do with the airbrush, and more. As time went by I got more used to working with these two programs rather than Photoshop. I do use Photoshop a lot, though, for sketching and for applying final effects and textures to my artwork.

I work mostly with the Pen tool in Illustrator. I use it to draw shapes based on the sketch, and to create additional shapes to add shadows and highlights to a piece. I am a big fan of using clipping masks; again, this is similar to something I used to do with the airbrush that I enjoyed but found extremely tedious. I tend to work with quite a few layers set to Multiply to build up soft shadows, and several in Screen or Soft Light for highlights (although this may not be necessary with the newer gradient features in CS5).

| A New Dimension |
(for Photoshop CS5
Extended version users)

charting your course

Photoshop has always been known as a 2D image manipulation program, but that has changed. Photoshop CS5 Extended can support transformation, material editing, and texture mapping on simple three-dimensional (3D) objects available within the program or imported from 3D authoring programs. The world of 3D modeling and animation can be a full-time study; in this chapter you'll explore some basic concepts and discover what Photoshop CS5 Extended has to offer.

goals

In this chapter you will:

► *Transform objects in three dimensions*
► *Practice moving in camera view*
► *Place materials and textures onto an object*
► *Explore the 3D scene properties panel*
► *Convert a 2D image into a 3D model*
► *Import a 3D model*

X, Y, AND Z

In traditional 3D (three-dimensional) modeling and animation authoring programs, such as DAZ Bryce, Autodesk's Maya and 3ds Max, Softimage, or NewTek Lightwave, you model and animate objects in a virtual space made up of three axes: X, Y, and Z. When working in the 3D default view in Photoshop, the ground plan (horizontal orientation) is made up of the X (red) and the Y (green) axes and the vertical orientation (up and down) is the Z-axis (blue). The three axes can be represented by placing your hand palm up and extending the middle finger straight up. See Figure 12–1.

FIGURE | 12–1 |

The default positioning of the three axes in Photoshop are Z (blue) on the vertical plane and X (red) and Y (green) on the horizontal plane.

FIGURE | 12–2 |

Photoshop places a 3D object on its own layer in the Layers panel.

Photoshop Extended simulates working in three dimensions with tools and commands that transform (scale, rotate, move), apply materials and textures, change the lighting or render modes (from solid to wireframe, for example) to pre-constructed 3D models. Photoshop places 3D models on a separate "3D Layer," a discrete entity in the Layers panel that behaves like any other layer. It can have effects and blending modes applied to it, be masked, and so on. See Figure 12–2.

There are numerous primitive 3D shapes available in Photoshop that you can add to your 2D scenes, such as cone, cylinder, sphere, donut, soda can, etc. However, you can also open and work with 3D files (.u3d, 3ds, .obj, .kmz [Google Earth], and .dae [Collada] file formats) created in programs like Adobe Acrobat 3D version 8, or Autodesk's 3ds Max or Maya. However, to edit a 3D model itself (alter its polygonal structure, for example), you must use a traditional 3D authoring program.

LESSON 1: TRANSFORMING IN X, Y, AND Z

In this lesson, you'll practice moving, scaling, and rotating a 3D object and then practice orbiting around the object in camera view.

Creating and Moving a 3D Object

1. In Photoshop choose File > New, call it **my_cube** and under Preset select the Default Photoshop Size. Click OK.

2. Choose the 3D Workspace option. See Figure 12–3.

3. From the menu bar choose 3D > New Shape from Layer > Cube. Note that there are plenty of other simple 3D Objects to choose from (Donut, Hat, Soda Can), but those are for you to play with later. See Figure 12–4.

FIGURE | 12–3 |

Select the Advanced 3D Workspace.

FIGURE | 12–4 |

The 3D options from the menu bar.

FIGURE | 12–5 |

An example of a 3D Preferences warning.

FIGURE | 12–6 |

The 3D Preferences window.

> Note: *If you get a "To speed-up the 3D import ..." warning, choose Continue (see Figure 12-5). However, in the future if you need to adjust 3D Preferences, such as rendering options, RAM and file loading usage, and 3D Overlay colors, choose Photoshop > Preferences > 3D (Mac) or Edit > Preferences > 3D (Windows). See Figure 12-6.*

4. In the toolbox, select the 3D Object Rotate tool. See Figure 12–7.

5. An interactive indicator representing the three axes appears at the top left of your workspace (if the 3D axis indicator is not visible, choose View > Show > 3D Axis). You will play with this 3D axis indicator to perform transformations on the object. Click on the gray bar at top of the axis indicator and drag it over the center of the cube shape. See Figure 12–8 (on the next page).

FIGURE | 12–7 |

Select the 3D Rotate tool from the toolbox.

FIGURE | 12–8 |

Position the 3D axis indicator over the cube.

> **Note:** *It's not necessary to move the 3D axis indicator over the object to have it work effectively; this is simply to better illustrate how moving, scaling, and rotating the object (which originates from its center in this instance) will be affected on the x, y, and z axes. While you are practicing, be sure the cube is set at the "Default" position so it matches the steps and visuals in this lesson. See Figure 12–9.*

6. Let's first play with moving the object. On the indicator the blue arrow represents the "z" axis, the green arrow the "y" axis, and the red arrow the "x" axis. Click on the cone-like shape at the top of the z axis indicator (placing your mouse over it changes it from blue to yellow) and drag up and down. See Figure 12–10. With this method, you are moving the object in virtual space along the "z" axis.

7. Click the Home button to return the object to its initial position. See Figure 12–11.

FIGURE | 12–9 |

Be sure the cube is set to the default position.

8. Click on the cone of the x-axis indicator (placing your mouse over it changes it from red to yellow) and drag right and left. You are moving the object along the x-axis of virtual space. See Figure 12–12.

9. Click the Home button again to start over. Refer to Figure 12–11 again.

10. Click on the cone of the y-axis indicator (placing your mouse over it changes it from green to yellow) and drag left and right. You are moving the object along the y-axis of virtual space. See Figure 12–13.

11. Click the Home button again.

FIGURE | 12–10 |

Move the object along the z-axis.

FIGURE | 12–11 |

Click the Home button to return the object to its initial position.

FIGURE | 12–12 |

Move the object along the x-axis.

FIGURE | 12–13 |

Move the object along the y-axis.

Scale the Object

1. To scale an object uniformly, move your mouse over the cube in the middle of the axes indicator until it turns yellow, click on it, and drag up and down. See Figure 12–14.

2. Click the Home button.

3. Click on the blue cube on the z-axis and drag up and down to scale along the z plane. See Figure 12–15.

4. Click the Home button.

FIGURE | 12–14 |

Click and drag up or down on the center of the axis indicator to scale the object uniformly.

FIGURE | 12–15 |

Scale along the z-axis.

FIGURE | 12–16 |

Scale along the x-axis.

FIGURE | 12–17 |

Scale along the y-axis.

5. Click on the red cube on the x-axis and drag right and left to scale along the x plane. See Figure 12–16.

6. Click the Home button.

7. Click on the green cube on the y-axis and drag left and right to scale along the y plane. See Figure 12–17.

8. Reset to Home again.

Rotate the Object

1. Now, practice rotating the object. Click on the elongated blue rectangular shape between the cube and cone shape on the z-axis (placing your mouse over it changes it to a yellow circle that wraps around the center of the axis indicator). Drag the mouse in a circular motion and note that the degree of rotation is tracked by a dark blue highlight. See Figure 12–18.

> **Note:** *While the rotation is being initiated from the z-axis, its path is circling around the x-axis. This is noted numerically in the x orientation field on the options bar. See Figure 12–19.*

2. Click the Home button to return to the cube's original position.

3. Next, click on the elongated red rectangular shape between the cube and cone shape on the x-axis (placing your mouse over it changes it to a yellow circle that wraps around the center of the axis

FIGURE | 12–18 |

Rotation of the object.

indicator). Drag the mouse in a circular motion and note that the rotation is tracked by a dark red highlight. See Figure 12–20. Also, note the numeric rotation in the y-orientation field on the options bar.

4. Reset back to Home.

5. Next, click on the elongated green rectangular shape between the cube and cone shape on the y-axis (placing your mouse over it changes it to a yellow circle that wraps around the center of the axis indicator.). Drag the mouse in a circular motion and note that the rotation is tracked by a green highlight. See Figure 12–21. Also, note the numeric rotation in the z-orientation field on the options bar.

6. Click the Home button again. Now that you've explored moving, scaling, and rotating the object in each dimension, you can practice multiple transformations with more confidence.

Note: *You have been practicing transformations on a 3D object using the axis indicator. You can also transform by clicking a specific 3D tool in the toolbox or options bar. See Figure 12–22 and Figure 12–23 (both on the next page). Move the axis indicator away from the scene by clicking on its gray bar, and try each 3D tool to familiarize yourself with this method of transforming. Options include:*

- ▶ **3D Object Rotate** – *constrains the rotation of an object around the X, Y, or Z-axis*
- ▶ **3D Object Roll** – *rolls an object two-dimensionally in the front-facing view*
- ▶ **3D Object Pan** – *moves an object right/left and/or up/down*
- ▶ **3D Object Slide** – *moves an object with perspective right/left and/or away/toward*
- ▶ **3D Object Scale** – *scales an object uniformly*

Also explore what happens when you change the position of the object, which alters its default view as you apply transformations, such as Left, Right, Top, Bottom, Back, and Front views of the object. Refer to Figure 12–9.

FIGURE | 12–19 |

Rotation initiated from the z-axis orients around the x-axis, as shown in the numeric orientation field for the x-axis.

FIGURE | 12–20 |

Rotation of the object around the y-axis.

FIGURE | 12–21 |

Rotation of the object around the z-axis.

FIGURE | 12–23 |

You can also select a 3D tool, such as the 3D Object Scale tool, from the options bar.

FIGURE | 12–22 |

Select a 3D tool, such as the 3D Object Scale tool, from the toolbox.

Moving in Camera View

In the first part of this lesson, you practiced transforming the actual object; in this section you will practice moving around the object as if you were viewing it through a video camera.

1.   Let's explore the camera view with a different object. Close and don't save the **my_cube** file you were working on previously. In Photoshop choose File > New, call it **my_hat**, and under Preset select the Default Photoshop Size. Choose OK.

2.   Check that the 3D Workspace option is selected. Refer to Figure 12–3.

3.   From the menu bar, choose 3D > New Shape from Layer > Hat. Leave the axis indicator away from the scene; we will play with each camera view by selecting the tools from the toolbox or options bar, rather than using the indicator. See Figure 12–24.

4.   In the toolbox, select the 3D Rotate Camera tool. See Figure 12–25 and note the little video camera visual in the upper-right corner of the tools icon. Place your cursor over the object and click and drag up/down and right/left; imagine you are an acrobatic camera operator orbiting around the object in all directions.

FIGURE | 12–24 |

A 3D hat object – leave the axis indicator away from the scene.

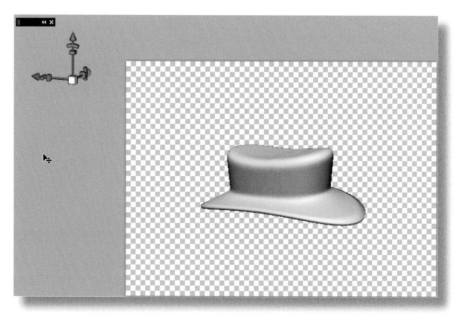

5. Click on the Home button.

6. Try the other Camera movement tools by selecting each one from the toolbox or the options bar. Remember to click the Home button between each movement to set the camera back to its default position. See Figure 12–26.

Options include:

- ▸ **3D Rotate Camera** to easily view all sides of the object, the tool adds a spinning action to the camera's motion

- ▸ **3D Roll Camera** rolls/tilts the camera two-dimensionally in the front-facing view

- ▸ **3D Pan Camera**– moves the camera right/left and/or up/down

- ▸ **3D Walk Camera** – simulates a viewer walking right/left and/or away/toward the object

- ▸ **3D Zoom Camera**– simulates a viewer walking away/toward the object

FIGURE | 12–25 |

Select the 3D Rotate Camera tool – note the video camera icon next to the tool's icon.

7. Close the **my_hat** file. There is no need to save it.

FIGURE | 12–26 |

Select other camera view options from the toolbox or options bar.

LESSON 2: MAPPING A TEXTURE AND ADJUSTING MATERIAL SETTINGS

In this lesson, you'll map a logo to a 3D wine bottle model and adjust its material settings.

1. In Photoshop choose File > New, call it **my_bottle**, and under Preset select the Default Photoshop Size. Choose OK.

2. Choose the 3D or Reset > 3D Workspace option. Refer to Figure 12–3.

3. From the menu bar choose 3D > New Shape from Layer > Wine Bottle.

4. Select the **Filter By: Whole scene** option in the 3D Panel. See Figure 12–27.

5. Select the 3D Camera Zoom tool. See Figure 12–28 (on the next page). Over the wine bottle, click and drag down with the tool to zoom in closer to the object.

FIGURE | 12–27 |

In the 3D Panel choose the **Filter By: Whole scene** option.

FIGURE | 12–28 |

Select the 3D Zoom Camera tool.

6. Let's map a label around the wine bottle—a 2D image of the wine label you explored in Adventures in Design: Wine Box Composition. From the Scene List in the 3D panel choose the **Label_Material** layer; the panel changes to the Material options mode. See Figure 12–29.

Note: *The way we perceive the material or texture of an actual object is related to how light hits its surface. In the virtual world it's the same. However, in the virtual world we can control this effect in Photoshop's 3D (Materials) panel, where we can adjust surface characteristics such as Ambience, Refraction, Diffusion, Bump textures, Glossiness, Opacity, and Reflectivity as we see fit. In this short chapter on 3D, we will not cover the specifics of each characteristic, but feel free to play with the options. Note, however, that many of the options will not be visible directly in Photoshop; they must be rendered into a final image. See Rendering options in the Exploring on Your Own section at the end of this chapter.*

7. Under the Diffuse options choose Load Texture. See Figure 12–30. Open the **wine_label.jpg** found in the **chap12_lessons/ lesson2** folder.

FIGURE | 12–30 |

Select the Load Texture option.

FIGURE | 12–29 |

Choose the **Label_Material** layer.

Note: *In the Diffuse options submenu (and the other surface characteristic sub-menus) there is an option to create a New Texture. New Texture creates a blank document in Photoshop in which you can draw and paint your own texture directly in the program and map it onto the object. To load the New Texture, choose the Open Texture option (also in the submenu). In this lesson, however, we opened a texture that is a premade image in the JPEG format using the Load Texture option. Refer to Figure 12–30 again.*

FIGURE | 12–31 |

The wine bottle with the label mapped onto it.

FIGURE | 12–32 |

Select the **Glass_Material** layer.

8. Use the 3D Object Rotate tool to orbit the object and see how the label has wrapped around the object. See Figure 12–31.

9. Now, choose the **Glass_Material** layer in the 3D panel. See Figure 12–32.

10. Adjust the Opacity setting to 80%. (As an alternative to typing the percentage manually into the Opacity field, you can use the "scrub" feature to adjust the setting by clicking directly on or below the word "Opacity" and dragging left or right. See Figure 12–33.)

11. If you would like a different color glass—other than the default green—click on the Diffuse color box and choose a new color. See Figure 12–34 (on the next page).

12. Choose File > Place and open **table_chairs.jpg** in the **chap12_lessons/lesson2** folder. Press Enter or Return on the keyboard to confirm the placed object.

FIGURE | 12–33 |

Set the Opacity by clicking on or below the word "Opacity," and scrubbing the arrow left or right.

FIGURE | 12–34 |

Choose a Diffuse (main) color for the objects glass material.

13. In the Layers panel, drag the **table_chairs** layer below the Background layer, which contains the wine bottle object.

14. Select the Background layer and position the wine bottle on the table using the 3D transformation tools (scale, pan, and rotate). See Figure 12–35. It's not a perfect match to the table photo, but you get the idea.

FIGURE | 12–35 |

An example of the 3D bottle positioned within a 2D photo.

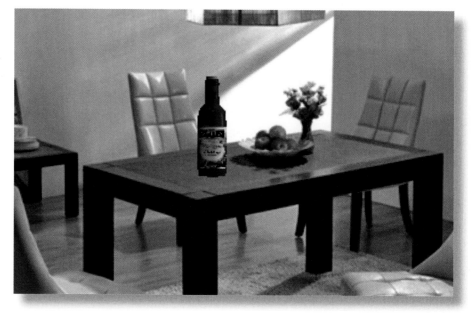

15. Let's adjust the lighting a little. Choose the **Filter By: Lights** option in the 3D panel. See Figure 12–36 (on the next page).

16. Under Infinite lights in the layers, choose the **Infinite Light 1** layer.

17. Set the intensity setting to 1.55, then choose the Light Rotate tool. See Figure 12–37. Click and drag the tool on the scene to adjust the light so that it appears to be coming from the same direction as the light in the rest of the room.

18. Save your scene.

FIGURE | 12–37 |

Rotate the light.

FIGURE | 12–36 |

Select the **Filter By: Lights** option in the 3D panel.

TURNING 2D IMAGES INTO 3D OBJECTS

In Photoshop, you can convert images or photographs into dimensional objects with the 3D Postcard, Mesh from Grayscale, Volume from Layers, and Repoussé commands.

3D Postcard creates a perspective effect on the image or converts an image or photograph into a repeated grid for tiling and texturing.

Mesh from Grayscale converts a grayscale image into a 3D mesh. The various levels of gray, black, and white in the image determine the depth of the 3D conversion. It works great for terrain-like effects. This is a simplified version of depth mapping or bump mapping.

Volume from Layers converts selected layers into a 3D volume. This feature is still quite buggy and requires a high-end video card and a recommended 256 MB of video RAM.

Repoussé, as specified in the Photoshop help files, is a term that describes a metalworking technique in which object faces are shaped and patterned by hammering on the opposite side. In Photoshop, the Repoussé command converts 2D objects into 3D meshes, which you can precisely extrude, inflate, and reposition in 3D space.

FIGURE | 12–38 |

Select the 3D Object Rotate tool to rotate the postcard.

FIGURE | 12–39 |

The 3D postcard in a perspective view.

LESSON 3: EXPLORING THE 3D POSTCARD FEATURE

In this lesson, you learn how the 3D Postcard feature can alter the perspective plane of a 2D image that is then mapped into another 2D scene.

Transforming a 2D image

1. Choose File > Open and open the **lisbon_framed.tif** found in the **chap12_lessons/lesson3** folder.

2. From the menu bar, choose 3D > New 3D Postcard from Layer.

3. Select the 3D Object Rotate tool from the toolbar. See Figure 12–38.

4. Click and drag on the image to rotate it into various perspective views. See Figure 12–39. Try the other 3D transformation tools (pan, scale, etc.) by selecting them in the options bar, the toolbox, or using the axis indicator. That's the essence of what the postcard feature can do, but let's see how it works in a scene.

5. Close the **lisbon_framed.tif**—don't save it.

Using the Postcard Feature in a Scene

1. Choose File > Open and open **chap12L3.psd** found in the **chap12_lessons/lesson3** folder. This scene should look very familiar; it's the first lesson you did in this book (you've come a long way since then!). One difference, however, is the Lisbon photo you played with in the previous section of this lesson is positioned over the bed. It appears out of place, because the perspective and lighting on the photo don't quite match the rest of the room. Let's fix this.

2. Choose the Reset 3D workspace.

3. Highlight the **framed_photo** layer in the Layers panel.

4. From the menu bar, choose 3D > New 3D Postcard from Layer.

5. Use the 3D Object Rotate tool, 3D Object Pan tool, and 3D Object Scale tool to adjust the photo so that it is aligned in the same perspective as the rest of the scene. See before and after in Figure 12–40.

6. In the Layers panel, set the blending mode for the Lisbon photo to Soft Light. See Figure 12–41. This blends the photo better into the scene; however, zoom in close and notice there is a white border artifact around the photo. Let's correct this.

7. Be sure the **framed_photo** layer is selected. In the 3D panel, choose the **Filter By: Materials** option. See Figure 12–42.

FIGURE | 12–40 |

Use the 3D object tools to align the photo in the scene as shown in the "after" example.

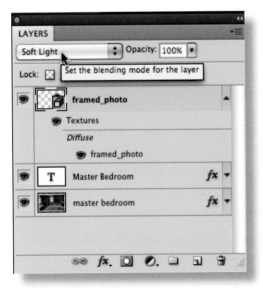

FIGURE | 12–41 |

Set the layer blending mode for the photo to Soft Light.

FIGURE | 12–42 |

Select the **Filter By: Materials** option.

8. Click on the Diffuse color box to open the Color Picker. Move the cursor (which is actually the Eyedropper tool) over the dark frame of the photo and click to select the dark brown color. Select OK. See Figure 12–43 and Figure 12–44.

9. Choose View > Fit on Screen to admire the finished image—well done!

10. Save, if you'd like.

FIGURE | 12–43 |

Click the Diffuse box to open the Color Picker.

FIGURE | 12–44 |

Take a sample of the color in the image with the Eyedropper tool.

LESSON 4: EXPLORE NEW MESH FROM GRAYSCALE (DEPTH MAPPING)

Photoshop uses a technique called depth or height mapping—often found in 3D authoring programs to create terrains and landscapes—to translate a 2D image into a three-dimensional object. A depth map is a map (image) that includes depth information for every pixel. In Photoshop, this depth information is created by the variations of gray in a grayscale image (kind of like how it determines color levels in an image using a histogram, as learned in Chapter 6). In this lesson, you explore depth mapping using Photoshop's New Mesh from Grayscale command.

1. Open the file **depth_map_normal.psd** in the **chap12_lesson/lesson4** folder. This was a color image that I converted to grayscale for use in this lesson: Image > Mode > Grayscale.

2. Choose 3D > New Mesh from Grayscale > Plane. See Figure 12–45.

3. Select the 3D Object Rotate tool in the toolbox. Rotate the object to view its new three-dimensional state—amazing! See Figure 12–46.

3D View Window Help

New Layer from 3D File...

New 3D Postcard From Layer
New Shape From Layer   ▶
New Mesh From Grayscale   ▶   Plane
New Volume From Layers...   Two-Sided Plane
Repoussé   ▶   Cylinder
                                                Sphere
Render Settings...

FIGURE | 12–45 |

Create a new mesh from a grayscale image.

4. Let's do some compare and contrast on three of the same images with varied levels of color. Open the file **depth_map_light.psd**.

5. Apply the 3D > New Mesh from Grayscale > Plane command.

6. Open the file **depth_map_dark.psd** and again apply the New Mesh from Grayscale > Plane command.

7. From the Application bar, select 3-up under the Arrange Documents options, and note the variation of surface texture resulting from the color differences in each image. See Figure 12–47.

8. Now, select each file and use the 3D Object Rotate tool to rotate each object so you can see the depth differences in each object. See Figure 12–48.

9. Close the files or play with them further. This ends the lesson.

FIGURE | 12–46 |

The image transformed into a 3D mesh.

FIGURE | 12–47 |

Note that each object has different levels of grayscale.

FIGURE | 12–48 |

Rotate each object to see the various levels of depth that were created based on the variations of gray color in the object.

GUIDED PROJECT: IMPORTING A 3D OBJECT

In this project, you import a 3D object, add materials and texture maps to it, and place it within a 2D scene. You can import preconstructed 3D objects in the following formats: .u3d, 3ds, .obj, .kmz, and Collada. Via the Web, many 3D objects can be found for royalty-free usage at little or no cost; for example, visit *http://www.the3dstudio.com/*. Keep in mind that 3D files can be very large; they can take some time to download and require significant amounts of RAM to render efficiently in Photoshop.

1. Choose File > New, call it **3D_import** and under Preset select the Default Photoshop Size. Choose OK.

2. Reset the 3D Workspace in the Application Bar.

3. Choose from the menu bar 3D > New Layer from 3D File and open the model in **chap12_lessons/project/mini_obj.obj.** It's quite large (23 MB without any textures applied), so it might take some time to open.

> Note: *This Mini Cooper model is compliments of Gilles Tran's web site: Oyonal - 3D Art and Graphics Experiments (http://www.oyonale.com/modeles.php?page=58).*

4. Use the 3D Rotate Camera tool to orbit around the model to check out its detail.

5. In the 3D (Scene) panel, select the **Body** layer and change its diffuse color.

6. Select the **Glass** layer and change its opacity to 10%. Feel free to change the window color by adjusting the diffuse color.

7. Select the **Headlight** layer, change the diffuse color to a bright yellow and set the opacity to about 50%.

8. Save the file in your lessons folder.

9. Rotate the car so you can see the front of it and zoom in close with the 3D Zoom Camera tool. See Figure 12–49.

10. Select the **Plate** layer and under the Diffuse submenu choose Load Texture. Open the **lplate.jpg** found in the **chap12_lessons/project/texture_images** folder. The European-style license plate should map to the plate model on the front of the car.

11. Select the **Emblem** layer under the Diffuse submenu choose Load Texture. Add the **mini_emblem.jpg** found in the **project/texture_images folder**.

12. At this point select any other layers in the 3D Panel and adjust colors as you see fit.

13. Choose File > Place and add a country road image (or any other image you like) to the scene. The country road image, used with permission from *http://www.freefoto.com/*, can be found in **chap12_lessons/project/country_road.jpg**. Scale the image to fit the scene size, then double-click on the image to apply it to the document.

14. Move the **country_road** layer below the **mini_obj** layer.

15. Orient and scale the Mini Cooper to fit in the scene. Adjust its lighting if necessary. See Figure 12–50.

FIGURE | 12–49 |

Use the 3D Zoom tool to zoom in closer to the object. Mini Cooper model is courtesy of Gilles Tran.

FIGURE | 12–50 |

An example of a 2D photo placed behind the 3D object.

SUMMARY

The 3D tools in Photoshop CS5 Extended are basic yet useful, and this chapter only brushed the surface of the features currently available. I suspect they will become more extensive and robust in future editions of Photoshop. For now, the features highlighted here provide artists a way to import and add 3D objects to their 2D artwork—an option never before available without access to an extensive 3D authoring program.

Now that we are at the end of this book, it is up to you to continue exploring the magic of Photoshop. As you undertake this graphic design adventure, keep in mind the words of the great magician Harry Houdini: "Don't lose confidence in an effect because it has been presented many times before. An old trick in 'good hands' is always new. Just see to it that yours are 'good hands.'"

► IN REVIEW

1. Explain the concept of x, y, and z.

2. A 3D model can be transformed in Photoshop. Define transform.

3. What does the 3D Object Pan tool do? What does the 3D Pan Camera tool do?

4. What's the difference between the 3D Object Scale tool and the 3D Zoom Camera tool?

5. What does the New Mesh from Grayscale command do?

6. List at least three surface characteristics that can be altered on a 3D object in Photoshop.

7. What does the Load Texture command do?

8. Name at least three software programs where you can model and animate 3D objects.

9. Where can textures be created to map onto 3D objects?

10. What's rendering (see Exploring on Your Own at the end of this chapter)?

► EXPLORING ON YOUR OWN

1.   Rendering is the process of computing, pixel by pixel, one or more 2D images from 3D scene data, from the viewpoint of a simulated camera (from: *http://www.mentalimages.com*). Play with the rendering options in the 3D Panel. Create a new file. Choose 3D > New Shape From Layer, and select any of the premade 3D objects. In the 3D (Scene) Panel, explore the rendering options. See Figure 12–51.

FIGURE | **12–51** |

Explore the rendering options for a 3D object.

Note: *If your video card does not meet the minimum requirement for hardware-accelerated 3D rendering, a warning message will display.*

---

2.   Study texture mapping and read this informative article: 'Teaching Texture Mapping Visually', by Rosalee Wolfe: *http://www.siggraph.org/education/materials/HyperGraph/mapping/r_wolfe/r_wolfe_mapping_1.htm*.

3.   View a video on mapping 2D images onto 3D models in Photoshop at *http://www.adobe.com/designcenter/video_workshop/?id=vid0020*.

4.   Make your own textures with texture-making software, or in Photoshop. Or, find free textures online to map onto your objects.

     ► Texture Maker for Windows: *http://www.texturemaker.com/download.php*
     ► StarfishX for Mac and Windows: *http://homepage.mac.com/mscott/starfishx/starfishx.html*